D1548546

TECHNICAL COLLEGE OF THE LOWCOUNTRY.
LEARNING RESOURCES CENTER
POST OFFICE BOX 1288
BEAUFORT, SOUTH CAROLINA 29901-1288

FRIEDRICH NIETZSCHE

Modern Critical Views

These and other titles in preparation

Modern Critical Views

FRIEDRICH NIETZSCHE

Edited and with an introduction by
Harold Bloom
Sterling Professor of the Humanities
Yale University

TECHNICAL COLLEGE OF THE LOWCOUNTRY
LEARNING RESOURCES CENTER
POST OFFICE BOX 1288
BEAUFORT, SOUTH CAROLINA 29901-1288

CHELSEA HOUSE PUBLISHERS ◊ 1987
New York ◊ New Haven ◊ Philadelphia

TECHNICAL COLLEGE OF THE LOWCOUNTRY
LEARNING RESOURCES CENTER
POST OFFICE BOX 1288
BEAUFORT, SOUTH CAROLINA 29901-1288

© 1987 by Chelsea House Publishers,
a division of Chelsea House Educational Communications, Inc.,
    95 Madison Avenue, New York, NY 10016
    345 Whitney Avenue, New Haven, CT 06511
    5014 West Chester Pike, Edgemont, PA 19028

Introduction © 1987 by Harold Bloom

All rights reserved. No part of this publication may be
reproduced or transmitted in any form or by any means
without the written permission of the publisher.

Printed and bound in the United States of America

∞ The paper used in this publication meets the minimum
requirements of the American National Standard for
Permanence of Paper for Printed Library Materials,
Z39.48-1984.

Library of Congress Cataloging-in-Publication Data
Friedrich Nietzsche.
    (Modern critical views)
    Includes index.
    1. Nietzsche, Friedrich Wilhelm, 1844–1900.
I. Bloom, Harold. II. Series.
B3317.F82   1987   193   86-34318
ISBN 1-55546-278-2 (alk. paper)

Contents

Editor's Note

This book brings together the best essays available in English upon those aspects of Nietzsche's writings that chart the "ghostlier demarcations, keener sounds" between philosophy and literature. I am grateful to Thomas Keenan for his informed aid in editing this volume. The critical essays are reprinted here in the chronological order of their first publication in English.

My introduction centers upon *On the Genealogy of Morals,* and argues that the ascetic spirit and the aesthetic stance so fuse in that work as to become a virtual identity, despite Nietzsche's own, highly overt argument. The late G. Wilson Knight, imaginative critic of Shakespeare and of the Romantics, commences the chronological sequence with his introduction to *Zarathustra,* which he sees as presenting the doctrine of the Overman without endorsing that doctrine (or the Overman's acts).

Maurice Blanchot, author of critical fictions and fictive criticisms, follows with a meditation upon Nietzsche and nihilism, which Blanchot judges to be a dialectical relation, in that reversal always governs Nietzsche's vision of the uncanny transformations of value into nihilism, and then back again.

In an exegesis of Nietzsche's "experience" of Eternal Recurrence, Pierre Klossowski emphasizes the *intensity* of the philosopher's awakening surprisingly akin, I would note, to Walter Pater's "privileged moment" or secular epiphany.

The late Paul de Man, our most distinguished reader of Nietzsche's stance on the frontier between literature and philosophy, is represented here by his pathbreaking study of Nietzsche's theory of rhetoric. A very different reading of Nietzsche is given by Gilles Deleuze, who balances the active and reactive elements in Nietzsche's theory of interpretation, or the Will to Power over texts.

Jacques Derrida, perhaps the contemporary French person-of-letters most identified with Nietzsche, thinks through Nietzsche's politics of the self, or the role of "the proper name" in the education of the self. Again very different is the approach of Alexander Nehamas, who analyzes Nietzsche's attempts to assimilate life and cognition to literature, and judges that the endeavor could not succeed.

Werner Hamacher, examining Nietzsche's figure of the mask, seeks to clarify Nietzsche's sense of the identity of an individual. I myself am most persuaded by Richard Rorty's pragmatic exposition of Nietzsche's awareness of the contingency of selfhood, an awareness akin to that of the strong poet who triumphs in an agon with tradition, while knowing that tradition cannot be wholly defeated, since it imposes the contingency that authentic strength cannot evade.

In this book's last essay, published here for the first time, Richard Drake reads *Zarathustra* as a study in psychogenesis, and presents a powerful interpretation of Nietzsche's prophetic phantasmagoria.

Introduction

Origin and purpose, for the sake of life, must be kept apart; that fierce admonition is central to Nietzsche. Can they be kept apart, for very long, in an individual psychology? Nietzsche's true strength was as a psychologist, but he finally asked of us what no psychologist rightfully can expect, since the cyclic return of aim or purpose to origin is not to be evaded, a dark lesson taught by poets and speculators throughout recorded time. Beginnings have more than prestige; they foster the perpetual illusion of freedom, even though to invade that illusion generally results in dying.

Nietzsche's deepest teaching, as I read it, is that authentic meaning is painful, and that the pain itself is the meaning. Between pain and meaning comes memory, a memory of pain that then becomes a memorable meaning:

> "How can one create a memory for the human animal? How can one impress something upon this partly obtuse, partly flighty mind, attuned only to the passing moment, in such a way that it will stay there?"
>
> One can well believe that the answers and methods for solving this primeval problem were not precisely gentle; perhaps indeed there was nothing more fearful and uncanny in the whole pre-history of man than his *mnemotechnics*. "If something is to stay in the memory it must be burned in; only that which never ceases to *hurt* stays in the memory"—this is a main clause of the oldest (unhappily also the most enduring) psychology on earth. One might even say that wherever on earth solemnity, seriousness, mystery, and gloomy coloring still distinguish the life of man and a people, something of the terror that formerly attended all promises, pledges, and vows on earth is *still effective:* the past, the longest, deepest and sternest past, breathes upon us and rises

1

up in us whenever we become "serious." Man could never do without blood, torture, and sacrifices when he felt the need to create a memory for himself; the most dreadful sacrifices and pledges (sacrifices of the first-born among them), the most repulsive mutilations (castration, for example), the cruelist rites of all the religious cults (and all religions are at the deepest level systems of cruelties)—all this has its origin in the instinct that realized that pain is the most powerful aid to mnemonics.

I hesitate to name this as Nietzsche's most fundamental insight, but I myself always remember it first when I think of Nietzsche. That the hurt itself should be the *logos,* the link of meaning that connects character and feeling, is the implicit teaching of all religions, which indeed are "systems of cruelties" as Nietzsche calls them, and I am certain he would have placed Marxism and psychoanalysis among them. But I fear that Nietzsche's insight is darker and more comprehensive than that. It embraces all literature as well, since what *On the Genealogy of Morals* goes on to call "the ascetic spirit" might as well be called "the aesthetic spirit" also, or the ascetic/aesthetic ideal:

That this idea acquired such power and ruled over men as imperiously as we find it in history, especially wherever the civilization and taming of man has been carried through, expresses a great fact: the *sickliness* of the type of man we have had hitherto, or at least of the tamed man, and the physiological struggle of man against death (more precisely: against disgust with life, against exhaustion, against the desire for the "end"). The ascetic priest is the incarnate desire to be different, to be in a different place, and indeed this desire at its greatest extreme, its distinctive fervor and passion; but precisely this power of his desire is the chain that holds him captive so that he becomes a tool for the creation of more favorable conditions for being here and being man—it is precisely this *power* that enables him to persuade to existence the whole herd of the ill-constituted, disgruntled, underprivileged, unfortunate, and all who suffer of themselves, by instinctively going before them as their shepherd. You will see my point: this ascetic priest, this apparent enemy of life, this *denier*—precisely he is among the greatest *conserving* and yes-creating forces of life.

With singular contempt, Nietzsche keeps repeating that, in the case of an artist, ascetic ideals mean nothing whatever, or so many things as to amount to nothing whatever. This is part of his polemic against his once-idealized Wagner, but it is also the defense of a failed poet who could not acknowledge his failure, as *Zarathustra* dreadfully demonstrates. The desire to be different, to be elsewhere, is the one motive for metaphor in Nietzsche, and perhaps in everyone else as well. If it leads to a Moses, then it leads to a Goethe also. The antithetical spirit in Nietzsche, his own version of the ascetic and the aesthetic, drives him towards what I venture to call a *poetics of pain*, which has to be read antithetically, as meaning nearly the reverse of what it appears to say:

> *Art*—to say it in advance, for I shall some day return to this subject at greater length—art, in which precisely the *lie* is sanctified and the *will to deception* has a good conscience, is much more fundamentally opposed to the ascetic ideal than is science: this was instinctively sensed by Plato, the greatest enemy of art Europe has yet produced. Plato versus Homer: that is the complete, the genuine antagonism—there the sincerest advocate of the "beyond," the great slanderer of life; here the instinctive deifier, the *golden* nature. To place himself in the service of the ascetic ideal is therefore the most distinctive *corruption* of an artist that is at all possible; unhappily, also one of the most common forms of corruption, for nothing is more easily corrupted than an artist.

The agon between Plato and Homer here is misread, creatively or strongly, as a struggle between the ascetic and the aesthetic, rather than as the struggle for aesthetic supremacy Nietzsche elsewhere declared it to be. But Nietzsche's superb irony makes my attempt to "correct" him a redundancy; what artists have not shown such *corruption* in which they place themselves in the service of the ascetic ideal? Indeed, what other option have they, or we, according to Nietzsche? Which is to say: how are we to read the final section of the *Genealogy*?

> Apart from the ascetic ideal, man, the human *animal*, had no meaning so far. His existence on earth contained no goal; "why man at all?"—was a question without an answer; the *will* for man and earth was lacking; behind every great human destiny there sounded as a refrain a yet greater "in vain!" *This* is precisely what the ascetic ideal means: that something was *lacking*, that man was surrounded by a fearful *void*—he did not know how to justify, to account for, to affirm himself; he *suffered* from the problem of his meaning. He also suffered otherwise, he was in the main a sickly animal: but his problem was *not* suffering

itself, but that there was no answer to the crying question, *"why do I suffer?"*

Man, the bravest of animals and the one most accustomed to suffering, does *not* repudiate suffering as such; he *desires* it, he even seeks it out, provided he is shown a *meaning* for it, a *purpose* of suffering. The meaninglessness of suffering, *not* suffering itself, was the curse that lay over mankind so far—*and the ascetic ideal offered man meaning!* It was the only meaning offered so far; any meaning is better than none at all; the ascetic ideal was in every sense the *"faute de mieux" par excellence* so far. In it, suffering was *interpreted;* the tremendous void seemed to have been filled; the door was closed to any kind of suicidal nihilism. This interpretation—there is no doubt of it—brought fresh suffering with it, deeper, more inward, more poisonous, more life-destructive suffering: it placed all suffering under the perspective of *guilt.*

But all this notwithstanding—man was *saved* thereby, he possessed a meaning, he was henceforth no longer like a leaf in the wind, a plaything of nonsense—the "sense-less"—he could now *will* something; no matter at first to what end, why, with what he willed: *the will itself was saved.*

We can no longer conceal from ourselves *what* is expressed by all that willing which has taken its direction from the ascetic ideal; this hatred of the human, and even more of the animal, and more still of the material, this horror of the senses, of reason itself, this fear of happiness and beauty, this longing to get away from all appearance, change, becoming, death, wishing, from longing itself—all this means—let us dare to grasp it—*a will to nothingness,* an aversion to life, a rebellion against the most fundamental presuppositions of life; but it is and remains a *will!* . . . And, to repeat in conclusion what I said at the beginning: man would rather will *nothingness* than *not* will.

To give suffering a meaning is not so much to relieve suffering as it is to enable meaning to get started, rather than merely repeated. What Nietzsche shares most deeply with the Hebrew Bible and with Freud is the drive to find sense in everything, to interpret everything, but here Nietzsche is at his most dialectical, since he knows (and cannot accept) the consequences of everything having a meaning. There could never be anything new, since everything would have happened already. That is the Hebrew

Bible's loyalty to Yahweh, its trust in the Covenant, and finally that is Freud's faith in the efficacy of interpretation. And that is also Nietzsche's most profound argument with the Hebrew Bible.

"Man . . . suffered from the problem of his meaning" and then yielded to the ascetic ideal, which made the suffering itself into the meaning, and so opened the perspective of guilt. Rather than be void of meaning, man took the void *as* meaning, a taking that saved the will, at a fearful cost. Nietzsche has no alternative but to accuse the poets of nihilism, an accusation in which he himself did not altogether believe. But his association of memory, pain, and meaning is unforgettable and productive, suggesting as it does an antithetical poetics not yet fully formulated, yet lurking in his forebodings of an uncannier nihilism than any yet known.

II

"We possess art lest we should perish of the truth." If a single apothegm could sum up Nietzsche on the aesthetic, it would be that. Poetry tells lies, but the truth, being the reality principle, reduces to death, our death. To love truth would be to love death. This hardly seems to me, as it does to Gilles Deleuze, a tragic conception of art. The world is rich in meaning because it is rich in error, strong in suffering, when seen from an aesthetic perspective. Sanctifying a lie, and deceiving with a good conscience, is the necessary labor of art, because error about life is necessary for life, since the truth about life merely hastens death. The will to deceive is not a tragic will, and indeed is the only source for an imaginative drive that can counter the ascetic drive against life. But these antithetical drives, as in Freud's *Beyond the Pleasure Principle,* form the figure of a chiasmus. Nietzsche is scarcely distinguishable from the Pater of *Marius the Epicurean,* who also so mingles the ascetic and the aesthetic that we cannot undo their mutual contaminations, at least in the strong poet.

Richard Rorty makes the crucial observation that only the strong poet, in Nietzsche, is able to appreciate his own contingency, and thus to appropriate it:

> The line between weakness and strength is thus the line between using language which is familiar and universal and producing language which, though initially unfamiliar and idiosyncratic, somehow makes tangible the blind impress all one's behavings bear.

Rorty goes on to say that Nietzsche does not avoid an "inverted Platonism—his suggestion that a life of self-creation can be as complete and as autonomous as Plato thought a life of contemplation might be." In some terrible sense, Nietzsche did live his life as though it were a poem, and found a value in the idea of his own suffering, a value not unrelated to his adversary, the ascetic ideal. In his own terms, Nietzsche was one of the corrupted strong poets, but such corruption is indistinguishable from strength, even as the ascetic and the aesthetic spirits do blend together. More even than Pater, Nietzsche is an aesthete, giving everything to perception, and finding valid perception only in the arts. Yet Nietzsche, unlike Pater, has his own kind of uneasy conscience at his own aestheticism.

Does Nietzsche offer any mode of understanding reality that does not depend upon literary culture? Clearly not, and that seems to me his difference from all previous psychologists and philosophers. Though he insisted that he was wiser than the poets, he never presented us with that wisdom. If you are going to be the poet of your own life, then you are going to share, at best, the wisdom of the strong poets, and not of the philosophers, theologians, psychologists, or politicians. I think that Nietzsche's true strength, his originality, was that he did realize the cognitive implications of poetic wisdom. To call our cosmos the primordial poem of mankind, something that we have composed ourselves, sounds like Shelley, but is Nietzsche:

1046 (1884)

1. We want to hold fast to our senses and to our faith in them—and think their consequences through to the end! The nonsensuality of philosophy hitherto as the greatest nonsensicality of man.

2. The existing world, upon which all earthly living things have worked so that it appears as it does (durable and changing *slowly*), we want to go on building—and not criticize it away as false!

3. Our valuations are a part of this building; they emphasize and underline. Of what significance is it if entire religions say: "all is bad and false and evil"! This condemnation of the entire process can only be a judgment of the ill-constituted!

4. To be sure, the ill-constituted can be the greatest sufferers and the most subtle? The contented could be of little value?

5. One must understand the artistic basic phenomenon that is called "life"—the building spirit that builds under the most unfavorable conditions: in the slowest manner——A demonstration of all its combinations must first be produced afresh: it preserves itself.

Walter Pater would have had no difficulty in endorsing this; his own emphasis upon sensation and perception as constitutive of his kind of reality would be wholly consonant with Nietzsche, except that Pater is overtly and candidly solipsistic. Nietzsche, rebellious student of Schopenhauer, might not have agreed with his mentor (or with Wittgenstein) that what the solipsist means is right.

What the poet means is hurtful, Nietzsche tells us, nor can we tell the hurt from the meaning. What are the pragmatic consequences for criticism of Nietzsche's poetics of pain? To ask that is to ask also what I am convinced is the determining question of the canonical: what makes one poem more memorable than another? The Nietzschean answer must be that the memorable poem, the poem that has more meaning, or starts more meaning going, is the poem that gives (or commemorates) more pain. Like Freud's ghastly Primal History Scene (in *Totem and Taboo*), the strong poem repeats and commemorates a primordial pain. Or to be more Nietzschean (and more Paterian), the strong poem constitutes pain, brings pain into being, and so creates meaning.

The pain is the meaning. I find this formulation peculiarly and personally disturbing because, ever since I was a small boy, I have judged poems on the basis of just how memorable they immediately seemed. It is distressing to reflect that what seemed inevitable phrasing to me (and still does), was the result of inescapable pain, rather than of what it seemed to be, bewildering pleasure. But then the Nietzschean Sublime, like the Longinian and the Shelleyan, depends upon our surrendering easier pleasures in order to experience more difficult pleasures. Strong poetry is difficult, and its memorability is the consequence of a difficult pleasure, and a difficult enough pleasure is a kind of pain.

Rorty is right, I think, in associating Nietzsche's poetics with the acceptance of contingency, to which I would add only that it is very painful to accept contingency, to be the contained rather than the container. The uneasy fusion of the aesthetic and ascetic spirits (I would prefer to call them stances) figures again in Nietzsche's ability to compound with facticity. Stevens's Nietzschean "The Poems of Our Climate" ends with a return to the primordial poem of mankind, to what had been so long composed, and so ends with the Nietzschean exaltation of the aesthetic lie, lest we perish of the truth:

> Note that, in this bitterness, delight,
> Since the imperfect is so hot in us,
> Lies in flawed words and stubborn sounds.

G. WILSON KNIGHT

The Golden Labyrinth: An Introduction to Thus Spake Zarathustra

> The surest virtues thus from passions shoot
> Wild nature's vigour working at the root.
> —POPE, Essay on Man

> Thou goest thy way of greatness: now is that become thy final refuge
> which hath been hitherto thine extremest peril.
> —Thus Spake Zarathustra

In Nietzsche's *Thus Spake Zarathustra* the main tensions of European poetry reach a self-conscious resolution drawing level with that of the New Testament itself. The book is accordingly far from easy:

> I go new ways, a new speech is in my mouth; I am wearied, like
> all creators, of old tongues.

Nietzsche scarcely, I think, recognises how precisely he is translating into conceptual thought and direct, if symbolically expressed, doctrine, the diverse energies of Renaissance literature. These in translation seem startling and paradoxical, and only yield full value to a sensitive and unprejudiced intelligence. Thus Nietzsche needs "clear smoothe mirrors" for an audience or the teaching will be, as indeed it has been, "distorted." Yet he himself, or Zarathustra—it comes to nearly the same thing—expresses no static scheme, the meditations moving with a steadily modulated interplay of doubts and certainties, of cutting satire and poetic song. Zarathustra is himself uncertain whether he is "one that promiseth or one that fulfilleth." He can be

From *Christ and Nietzsche: An Essay in Poetic Wisdom.* © 1948 by Staples Press.

humble enough, knowing himself a "cripple" upon the bridge to the future; but his single aim is to make men whole. It is, indeed, terrible to him to see them "broken in pieces" and "scattered as upon a battlefield and a shambles," mere "fragments" only. Therefore he says:

> My whole imagination and endeavour is this—to assemble and bring together that which is fragment and riddle and grisly accident.

He writes from, and works to recreate in others, the perfectly integrated consciousness, claiming to offer man that purpose and divine at-homeness which his split and bleeding intelligence cannot focus.

The book penetrates the most difficult of all fortresses, for the integration offered is all but completely presented, though without ever forgetting the evils and agonies of mortality, in positive terms:

> And many a one that cannot see the sublime in mankind calleth it virtue to see too well what is base: thus he calleth his evil eye virtue.

The antithetical impulses of love and power probably attain a synthesis more coherently reasoned and convincingly set forth than in any other work of explicit teaching outside the New Testament itself. As in the New Testament, the doctrine is one maturing directly from the poetic, not the philosophic, consciousness: therein is its unique value and difficulty. It deals not in concepts so much as forces, which themselves next wind into the eternal. The adventure is strange and daring, but the result achieved holds a finality beyond theory.

My aim is to elucidate Nietzsche's book by showing his directions: it is so fatally easy to receive a thought without the angle of its purpose. Nietzsche's artistry is far finer in the pointing of his phrases than in the organisation of his book as a whole. There is little meaning in his structure; each disquisition relies on itself alone; his repetitions are seldom elucidations. Once, however, we get the spinal, upright, pointing all falls into place; we know why this or that ribbed meaning pushes sideways, feel the beating heart of the main symbolisms, love the satin flesh-texture of its sensuous detail, and finally understand the captaincy of its eye and the whole body's forward directional poise.

But, though superbly positive as a whole, the doctrine is conditioned by a facing of all those fears and conflicts which it transcends. Zarathustra can be himself afraid. His teaching concerns something very intimate, involving the inmost quiver and luxury of the sensuous imagination. In "The Stillest Hour" he admits that he knows, but will not, dare not, speak the secret truth; and asks forgiveness; he feels unworthy, lacks the "lion's voice of command," is ashamed; and, though told not to care for himself, to become like a child without shame, yet ends knowing he has failed. He is not yet "ripe," is self-conscious, setting "hedges" about his thoughts lest "swine and libertines" break in. Some semi-sexual sanctity is in question; he lacks the last "lion-insolence and wantonness" to call up that "abysmal," burrowing, thought which he has, however, *always carried with him,* and which he will one day find courage to deliver. Thus the man who is perfectly well able is not yet willing to be true, to be utterly himself. In "The Convalescent" this conflict is peculiarly fierce: his own thought terrifies, he cries "Horror!" over and over. He passionately warns others to keep their "reasons" secret, since today "is of the rabble" and the creator, being a mother, must, as in childbirth, bring forth some dirt with every new life. Like any poet, he takes pains to render his message presentable, even though this forces a certain falsification; he will rather die than confess his "midnight" speculations or, as we should say, fantasies. And yet only he who shall have "courage enough" to liberate man, saying "thus shall ye flow, ye great and small streams," shall be "lord of the earth": which is a speech for "subtle ears." Some virtue peculiarly personal, sweet and "unutterable" is involved; something which once brought "mockery" on him, since when he has faltered.

Now Zarathustra's shame-virtue complex is related to his doctrine of Recurrence, which causes him at first both fear and horror, though its connection with shame is less obvious. It seems that some sensuous enjoyment of evil in midnight fantasy (where good and evil coalesce under the concepts "midnight" and "eternity") is the originating source and heart of that wholesale acceptance and love of all life which stamps even its present miseries with eternal status in joy. Zarathustra moves from horror of Recurrence to a holy rapture. Once he contrasts (1) his happy and creative superman-gospel with (2) this darker, immediate, compulsion apparently entwined with some secret vice which is yet the germ of noblest, because all-loving, insight. As so often, rational creativeness relates to time, perversion to eternity. Sexual fear is vivid where Zarathustra doubts his own "mountains" whilst being only too horribly conscious of his "valleys"; and states his reluctance—typical of such situations—to speak out whilst his first approaches lack recognition. Our various passages suggest more strongly a new technique of channeling, or in-gathering, sexual energy (e.g., especially "thus shall ye flow, ye great and small streams") than a philosophic exposition. Possibly this is the yet "greater matter" for which he will find courage

when his other difficulty is surmounted. We may accordingly suggest that
the triumph of his Recurrence doctrine is at once a proud resultant and a
discrete veiling of a secrecy he cannot, or will not, fully divulge; and that his
final ratification of the objective and contemporary world crystallises—as
such insight must—from a preliminary ratification of himself, unity being
glassed in unity.

Certainly a study of Zarathustra's meditations casts a light on the
semi-sexual inferiority-pain so insistent, and growing yet more so, in our
literature. You can see why Zarathustra lays so great an emphasis on psychological courage as an essential. With this regard must we read Nietzsche's
sparing use of military metaphors, resembling those of Jesus and St. Paul, as
when he urges his followers to be, if not "saints," "warriors" of "knowledge"—Blake's "mental strife"—or calls them his "brethren in war"; and
says how many an aspirant will, at the start, be fearful at the first sound of
"the loud roll of my drums." Though Zarathustra knows periods when he
himself quails, we are told that true courage is not absence but conquest of
fear, its expulsion by reliance on the higher power, the "lion in the spirit."
His gospel is frightening and he knows it, for he has grasped the one central
and shattering truth, which the Christian tradition, properly understood,
has, though perhaps without Nietzsche's purity of direct understanding,
also recognised, that "the most evil thing in man is necessary to the best of
him." Such realisation is basic always to the agonies of genius, cutting out
and up, as they must, new ways for man, as backwoodsmen of eternity:

> To be true—few indeed are able! And he that is able willeth not,
> as yet. But least of all are the Good able.
>
> Oh, these Good! *Good men never speak the truth;* for thus to
> be good is a sickness of the mind.
>
> They yield, these Good, they submit themselves, their heart
> repeateth what is said thereunto, their very soul obeyeth: but he
> that obeyeth *heareth not himself!*
>
> All that the Good call wicked must flow together that a truth
> may be born: O my brethren, are ye wicked enough for *this* truth?
>
> Rash daring, long mistrust, cruel nay-saying, disgust, a cutting
> to the quick—how rarely do *all these* come together! But from
> such seed truth is begotten!
>
> Heretofore hath all *knowledge* grown up with an evil con-
> science! Break, break, ye knowers, the ancient tables!

Such truth is not to be discovered but rather "born," created; is less perhaps
"knowledge" in a limited sense, than a psychological acceptance and re-

sulting action, a new orientation of human life. Zarathustra's message is one with his dramatic conflicts. "Rash daring" works against "long mistrust" to create the new advance. The critical faculty is present. "Nay-saying" suggests self-criticism, ethical inhibitions, social opposition, the whole burden and inertia of hostility within and without; while "a cutting to the quick" balances "disgust" in reference to the most private quiverings of personal joy and fear. All these contribute, the conflict being *itself* constituent and necessary to the creation. As Keyserling once suggested, in *From Suffering to Fulfilment,* the opposition encountered by genius is itself a necessary part of that genius. Nietzsche's uncompromising use of "good," "wicked," and "evil conscience" is therefore well advised. The conquest of ethical inhibition may well be utterly integral to the highest good. Both Socrates and Jesus were considered immoral and may have suffered preliminary moods of intense guilt. Those today who most sincerely desire a revitalisation of our Christianity must be prepared to feel horror at the first signs of any real advance. They should ask themselves this: is not their real desire for the old, safe, established Christianity, which is today little more than a conventional ethic, polished up, oiled, tinkered, and set going again, however weakly?

Zarathustra is himself a poet trying to trascend his calling. His nervousness is a commentary on the poet's job of objectifying, at once veiling and rendering more socially acceptable, and therefore immediately creative, the naked impulses prompting his work; the obscurity of much modern poetry being, in part at least, due to a new self-consciousness together with an integrity of purpose that sees and admits the twining roots in the psyche while remaining rightly diffident of a too direct expression which would, indeed, be the less potent and finally less inclusive; such so-called "directness" of expression being doubtfully authentic, as poetry is not. Zarathustra knows himself a poet, his power being one with the powers of great literature or great music; and feels how "all Being desireth to become speech, all Becoming desireth to learn speech of me," a sentence compactly defining poetic consciousness as the relation born by time to eternity, as a perpetual intercourse between them, as it were, so that poetry becomes at once echo and ringing command, or, as Middleton Murry in *Keats and Shakespeare* once finely phrased it, "Poetry is the immanent purpose of the universe become vocal." But, though he knows all this, Zarathustra remains dissatisfied:

> Thus I speak in smiles and, poet-like, halt and stammer: and, verily, I am ashamed that I must needs yet be a poet!

This thought lies deep in Zarathustra's musings.

For many reasons the poet, as such, is repudiated. The attack is developed in the section called "The Song of Melancholy," the song itself being sung by the Wizard (called a "play-actor"), who is insecurely attracted, purely for his "evil spirit's sake" (i.e., imaginatively), to Zarathustra and his doctrines, which appear as "some new and marvellous masquerade." This "spirit" or "magic devil," we are told, is especially "propitious" to all who have lost faith in the old gods but as yet found no new ones: the intellectual world of Matthew Arnold is suggested, indeed of the Renaissance widely considered. Poetry, however, remains a second-best, working from melancholy and gloom, "a devil of nightfall." Keats's *Ode to Melancholy* and Moneta's words in *Hyperion* explain the meaning. The poet is a dreamer, as in O'Shaughnessy's "We are the music makers and we are the dreamers of dreams . . ." Thus poetry, so entwined, it would seem, with the negations Zarathustra would surpass—the Wizard is shown as an *unreliable* disciple—is not only "an evil spirit of deceit and magic," because using fictions, but also a "melancholy devil." Shelley's "sweetest songs" that "tell of saddest thought" (in his *Skylark*) are suggested and repudiated after the manner of D. H. Lawrence. Shelley, who may be allowed to typify himself the poetic essence, often images that same or some related essence in metaphors of nakedness, with an insistence balanced by Nietzsche's various references; as with the "naked seraph" born of eternity-experience on earth in the additional lines to *Epipsychidion,* the transfiguration of Asia in *Prometheus,* and elsewhere. The image is used, too, with explicit reference to the more inward and secret mysteries of poetic art in his *Defence of Poetry:*

> Few poets of the highest class have chosen to exhibit the beauty
> of their conceptions in its naked truth and splendour; and it is
> doubtful whether the alloy of costume, habit, etc., be not nec-
> essary to temper this planetary music for mortal ears.

Poetry in interpretation of life "lays bare the naked and sleeping beauty which is the spirit of its forms." Again,

> Veil after veil may be undrawn and the inmost naked beauty of
> the meaning never exposed.

Now this "melancholy devil" of poetry which "constraineth" the Wizard to sing his song is personified, precisely as personified in Shelley's *Witch of Atlas,* as an hermaphroditic, Ariel-like, figure with these words: "He lusteth to show himself naked, whether as male or female I know not yet"; a physical image of the compulsion to give through self-revelation which reaches physical manifestation in the crucifixion of Christ, and is indeed implicit, sometimes directly physical, as in *Timon of Athens,* or purely confessional, as in *The Ancient Mariner* and *Sweeney Agonistes,* within all poetry; and may moreover be related directly to Zarathustra's mixture of shame and respect regarding those naked impulses from which poetry, in part, derives.

There follows the song, a melancholy self-analysis by the spirit of poetry. There is however no consistency. Poetry is attacked both for exhibitionism—the poet or "eternal feminine" in us "craveth onlookers"—and for hiding behind fictions. It does not, because it dare not and must not, tell the intimate, unnameable, truth. It is therefore "forced to lie," to be a "mask" for itself, strutting on "false word-stages." Poets are even charged with that lack of integration Pope treats in his study of Sporus. They have (1) too much "salt slime" in them and (2) tend to make "intellectual penitents," and must be grouped with "saints" and "world-redeemers." Zarathustra thus takes a sternly critical view of that dissociation and conflict in the personality which forces the resolution of poetic utterance. Nietzsche is not really attacking poetry so much as poets whose instability drives them towards that purely artistic integration with which he is not content: otherwise he would be writing a poem, play or novel instead of this book. Like the later Ibsen, he insists on life as taking precedence over art; *and yet that life itself must, to take such precedence, be a super-art.* Our song remembers the dynamic of poetry which (like Zarathustra) hates "petrified truths," and prefers "deserts" to "temples"; but it may incur the opposite charge of a purely animal vitality, being undisciplined, "wanton" as a "cat," sniffing the "primeval forest," full of "a sinful health," a non-human health, a thing of both "painted beauty" and "blood-lust." . . . Nietzsche here bitterly accuses poetry of enjoying cruelty. It is therefore an eagle "lusting for lambs" and raging "ruthlessly," like Zarathustra himself—for it is all a self-criticism—against what is "grey and sheep-like" and "well meaning"; against mediocrity. The poet's desires are "destructive," though hidden beneath "a thousand masks." A dormant sadism is felt within poetic creation: it tears both the "god" and "sheep" in man and "laughs in tearing," itself feeling the "bliss" of the panther and the eagle; wherein the entertainment quality of high tragedy is questioned. The poet "accuses life" and "wounded vanity" is "the mother of all tragedies." Once Zarathustra falls with mocking wrath upon the Wizard who has been enacting a bitterly cruel imitation of a cross-intoxicated devotee. The Wizard is an aspect of his own conscience. So Zarathustra wrestles with himself to find whether there be any impurity of negation, of destructiveness, within his own burning will to the supreme good: whether he, or Nietzsche, be guilty of enjoying his own cauterising criticisms of religion and society.

TECHNICAL COLLEGE OF THE LOWCOUNTRY
LEARNING RESOURCES CENTER
POST OFFICE BOX 1288
BEAUFORT, SOUTH CAROLINA 29901-1288

Nietzsche is reviewing the whole range of our discussion on the literature of evil and condemning it, not utterly, but, as it were, tentatively, as insidiously dangerous if not understood as pointing, as does, or should, the crucifixion of Christ too, beyond itself to the higher perfection, the one radiant and justifying positive. This is why he attacks poetry not as an easy retreat-mechanism—he is thinking on a much deeper level than that—but as often limited, even at its greatest, to that sense of tragic destiny so powerful in all great thinkers of our era. This he would transcend. Poetry and all its compassionate attendants would drag him from that other splendour, from the "day" and "rosy garlands"; would tempt him from daylight victory into its own moonstruck world. The opposition resembles that in *A Midsummer Night's Dream* when Theseus, chivalrous and kindly man of action, enters with the dawn on the moonlit night of those insubstantial dreams so close to the poetry he later explicitly repudiates. At the conclusion to *Hassan*, where the Golden Journey to Samarkand expresses the beyond-lust and even beyond-love quest, after the tortured horror, Ishak, the court poet, *has broken his lute:* the move is one beyond poetry. Pope and Ibsen—and Byron even more—in their later work vary between despisal and devotion for their artistic calling, just like Nietzsche, and are similarly at pains to create not a didactic poetry but a new didacticism, a new prophecy, a new life-way, itself based on the ethical transcendencies of great literature. Blake, Whitman and Lawrence were similarly engaged.

Therefore Nietzsche's attack is both a self-questioning and a self-counselling; a varying analysis of poetry and the final good interacting; an expression of poetry in the act of surpassing itself. Though all words, being words, are "lies to the light," though "all gods," yes and "supermen" too, he calls poets' "allegories" and "tricks," just "gaudy puppets," though poets lie "exceedingly" and "beyond measure"; yet Shelley's *Prometheus* foretold a day when language and song would be identical, and Zarathustra too confesses: "But Zarathustra also is a poet." The magic currency of words is nobly honoured. Within this currency poetry is a step, indeed *the* step, towards our aim: but, though "singing" is proper for the "convalescent," the "healthy man," that is, the Superman, will "speak." A fine truth, may, indeed, be reached through poetry ages before its expression in direct and simple prose becomes possible; and here Eliot's persistent quest for a prose idiom as a basis for poetic truth may be neatly placed. Zarathustra knows that his own poetry holds, in embryo, deepest wisdom, its synthesis redeeming both "chance" and the "past," "fusing" man's fragmentary nature into a living harmony, revealing the eternal patterns Shelley writes of in his *Defence of Poetry;* and is thus the "solver of riddles." More, it is created from the state, as Shelley too saw, from which flowers the only righteousness, a state in which the body's bliss "ravisheth the spirit":

> My brethren, give heed to each hour wherein your spirit would speak in images: there is the source of your virtue.

Not, we may notice, the hour of midnight fantasy. Poetry, though for convenience we may emphasize its dynamic energies, always fuses the nakedly instinctive with the traditional-respectable, it would gear the one on to the other, itself rising finally above the dynamic-static conflict, being both at once and yet neither. From the play of intellectual criticism upon primal jets of instinct imagination, in the Coleridgean or Shelleyan sense, arises. Though less than the greater being to which it points, and which all literature aims stumblingly to define, the poetic imagination remains the crowning wisdom of man; though it must always be fertilised by something more natural and earthy, perhaps more oceanic, of which the midnight fantasy, being itself imagination in embryo, will be a vitally important symptom.

Nietzsche's wisdom here is therefore itself throughout a poetic wisdom. With what poetic delicacy he handles the animal-spirit antinomy, seeing man as a "discord" and "hybrid of plant and ghost" to be resolved in the superman; thereby recalling Tennyson's comparison of man to just such a "discord," setting "dragons of the prime" against psalms rolled "to wintry skies" in *In Memoriam*. His impressionism very precisely reflects his doctrine of opposites: power and love, wisdom and life, eternity and creation. It is variously metallic and naturalistic, and many a paradox balances in tiny phrase a pregnant synthesis; such are "heavy" happiness, "laughing lions," "supple hardness," "merry malice," and sympathy hid behind a "hard shell." Talking of clouds, here suggestive of depression and ignorance, he says:

> And oft I longed that I might pin them fast with the jagged gold
> nails of the lightning.

This in miniature dramatises his technique, his will to catch the most subtle psychic fluidities and point them to a transcendent purpose. . . . There is no overemphasis on the metallic and hard. Impressionistically Nietzsche tends to the gentle, the soft, the sympathetic, with images both crisply forceful and of pulsing warmth. Reverence for the evanescent promptings of instinct is driven home through an image anyone repelled by his more daring intuitions might do well to ponder:

> It is over much for me even to keep mine own opinions; and
> many a bird taketh wing.

> And sometimes I find a stray bird in my dovecot, that is strange
> to me, and that trembleth when I lay my hand upon it.

This simultaneously describes and witnesses the deep morality, or ethic, if
such it can be called, of all artistic expression wherein unshaped instinct is
rendered utterly innocent by being serenely fitted to a living, and therefore
lovable, nature-symbol, such as the sea-side mountains which "lower their
muzzles to drink." Here is another:

> For I am particularly wicked in the morning: at that early hour
> when the pail clattereth at the well and the horses whinney warm
> breath in the grey alleys.

Such wickedness is clearly more profitable than a host of virtues. A delightful humour plays through many of Zarathustra's phrases: "I am Zarathustra
the Godless: I ever boil each event in mine own pot." Or again, he may
speak softly, with a whisper that swings centuries of man's spiritual history
across the page: "Thoughts which come on doves' feet rule the world."

My many poetic comparisons are evidence of the amazing range and
compactness of Nietzsche's comparatively short book. It concentrates the
massed meanings of Renaissance literature into one compact and purposeful
statement.

Zarathustra's alternate withdrawal to nature and return to man reflects
both the life of Christ and our Western poetic history, of which the great
archetype and precursor is Shakespeare's *Timon of Athens,* ancestor of
many satiric writers such as Swift, Pope, Byron, Tennyson and Tolstoy; and
also of rebels from society returning to natural solitudes, such as
Wordsworth, Byron's *Manfred,* Shelley, and Arnold's *Empedocles.*
Zarathustra's phrases often recall the many speeches in *Timon of Athens*
concerning beasts:

> Go not to men, but tarry in the forest! Go rather to the beasts!
> Why wilt thou not be as I am—a bear among bears, a bird
> among birds?

"More perils found I among men than among beasts" directly recalls a usual
Shakespearian thought:

> Timon will to the woods, where he shall find
> The unkindest beast more kinder than mankind.

Animals possess the integration man lacks: therefore "Would at least ye
were perfect as are the beasts." Disgust for man such as Apemantus's or
Swift's is important in Zarathustra's drama, and conquest of "the great

disgust" rated somewhat as Shakespeare must have rated it. He once confesses his hermit's hands are too cleanly for human society. The analogy to *Timon of Athens* is further pointed by the Fool called the "*Ape* of Zarathustra" playing precisely the part of *Ape*mantus in Shakespeare, both objectifying that ugly and cheap disgust to which the protagonist, though tempted, will not surrender. We are reminded of Timon's argument with Apemantus after his own retirement. So, in Shakespearian vein, the Ape is a "frog" and a "toad," with a "rotten, scummy swamp-blood in his veins" always eager to "croak and slander," who rages for revenge because none flattered him. Zarathustra is nauseated: "For love alone shall my bird of contempt and warning soar upwards; but not from the swamp!" He knows that "where one can no longer love one should pass by."

Timon retreating to the beasts has a reflection in *Robinson Crusoe*, a book making of island loneliness a way to self-discovery, vaguely resembling that in *The Tempest;* and Crusoe's family of animals have close analogies in Zarathustra's more symbolically important, yet very friendly, "beasts," his Serpent and Eagle. These in turn may be compared, too, to Prospero's creatures, the semi-reptilian Caliban and ethereal Ariel, and point on to other such symbolisms, that so favoured by Shelley of serpent and eagle battling in midair and Coleridge's use of sea snakes and albatross in *The Ancient Mariner*. So Zarathustra, like Timon, Prospero, and Robinson Crusoe, works out his destiny apart from man. Like Swift on returning from the Houyhnhnms he can murmur, "All these Higher Men, smell they, perchance, not sweet?"; so "Draw nigh, mine Eagle and my Serpent," and "Now only do I know and feel how I love you, my beasts. There is here no Shelleyan conflict between the eagle—the bird so honoured by Jeffers—and the serpent; nor any domination of them by their master, as Prospero's of Ariel and Caliban. The integration dramatised is a gentle interplay, a happy give-and-take. The Serpent is wisdom, the Eagle vision; or, again, physical, semi-sexual, prompting and intuition of the eternal. So these "proudest" and "wisest" creatures first appear not as hunter and "prey" but the one coiled lovingly about the other. Bodily promptings are considered infinitely wise beyond man's daylight intelligence, like the Serpent in Eden, "more subtle than all the beasts of the field," a phrase justified by current commentaries on the *Genesis* myth as describing not so much a fall as an advance. We may remember the honour accorded the serpent as an earth-king waiting to be crowned in Lawrence's *Snake,* and the serpent and eagle symbols in his book *The Plumed Serpent,* whose very title celebrates the synthesis always urgent also behind the author's very Nietzschean emphasis on spiritual ratification of (1) the human body and (2) the earth. The contrast of Saul and David in Lawrence's play *David* is a strictly Nietzschean conception.

Byron's general development, and *Manfred* especially, shows a similar withdrawal. Byron uses the serpent symbol continually, most powerfully of all in *Cain*. Manfred addresses both the eagle and the sun in phrases toning with *Zarathustra*. Manfred retires among mountainous solitudes; and such solitudes are explicitly related by Byron in *Childe Harold* to human genius. The importance of mountains in Greek drama and mythology, the Old and New Testaments, Dante, Rousseau, Goethe, Ibsen and many English poets of Byron's day, Wordsworth, Coleridge and Shelley, can hardly be overemphasised: they symbolise some towering experience or at the least aspiration enthralling the poetic consciousness, especially dominating European literature of the romantic period, and used today with power by Robinson Jeffers and Francis Berry. Nietzsche builds his book round a mountain retreat which he carefully relates to its usual poetic antithesis, water, while extending both in psychological terms. "Happy isles" are referred to more than once. Zarathustra's cave—caves are normally poetic symbols for an inward soul-retreat—for which he has left his home by a "lake" is, unlike Timon's, on a mountain: Shakespeare does nothing much with mountain-symbolism, except for Belmont set opposite watery Venice; and the mountain cave in *Cymbeline*. Nietzsche gives his mountain scenery and mountain air fine description. The symbols are clearly interpreted, as when Zarathustra climbs a hill above the sea on an island and meditates on his climbing, on the sea's depth, and the relation of the one to the other, together with the risks attending such altitudes. "Courage" can slay giddiness on the edge of abysses. His work is itself mountains: "I build up a mountain-range of ever holier mountains." His drama is set between (1) sea and swamp and (2) mountains and keen air, the respective realms of Coleridge's *Ancient Mariner* and, to group two poems, *Kubla Khan* and *Hymn before Sunrise in the Vale of Chamouni,* a rhapsody on Mont Blanc."One should not stir the swamp," says Zarathustra, "one should live in the mountains." Yet both have their rights and all highest mountains— an exact commentary on the symbolism of Ibsen's *Little Eyolf*—drop towards deepest water. Water represents, roughly, the instinctive and mountains the spiritual life: neither must be denied. He addresses deep midnight, searching in it for instinctive wisdom, calls himself a "bell-voiced toad," tracing territories of the mind to be associated with J. C. Powys; while often approaching Keats in worship of drowsy noons, heavy fertility and soft darkness, though not caring for the moon. "Like the sun" he loves "life and all deep seas." The sun, that "deep eye of joy," dominates and is splendid throughout, as in Byron; the sun and, used symbolically but powerfully, the lion, a beast denoting that psychic power urging the victory of the final message of integration at the "great noon."

. . . Zarathustra's poetic experience develops beyond all earthy-natural and watery excellences into eternity-symbolisms of orbits, the dance, circles in general, rings, domes and gold, following the usual poetic connotations. Especially interesting in view of its importance in Coleridge, Shelley, Yeats and Berry is the dome. This has, too, an Oriental impact, as in *Kubla Khan* and *Byzantium* (to be compared with Flecker's eastward journey to Samarkand), Shelley's Indian dreams, his Asia in *Prometheus,* the application of the term "Magian" to Manfred, Shakespeare's Cleopatra and Indian fairies, Wordsworth's affinities with Indian mysticism, and indeed that general tendency in our poetry to project wisdom through Oriental suggestion. Nietzsche's doctrine often resembles that of Confucius. Yet against all mystic fairylands and feminine-oriental lore, the masculine sun-powers must be proudly assertive too. That the sun is in German feminine helps to condition the synthesis. Notice how admirably Nietzsche's use of Zarathustra as his prophet combines both necessities, grouping the Oriental and meditative with, since to Zarathustra the sun was a symbol of deity, a certain leonine and golden strength.

Dante's movement from water and muddy marsh (in the *Inferno*) up a mountain (in the *Purgatorio*) to dance and brilliance (in the *Paradiso*) is implicit in Nietzsche's impressionism. Dante's poem is constructed throughout of circles; and a similar sense of ultimate harmony is felt here. *Zarathustra* is composed in terms of a poetic lore antedating and more basic than any one cultural approach. Its range is remarkable, circling round and winding into the poetic consciousness of all ages.

The book's artistic statement is thus true to the norm of at least the Western *imagination* (as opposed to its normal "thought") with a summing of the main psychic tendencies of ancient and modern literature. It helps us to place the titanic persons, whether good or bad, of Marlowe and Corneille; the strong men of romance from the Brontës onwards; the hero-worship of Carlyle, the "virility" of Lawrence, the evolutionary gospel of Bernard Shaw. But that is not all. The inferiority-sense in *Hamlet,* which later may be suspected in Swift and Pope, as men, and of gathering insistence recently in *Maud, The Playboy of the Western World, Nan, Hassan,* O'Neill's *Strange Interlude* and *The Great God Brown* and Eliot's *Prufrock* is, with the usual sexual undertones, strongly present in Zarathustra. Nietzsche's saint suffers poignantly from the loneliness of a Hamlet, of the Byronic heroes, of Tennyson in *The Palace of Art,* of the many "solitaries" of Wordsworth.

Here it is variously phrased—as a danger nourishing the "brute" within; as a preliminary to some distant worth, the "lonely ones" of today being the "chosen" of the "future"; or again, as in Hamlet and Eliot (at the end of *The Waste Land*) a "prison." Though there are dangers, solitude is basic to the main conception. Nietzsche's teaching of creative integration is closely Wordsworthian. Wordsworth's and Milton's uneasiness with women erotically approached, Marlowe's masculine aestheticism, as well as Shakespeare's favouring often of some idealistic masculine friendship culminating in the Sonnets and *Timon of Athens,* are newly elucidated in *Zarathustra.* Nietzsche's use of the word "whip" as an image of masculine control—the word is first spoken by a woman—is no more to be felt as a practical expedient than his war metaphors; we must, too, remember the book's supposedly Oriental setting and atmosphere (e.g., its camels, etc.); while both St. Paul's view of women and *The Taming of the Shrew,* where seriousness interpenetrates farce and Petruchio, as a stage figure, traditionally carries a whip, as does Ford in *The Merry Wives of Windsor,* may be remembered. We may recall the dangerous women of Euripides, Racine and Ibsen. Such emphases are one with poetry's normal balancing of masculine rights against the feminine-erotic, of reason against passion, Apollonian against Dionysian, with a view to spiritual power; are part of that dimly felt bisexual or supersexual integration—incorporating the willed idealism of a Corneille with the passionate abandon of a Racine—which Whitman and Nietzsche drive to an explicit and daylight doctrine.

That strain of demoniac revolt leading from *Faustus* and *Macbeth* through Milton's Satan to Heathcliff and Captain Ahab, with its Continental analogies in the satanism of Baudelaire, the tormented souls of Dostoyevski and half-fledged supermen of Ibsen, can only be seen in perspective from such a doctrine as Nietzsche's; which may be allowed, too, to resolve the striking enigma of Eliot's lines in *The Waste Land:*

> The awful daring of a moment's surrender
> Which an age of prudence can never retract
> By this, and this only, we have existed.

So in *The Family Reunion* the evil powers become at the last "angels." The dark revolt-substance is being turned gradually to the light, Goethe's cheery devil and the Byronic conflicts acting as pivots. The satanisms may, at their worst, be dark, as in the Machiavellian and profound, though most dangerous, mind-adventures of Wordsworth's *The Borderers* and Shelley's sadist tyrant in *The Cenci;* but against these are Byron's *Sardanapalus* and Shelley's *Prometheus,* where revolt is loving and radiant, and power sacrificial. Such as transmutation is, again, most beautifully apparent in the balance of Coleridge's two plays *Remorse* and *Zapolya,* wherein satanism, abysmal metaphysical speculation, and crime-guilt lead on, by a reversed use of the one set of symbols, to radiant heroism, sacrificial devotion, and the burning sun-powers of a transcendent chivalry.

In Ibsen likewise the dark things are gradually transmuted, his hero's soulmate becomes less satanic and more angelic, the recurring quest gets brighter, the meaning of his snowpeaks grows clearer. Today the golden quest is still being pursued: for what else is Yeats's mysterious creature in *Byzantium* heralded by the poet's cry, "I hail the superhuman"? What else, too, Eliot's deep record of self-purification by fire in his *Four Quartets,* with its conclusion, "The fire and the rose are one" recalling Nietzsche's many roses and his "Thou must be willing to burn thyself in thine own flame; how mayest thou be made anew unless thou first becomes ashes?" Where else shall we search out the meaning of the enigmatic yet compelling conclusion to Francis Berry's *Murdock?*

Nietzsche's sermon-drama includes and interprets all such transmutations. It spans with equal ease the dramas of Marlowe and Shaw, the poetry of Marvell and Bridges. It finally consolidates the various positions for which the literatures of both the ancient and the modern worlds have been battling. He wisely relates his Superman to the word "devil," knowing well what he is about: "I divine that ye would call my superman the devil." A weight is being lifted, a new direction cut out towards highest virtue and immortal powers. This is, precisely, what Ibsen in his last period was driving towards. As in Shakespeare, the power-thrust, in marriage to the love-quest, creates a death-vanquishing wisdom. Nietzsche throughout is explicitly formulating that swerve from an outward to an inner, yet cosmic, power of which Hamlet's substitution of a play for revenge action is an early symptom, and which Browning so finely develops in concentration on painters, musicians, poets and scholars as heroic material. Browning's challenge, built on a blend of power and love, draws him as close to Nietzsche in positive direction as Byron stands in creative conflict, though Browning can himself well characterise the conflict, as in *Bishop Blougram's Apology:*

> when the fight begins within himself
> A man's worth something. God stoops o'er his head,
> Satan looks up between his feet—both tug—
> He's left, himself, in the middle: the soul wakes
> And grows. Prolong that battle through his life!
> Never leave growing till the life to come!

A conflict of sexual energy and spiritual intuition is indicated in terms of "Satan" and "God," and the conflict itself regarded as good: Blake's "marriage of Heaven and Hell" and Goethe's placing of Mephistopheles in the universal scheme are important analogies. Growth is thus a steady enrichment through depth of conflict, with new evil as well as new good and continually more inclusive resolutions. This is the teaching within all literary creation; which, the more clearly it be recognised, the more inevitably, if paradoxically, it compels us not to destructions but, as in Nietzsche, to a delicacy which radiates power, and a sweetness mastering death.

The real devil for Nietzsche, and all such creative workers, is the pharisaic intelligence with its filming over of vital energies. He once discusses the "three most evil things," voluptuousness, lust of power, and selfishness, weighing them "well and humanly," and indicating their dual directions. The first may be either a torment of hell-fire or a "garden-joy of the earth," a procreative "gratefulness," a coition with one's *"strange"* other self, a "more than marriage." The second may be the self-torment of the tyrannic and cruel; and yet again, it can shatter all falsities and "whited sepulchres," and became a challenge, "the shining interrogative set against premature answers." It is the "supreme contempt" scorning "cities and empires." Power may, like voluptuousness, be lifted to purity and "self-content," a glowing love, an earth which is rosy heaven. Here the divine and human interlock as surely as in Christian doctrine; indeed, the whole book might be read as a Christology transplanted from history to flower afresh. So highest power, we are told, "stoopeth," descending from its heights of content with a "longing" which is "the virtue that giveth," an "unutterable" virtue; what St. Paul meant by *agapé*. It is an error to regard Nietzsche's gospel as limited to the aspiring, humanistic, *eros*. Power in *Zarathustra* is something inwardly gathered and next given out in generosity and sweetness. But neither of these gifts can flourish without respect to the third, and he ends by urging the right positive within all "selfishness," "the wholesome, healthy selfishness that floweth from a mighty soul," the "self-rejoicing soul." Such a passage is surely clear enough, urging that compulsion on man to face, respect, and transfigure his own instinctive self which poet after poet endures. So each lonely, thwarted, grandly demonic or miserably angelic hero, whether poet or protagonist, in the often painful annals of literary history, is given retrospectively a purpose and significance in Nietzsche's book. A whole mass of creative thinking, including the succession of Germanic philosophers too easily dismissed as obscure—it is partly the fault of a culture precluding honesty, especially sexual honesty, or their meanings would have been clearer—is here incorporated and rendered single and lucid. Each happy poem, love lyric or romantic drama, all erotic beauty and glittering merriment and deepest humour in our, or any other, literature, is placed; with, moreover, that vivid truth, so often neglected, of all poetry made plain, whereby each earthly glamour, each romantic delight, is invariably shown as in itself partial and an earnest, a momentary insight, of the deathless radiance into which it expands. All is concentrated, as light through a lens, the passive light of poetic wisdom through the ages turned to active and life-penetrating heat, a newly-conscious, cauterising, yet burningly creative command, at once scorching flame and golden wonder:

> White on a throne or guarded in a cave
>   There lives a prophet who can understand
> Why men were born; but surely we are brave
>   Who take the Golden Road to Samarkand.

That brave pilgrimage is the pilgrimage of poetry beyond poetry, and Zarathustra, or Nietzsche, more nearly than any teacher of the modern world, is that prophet.

Nietzsche sees himself as delivering a new gospel at direct variance with Christianity. He is, however, dominated, precisely as were Blake and Lawrence, by the tone quality of contemporary Christian observance. He cannot see the New Testament as a daring, supermoral, taboo-smashing book, as dangerous in its time as his own in ours, but only as it exists today, its bright meanings smeared over by false sanctimony and its steely challenge blunted by twenty centuries of ecclesiastical attrition. He cannot read the Old Testament without supposing an exactitude of acceptance necessary such as would make nonsense of Homer, Aeschylus, Dante, and Shakespeare; and his judgments are therefore as correct and pointless as Bernard Shaw's in his *Black Girl in Search of God,* blaming Jehovah for ambiguity of speech, failure in purpose, and unjust condemnation of man. He visualises the static and ghostly thought forms of a conventionalised teaching and attacks these as actualities. He sees Jesus as a "mob-orator" and "arrogant" advocate of "petty folk," trying to reduce human excellence to mediocrity; as one opposed to laughter and all for "weeping and gnashing of teeth," who came himself of the rabble, who therefore "loved not enough" and knew not how "to dance." The Christian God is as a "judge" who does not respect "love," and who in his youth built Hell. He is led astray by the fallen consciousness of a Puritanical Church, concentrating always on ethic, repeating but unable to think the smashing convictions of St. Paul's Epistles, and celebrating without living the romance of Jesus' Crucifixion; and forgets, if he ever knew, that the ecclesiastical conception of Hell is rather classic-medieval than Biblical and mainly Italian, probably because of Italy's volcanoes. Nietzsche's misconceptions stand as a living commentary both on the recurrent blindness of genius to that which most resembles itself and also on the decadence of Christianity in our time. There are, it is true, touches of a more generous insight, as when he feels Jesus noble enough to "revoke," as Lawrence makes Him revoke in *The Escaped Cock,* his supposedly defeatist doctrine had he lived, and admires his penetration of the false and Pharisaical. Nietzsche's attack is, properly, against the Church alone and the liturgical parody to the Hee-Haw of an Ass tells its own story: the ghostly, bloodless, nasalised and, normally, utterly unsexual instead of inclusively, and sexually impelled, supersexual tone of our Church tradition, has done its inevitable work: "They must sing better songs ere I learn disbelief in their saviour."

And yet he should at least be grateful to the Church for preserving the book on which his own style and many of his images are based. We come up against a curious paradox: *Zarathustra* bristles with Biblical parallels. We thus have "Pharisees," the Tree of Life, the Mount of Olives. Zarathustra observes the instinct of conventional morality to "crucify" the future of mankind in any one of creative, because original, virtue. His "I await a worthier one" recalls John the Baptist, his determination to strangle "even that strangler called sin" might have been spoken by St. Paul; as might too his "all is lawful," while his total message does not exclude Paul's reservation as to "expedience." His view of accepted goodness as a "whited worm-rottenness disguised beneath big words" and his

> Discover me that love that beareth not only all punishment but also all guilt! that justice that acquitteth all but the judge.

are echoes of Christ. So is this:

> But mine arms and my legs I spare not, my warriors I spare not: how then can ye be fit for *my* warfare?

Like Christ, he is troubled by people "crowding" to interrupt his "solitude" and is driven to declare "My kingdom is no longer of this world," with the characteristic addition, "I need new mountains." The concept of "eternal life" which is his own book's heart Nietzsche most unfairly repudiates as advanced by others: in restating a New Testament intuition, he often ignores in the passion of rediscovery—it is a worldwide failing which the greatest, it seems, cannot avoid—the obvious similarities. His marriage counsel is directly in line with Pauline doctrine and Church tradition, concentrating on its supreme creative responsibility. His superman gospel is a kind of Christology:

> Injustice and filth are cast at the solitary. But, my brother, if thou wouldst be a star, thou must shine upon them none the less.

Zarathustra is a universal lover: "Nowhere is there a soul more loving, readier to embrace, more all-embracing"; and again, "He loveth his enemies: this art knoweth he better than any that ever I saw"—though with the characteristic and delightful conclusion: "but he taketh vengeance therefore on his friends." Though attacking all defeatist pleasures in sacrifice, as well in great literature as in religious ritual, Zarathustra is himself the great apostle of true sacrifice, conceived as no reasoned "duty" but a "thirst," his whole integration-quest being a desire to make himself a worthy "gift," for "a giving virtue is the highest virtue"; "firstlings" are always "sacrificed" and the only happiness is to be an "anointed and consecrated" victim. This is St. Paul's sense of happy bondage, a joyful self-loss, an inexhaustible giving, a "honey-sacrifice" whose inmost suggested thrill may direct our understanding of Christ. Browning's Caponsacchi in *The Ring and the Book* may help us here. He is enraptured by a wild love pointing towards self-sacrifice:

> Death meant, to spurn the ground,
> Soar to the sky—die well and you do that.
> The very immolation made the bliss;
> Death was the heart of life, and all the harm
> My folly had crouched to avoid, now proved a veil
> Hiding all gain my wisdom strove to grasp.

He is like a "fly" who finds the "intense centre" of the flame to which it is drawn a "heaven." He would (in the manner of Crashaw)

> let come the proper throb would thrill
> Into the ecstasy and outthrob pain.

A similar masochistic positive is described in Shelley's *Epipsychidion;* and we can recall our long quotation from William James [elsewhere]. So "life and death" are to Caponsacchi only "means to an end," approaches to a higher dimension, *both* to be used by the "passion" called "mistress" of that man "whose form of worship is self-sacrifice." Nietzsche includes the best of both Browning and Shelley. The strength of his gospel derives from an indomitable will that man should store all riches in himself to shine with the "soft lustre" of that "highest virtue" which "giveth itself"; the virtue of the dedicated, of the artist, the saint, of God Himself. A strange sweetness flowers from this extraordinary book. Zarathustra is a St. Francis moved to "tears and song" by tiny beings of winged life, and all such simplicities among men. He is, like Timon, a universal lover; one who would prefer, Christ-like, to "pipe" his flock as does a shepherd, only wishing the impenetrability of man might allow the "lioness" of his "wisdom" to roar (like Bottom's lion) "tenderly."

Zarathustra works to release a stifled power which is also love: "much hidden kindness and power is never divined." His very acceptance of the satanic is a love, for he pities, not hates, the dark inconscient abyss, of which man is himself part, which man must help redeem, being himself potentially the only "meaning" of earth. So Zarathustra watches the sea and feels himself mystically to blame for the "dark monster's" sorrow, would by his own soul-energy redeem its agony and deliver it from "evil dreams":

> Oh, thou kind-hearted fool Zarathustra, thou too blindly confiding one! But thou wast ever so: ever drewest thou nigh familiarly to all that is terrible.
>
> Thou wouldst caress every monster. A whiff of warm breath, a little soft tuft on the paw—and forthwith thou wast ready to love and to coax it.
>
> Love is the peril of him that is most lonely—love for all *that doth but live!* Laughable indeed is my folly and humility in love!

How gentle always is the approach in *Zarathustra* to animal life; and I am reminded of Coleridge's Ancient Mariner suddenly recognising the beauty and pathos of "God's creatures of the great calm," before loathed, now blessing them from his heart. The whole book is soft, warm; however masculine its thought and steely-precise its images, a feminine gentleness pervades. Zarathustra is at least half a woman in intuition and sympathy, and can therefore the more readily both understand women and admire manly strength.

The emphasis on power is precisely conditioned by mental "humility" before creation and creative energy. After centuries of enervate Christianity Nietzsche's insistence on power as a way to grace balances that of Jesus who, after centuries of belief in a fierce tribal god, announces the rooted principle of love. The perfect love which casts out fear is itself a power; while perfected power, becoming cosmic, spills over in love. With neither can you be sure as to the process. In both a blend of love and power focusses eternity:

It is the Sign! said Zarathustra, and his heart was changed. And, verily, when it grew clear before his eyes, there lay a mighty yellow beast at his feet, and rested its head upon his knee and would not leave him for love, and did as an hound doth that findeth again his old master. But the doves were no less eager in their love than was the Lion; and whenever a dove brushed across the muzzle of the Lion, the Lion shook its head and wondered and laughed thereat.

This, "the laughing lion with the flock of doves" is the expected sign of Zarathustra's "hour." The symbolism may be grouped with that of the sequence from "spirit," through "camel" to "lion" and thence "at length" to a "child" which is Nietzsche's imagery of integration. We remember "a child shall lead them" in Isaiah's similar passage of universal synthesis, and "Except ye be converted and become as little children ye shall not enter into the Kingdom of Heaven" (Matt., 18:3). The similarity is patent, those before, the other after, the ages of Christendom and Renaissance humanism; and both a super-poetry.

And yet there is a divergence too. Nietzsche reiterates his rejection of the Christian God, regarding such an omniscient being as incompatible with creative adventure: "Shall his faith be taken from the creator, and from the eagle his flight in the realm of eagles?" This earthly world, he says, has through man a creative purpose which a self-sufficient and *absolute* deity necessarily precludes. His difficulty here corresponds to that which Milton's artistic genius so disastrously challenged in *Paradise Lost* by submitting his narrative to an absolute god; and which Pope accordingly reapproached with "the proper study of mankind is man" (*Essay on Man*, 2, 2) Nietzsche refuses to complicate his intuition of creative purpose with the theological dilemma of free will and predestination; and he is justified in that within the act of creation *both terms are implicit.* "God" thus to him means the denial of faith, hope, purpose; more, as he often asserts, God is retrospective, revengeful and cruel. Clearly, he is opposing, not the divine itself, but certain theological doctrines. He is merely working out a theology of his own: so "the womb of being" speaks to man, and Zarathustra addresses a rhapsody to Eternity, conceived as a woman, for marriage with whom his whole self thirsts and who throughout is felt to take precedence over Life, Wisdom and the Superman. His own theology is advanced in terms of marriage rather than the parental-filial relationship; that is the real difference, though both Christian thought and Dante hold, variously, erotic symbolism also. There is nothing in Nietzsche's scheme to preclude a Christian theology, comprehensively understood. Moreover, Zarathustra is not only all-loving; he is all-believing, the reverse of a sceptic; he is one who has "his prophetic dreams and signs in the heavens" and so "believes in believing."

Nor must we be deceived by Nietzsche's use of "evil," which can normally be equated with sexual stimulus regarded as the wellspring, as it surely is, of the creative life. His problem was probably the easier in that he seems to have been—certainly his book is—of the feminine, masochistic type; one senses slight inward experience of the sadistic, though he can diagnose a criminal's submission to "the bliss of the knife" as a symptom of that inward disease his teaching aims to cure. Probably Powys is right in supposing (in *The Pleasures of Literature*) that his experience of subjective evil was limited. There is no countenancing in his book of cruelty or oppression: it is precisely those elements in the Christian tradition concerned with the Cross (which he calls "the evillest of all trees"), Hell, divine wrath, and consequent defeatist spirituality that raise his anger. To put it bluntly, he sees official Christianity as a sadistic religion. To Zarathustra Christ himself is a too-violent, demagogic figure paradoxically delivering a doctrine of weakness; whereas he himself more nearly resembles the gentle, refined St. Francis.

As for his attacks on the moral order, Nietzsche is never counselling crude wickedness; the moral order, even the Christian tradition, is really being assumed, as a starting point, the necessary ground on which the new beyond-ethic doctrine must play out its dance; while "good" and "evil" are, though certainly "hints," yet hints only, the truth being far more subtle. His main point is that an established morality may, indeed always must, oppose the new good, the highest, because most original and most creative, virtue. This is not to water down the rich wine of his challenge, for two reasons. First, there is undoubtedly something we must call evil, some thrill *in the evil itself* ("How glowing guilt exalts the keen delight," Pope's *Eloisa to Abelard*) within the sexual stimulus, however blameless, even virtuous, its fruits; indeed, the more virtuous they be the greater the thrill in the "evil" concerned; and it is no less than this central characteristic of "fallen" mankind that Zarathustra deliberately sanctifies. Second, a new good is always likely to raise a revulsion and horror far in excess of anything caused by obvious wickedness; and one has only to think for a moment as to what a really new good, in our time, might conceivably be, to realise that this is so. Even though Nietzsche's strong doctrine may appear to some theologically limited, though we may in our present weakness have to add to it, fill out its meanings, by faith and prayer, yet where man's psychology is concerned he undoubtedly adds to, fills out the meanings of, the New Testament itself, which cannot be supposed to hold *all* the truth necessary for us, being almost wholly silent, except to a most sensitive poetic understanding, as to the sexual-creative impulses. A vigorous opposition is thus forced; more, it is salutary, for it levels the whole impact of the Renaissance imagination against what remains of our medieval heritage.

For the rest, there is little real divergence between *Thus Spake Zarathustra* and the New Testament. Nietzsche's strongest complaint is that "pious other worldlings" (following presumably Christ's teaching) counsel a pacific tolerance in a world where ruthless tyrannies and inhuman tortures are unchecked. There will be other differences, too, but Christ himself was an originator, smashing taboos and working direct from the creative source of life; and to be truly like him is to be likewise an originator and therefore necessarily in part different; and it is precisely this higher kind of likeness towards which Nietzsche drives. Such creative virtue was, clearly, Christ's own intention: he refused to lay down a neat system of ethics. The New Testament was itself composed from a creative excitement hard for us to recapture; we see it as static, completed, official, and past, while orthodox dogma is heavily weighted throughout by causative and backward thought; whereas Nietzsche would replace all this with a teaching forward and creative. Though both are at one in their upward, eternal, emphases, such is, in temporal terms, the main and striking difference. He offers a creative rather than a redemptive Christology, expecting, like Tennyson, "the Christ that is to be" (*In Memoriam*) and looking to an infinitely rich and divinely impregnated future as the meaning of earth.

Even so, his teaching complements, but cannot replace, Christianity. Nietzsche's book remains a book only, and in structure and fictional projection not even a supremely good book. In Christianity the drama of Christ transcends whatever interpretations we choose to give to his admittedly fragmentary doctrines. The very emphasis Nietzsche lays on courage, on the body, on deed as opposed to thought, on the misery of being "merely a poet," points straight and uncompromisingly to Christ's unswerving and heroic course as a talisman outspacing all categories of verbal doctrine, all flashing coinage of prophecy; which does not mean that Nietzsche, after two thousand years of human—and, for all we know, divine—experience and speculation, may not have the best of it, here and there, where vital truth is concerned.

Zarathustra's message is never finally delivered. The book ends with the coming of the "great noon." It is itself rather a laboratory of integration; a great drama of gradual acceptance and transmutation, a superb *katharsis;* and also an elaborate definition of real, as opposed to illusory, free will, corresponding to Ibsen's definition in *Emperor and Galilean* of the founder of the "Third Empire" as "the free necessity" and the "third great freed-man under necessity." So we watch the prophet at work with himself, in all his moods, creatively unfurling, like a flower, and going out at the last prepared, at the "great noon" of his destiny, to announce his message.

What is that further message to be? *Thus Spake Zarathustra* is a self-contained work of art, with the checks and counterchecks proper to its kind, and therefore a validity beyond its author's personal thinking. It presents the doctrine of the Superman without committing itself to the Superman's doctrine, or his acts. It expounds the prerequisites of his advent; his acts, by definition, must be strange, new, inconceivable, authentic; and Nietzsche may be no more able to describe them than we ourselves. Nevertheless, it would seem that Zarathustra must preach, with certain necessary modifications and expansions, something remarkably like the Gospel of Christ; more, must live the story of Christ.

These mountain meditations correspond closely to Christ's temptations in the wilderness (for Zarathustra has many temptations); where too you have vague thoughts of assertion, of creative ambition, of sickly towering solitude strongly subdued, as here they are delicately softened, to some yet deeper, eternal, compulsion. We need suppose no primary difference. Alone in our world-literature these two books have explicitly driven human integration to a death-conquering wisdom and strength. Christ wielded power greater than death; and Nietzsche, quite apart from his central concentration on "eternity" and "recurrence"—itself an immortality whereby man is "recreated"—suggests in passage after passage that his gospel is one that laughs at all "chambers of the dead." Again,

> Now it cometh to pass that solitude itself waxeth overripe and bursteth as a grave that can no longer contain its dead. Everywhere one seeth them that are risen.

And again:

> Ye Higher Men, redeem the graves, awaken the corpses! Ah, why gnaweth yet the worm? The hour draweth nigh, draweth nigh.

So his impressionism works to reveal that "invulnerable" essence of the integrated personality that is "unburiable" and "blasteth rocks."

Zarathustra preaches no earthly domination alone, but eternity-power, such as we approach also through great music and that Shakespearian drama where again unbreakable personality wins from tragedy resurrection and revelation. But he is the preacher also of the dance and rosy garlands, as surely as Dante; and he is all humour incarnate and philosophic; and he is a wondrous, and lovable, apostle of golden sin. In the recurring challenge of gospel against law there are always dangers; one must be prepared to recognise sexual perversion as the workshop of the eternal as surely as sexual normality is the workshop of time. We must have faith in God, Pope's "god within the mind" (*Essay on Man*), who prompts all desires and all instinctive checks. The day has passed for reliance on a vicarious sacrifice. Here is the alternative:

> Ready for myself and for my most secret will; a bow burning for its arrow; an arrow burning for its star—
> A star, ready and ripe in its noon, glowing, pierced, blessed, by the annihilating arrows of the sun.
> A sun itself and an inexorable sun-will, ready to annihilate in victory!

Zarathustra's lines blend the militant resonance of St. Paul with the deeper certainties of the Gospels. The words twang and speed unerringly to their mark. We must learn to face again the deep and enduring wisdom of Christ's words: "Unless your righteousness shall exceed the righteousness of the scribes and pharisees, ye shall in no case enter into the Kingdom of Heaven" (Matt. 5.20). Or, as Zarathustra puts it, in his meditation "On Virtue that Giveth":

> Verily, it is a new good and evil—verily a stirring of new deeps, the voice of a new fountain!
> It is power, this new virtue: a master thought it is, and round about it a subtle soul: a golden sun, and round about it the Serpent of Knowledge.

Such is the "power" of new "value" born from old "good and evil"; and "herein," we are told (in the section "On Self-Surmounting"), "is your *secret* love, the shining, the trembling, the overflowing of your soul." "Be ye therefore perfect, even as your Father which is in Heaven is perfect" (Matt. 5.48): such perfection is a perfection that breaks the shell of earthly existence, as we know it. Christ, said St. Paul, was to be the firstborn of a great brotherhood (Roms. 8.29); but that brotherhood must be one not merely of imitation. If *Thus Spake Zarathustra* seems too confident, too independent of the mournful Cross of a decaying Christianity, that is because it works not to increase our faith in any exemplar whatsoever, however great, however sacred, but rather to compel mankind to make from itself many new invulnerable Christs.

MAURICE BLANCHOT

Reflections on Nihilism: Crossing of the Line

Nietzsche's thought remains associated with Nihilism, a word he no doubt borrowed, ironically from Paul Bourget. [Jean Granier (*Le Problème de la vérité dans la philosophie de Nietzsche*, Éd. du Seuil) cites diverse sources for this term: Jacobi, Jean-Paul, Turgenev, Dostoyevski, and Paul Bourget. We should add others, but it does not matter. Not only is the word flat, but it is self-contradictory as well, in that it pretends to be systematic. Yet the contradiction only causes an accusation of dryness or aridity, the semantic play between nothingness and nothing shows that it is apparently difficult to deny what has not first been affirmed. In any case, the term's lack of depth does not simply render it inactive. Descartes, Kant, Hegel, and Bergson, for example, not only refused to think of nothingness apart from being, but were irritated with it for several reasons. (Hegel, perhaps, is the exception. In a supreme act of mischievousness, Hegel identifies it with the immediate, and thus turns immediacy into nothingness.) For one, it is the sign of the will's fullness (thus, a mark of perfection); for another, it is either the absence of a concept or an empty concept with no object; and for another, it is a void without object or concept—i.e., it is merely a word or the illusion of a word. At best, it is little more than a vestige—which, perhaps, is something. All these reductions (founded on the hidden demands of continuity and plenitude) have served for nothing, therefore, not even for deciding whether a language that holds onto this nothing has something to say, or, on the contrary, has nothing to say. It hasn't even been decided whether or not *no thing* might not precede language itself.]

From *The New Nietzsche: Contemporary Styles of Interpretation,* edited by David B. Allison. © 1977 by David B. Allison. Delta (Dell Publishing Company), 1977.

Nonetheless, he examined [the word Nihilism] enthusiastically and fearfully; sometimes by simple and radical statements, at other times by an uncertain, hesitating approach, in an impossible kind of thought. In short, it stands like an extreme that cannot be gotten beyond, and yet it is the only true path of going beyond; it is the principle of a new beginning. These oscillations are not to be attributed to Nietzsche's unstable genius or character, to his own "shortcomings." They are the very sense of his thought. Certainly the question: "What is Nihilism?" can be answered without difficulty, and Nietzsche has given many clear responses, such as the following: "That the highest values are devalued." He no less clearly indicates the origin of this degradation: "God is dead." But while Nietzsche has given a sort of tiresome celebrity to this dramatic event, he does not have the personal phenomenon of unbelief in mind. Kierkegaard's Christianity and, more specifically, Dostoyevski's, like Nietzsche's atheism or the young Marx's ("I hate all gods"), belong to that turning point in the history of the world from which the divine light has withdrawn. God is dead. God: this means God, but also everything that, in rapid succession, has tried to take its place—e.g., the ideal, consciousness, reason, the certainty of progress, the happiness of the masses, culture, etc. Everything not without value nevertheless has no *absolute* value of its own—there is nothing man can rely on, nothing of any value other than the meaning given to it in an endless process.

That analysis can no longer move us, so familiar has it become. What would Nihilism be? A mere humanism! Or the recognition of the fact that (deprived or freed of the ideal of some absolute meaning conceived on the model of God) from now on, man must create the world and give it meaning—and from the start, this is an immense, intoxicating task. Nietzsche, with a joy only he felt so purely and expressed so fully, has seen in this movement of infinite negation, which withdraws every solid foundation from us, the opening onto a suddenly boundless space of knowledge: "At last the horizon seems open once more . . . every hazard is again permitted to the discerner; and the sea, *our* sea, again lies open before us . . . There is yet another world to be discovered—and more than one! Embark, philosophers!" [*The Gay Science*]. We could fill pages with citations. Nietzsche is inexhaustible in expressing this happiness to know and to search freely, infinitely, and at all risks, without having the sky as boundary, or even truth, the all-too-human truth, as measure. We cannot read him without being taken up with him by the pure movement of this search. What disparages him is the fact that he became insensitive to this movement, a movement that is in no way a call to some vague, irrational awareness, but the affirmation of a rigorous knowledge—"clear, transparent, manly"—the kind that is manifest in the natural sciences. "And that is why: long live physics! And even more, what compels us to arrive at that: our probity!"

Here, then, is a first approach to Nihilism: it is not an individual experience or a philosophical doctrine, nor is it a fatal light cast over human nature, eternally vowed to nothingness. Rather, Nihilism is an event achieved in history, and yet it is like a shedding off of history, a moulting period, when history changes its direction and is indicated by a negative trait: that values no longer have value by themselves. There is also a positive trait: for the first time, the horizon is infinitely opened to knowledge—"All is permitted." When the authority of old values has collapsed, this new authorization means that it is permitted to know all, that there is no longer a limit to man's activity. "We have a still undiscovered country before us, the boundaries of which no one has seen, a beyond to all countries and corners of the ideal known hitherto, a world so over-rich in the beautiful, the strange, the questionable, the frightful . . ." [*The Gay Science*].

Nietzsche, we are told, had only a mediocre acquaintance with the sciences. That is possible. But, in addition to the fact that he had been professionally trained in a scientific method, he knew enough of it to have a presentiment of what science would become, to take it seriously and even to foresee—not to deplore—that from now on all the modern world's seriousness would be confined to science, to the scientist, and to the prodigious power of technology. On one hand, he saw with striking force that since Nihilism is the possibility of all going beyond, it is the horizon for every particular science as well as for the maintenance of scientific development as such. On the other hand, he saw no less clearly that, when the world no longer has any meaning, when it only bears the pseudo-meaning of some nonsensical scheme or another, what can alone overcome the disorder of this void is the cautious movement of science, its power to give itself precise rules and to create meaning (but of a limited and, so to speak, operational kind)—a power, therefore, to extend its field of application to the furthest limits or to restrict it immediately.

Agreed. And that, once more, is reassuring. The moment Nihilism outlines the world for us, its counterpart, science, creates the tools to dominate it. The era of universal mastery is opened. But there are some consequences: first, science can only be nihilistic; it is the meaning of a world deprived of meaning, a knowledge that ultimately has ignorance as its foundation. To which the response will be that this reservation is only theoretical; but we must not hasten to disregard this objection, for science is essentially productive. Knowing it need not interpret the world, science transforms it, and by this transformation science conveys its own nihilistic demands—the negative power that science has made into the most useful of tools, but with which it dangerously plays. Knowledge is fundamentally dangerous. Nietzsche has given the bluntest formulation of this danger: "We experiment on truth! Perhaps humanity will be destroyed by it! Well, so be it!" That is what the scientist is liable to say and *must* say, if he renounces the hypocrisy of deploring the catastrophe that is one of science's results—for a universe cannot be constructed without having the possibility of its being destroyed. Destruction and creation, when they bear on the essential, are hardly distinguishable, Nietzsche says. The risk, then, is great. Moreover, in its temperance and integrity, science bears this very contradiction within itself: it can produce a world in which scientists no longer would continue to exist as such, and in which work would no longer be permitted pursuant to the objectivity of knowledge, but in accordance with the arbitrary sense of some new world. In other words, by making science possible, Nihilism becomes the possibility of science—which means that the human world can be destroyed by it.

Another consequence is the following: to the void of Nihilism, there corresponds the movement of science; to the achievement of science, the domination of the earth. The greatest force of overcoming is set in motion. Now, what happens to man when this transformation is realized and history turns? Does he become transformed? Is he set to go beyond himself? Is he ready to become what he is, a clear-headed man who can depend on nothing and who is going to make himself master of all? No. Man, such as he is, the bourgeois at the end of the nineteenth century that Nietzsche knew, is a man of small aims, of small certainties, evil and inadequate; he still knows nothing of the event that is in the process of being achieved by his intervention, an event beyond him, so to speak, an event that is going to give to him infinite powers and impose on him as extreme an obligation as he has ever had, since he must freely create the meaning of the world and himself in proportion to this world without measure.

I pass over the succession of overthrows, "the formidable logic of terror," and the immense wars that Nietzsche foresaw to be the prerogative of the twentieth century, all of which stem immediately from the following imbalance: present-day man believes himself to be definitive, stable in his nature, happy in the small circle closed around himself, resigned to the spirit of revenge; yet, pushed by the impersonal force of science and by the force of that event which liberates him from values, he possesses a power in excess of himself—even without his trying to surpass himself in that power. Present-day man is man of the lowest rank, but his power is that of a being who is already beyond man: how would this contradiction not harbor the greatest danger? Now, instead of resting content with the conservative attitude and condemning knowledge, in order to safeguard the eternal in man (i.e., the man of his time), Nietzsche sides with science and the whole question of overcoming, which shall be humanity's future evolution.

In several commentaries, Heidegger has indicated that such was the meaning of the Overman: the Overman is not the man of today raised even to disproportion, nor a species of man who would reject the human only to make the arbitrary his law and titanic madness his rule. He is not the eminent functionary of some Will to Power; no more is he the enchanter, destined to introduce paradisical bliss on earth. The Overman is he alone who leads man to be what he is: the being who surpasses himself, who affirms the necessity to pass beyond himself and to perish in this crossing.

If such is the case (but is it?), we see why the Overman could be considered as the first decisive affirmation to follow the extreme negation of Nihilism—without himself, however, being anything other than this consequent negation: the Overman is the being who has overcome the void (created by the death of God and the degradation of values) because he could find the power of overcoming in this void, a power that for him has become not only power, but will—the will to overcome himself. Freed of all that thrusts or turns aside, of all that pulls down the will in its capacity to will, free of all reactive will, there is no longer anything negative in what he wills: by a free act, he dictates and decides the extent of his destiny.

However, the figure of the Overman, even interpreted in this way, remains ambiguous. As the end of human evolution, self-surpassing is thereby denied in this figure. And if this figure is *not* the end, it is because there is still something to overcome. Its will, therefore, is not free of all external meaning: its will is still Will to Power. With the Overman, Nietzsche had a fine presentiment of a man who is indistinguishable from present-day man except by negative characteristics, and because of this, he is qualitatively different—poorer, simpler, more moderate, more capable of sacrificing himself, slower in his resolution, quieter in his speech. Nonetheless, it is his essential trait, the will, that would make the Overman the very form of Nihilism, rigorous and austere—for, according to Nietzsche's clear statement, "The will loves even more to will nothingness than not to will." The Overman is the one in whom nothingness makes itself be willed and who, free for death, maintains this pure essence of will in willing nothingness. That would be Nihilism itself.

Enthusiastically and with categorical clarity, Zarathustra announces the Overman; then, he anxiously, hesitatingly, fearfully announces the

thought of Eternal Return. Why this difference of tone? Why is the thought
of the Eternal Return, thought of the abyss, in the very person who pro-
nounces it unceasingly deferred and put off, as if it were the detour of all
thought? There is its enigma and, no doubt, its truth. I should also like to
point out that, for a long time, nearly all the commentators, whether they
were on right or left (Bäumler, the official Nazi interpreter of Nietzsche,
eliminated the theory of the Eternal Return), have been hindered by this
"doctrine," which seemed arbitrary, useless, mystical, and, furthermore,
very antiquated, since it already lay about in Heraclitus. That a modern man
could come to such an idea is, strictly speaking, conceivable. But even if he
were seized by such a terror in his approach, even if he were to see this idea
as the heaviest, most anguishing, and most proper thought to overturn the
world, even then there was an absurdity everyone hastened to avoid by
thinking that the idea derived all its force precisely from the ecstatic vision
in which Nietzsche had grasped it. One of the changes in Nietzschean
interpretation is that this idea is taken seriously. Karl Löwith, to whom we
do owe some important books, has contributed a great deal to making us
more attentive to this idea. Also, no doubt, the very spirit of our age has led
us to reflect on time, on the circularity of meaning, and on the end of
history: to reflect on the absence of being as a recommencement.

Thought of the Eternal Return remains strange in its antiquated absurdity. It represents a logical vertigo. Nietzsche himself could not escape this.
It is nihilistic thought *par excellence;* it is how Nihilism surpasses itself
absolutely by making itself definitively insurpassable. Thus, such a thought
is more capable of enlightening us as to the kind of trap that Nihilism is
when the mind decides to approach it head-on. Nietzsche (or Zarathustra)
has said with perfect clarity that when the will becomes liberator, it lashes
out against the past. The rock of accomplished fact, which the will (however
powerful and willful it is) cannot displace, that is what transforms all sen-
timent into *ressentiment.* The spirit of revenge consists in the movement that
turns the will back into a counter-will, a willing-against: this occurs when
the former, the will, stumbles on the "it was." Now, so long as man is
characterized by *ressentiment,* he will remain on the level of his present
sufficiency, seeking only to lower all earthly things, himself, and time in the
name of some absolute ideal—far from the highest hope. He must no longer
be limited, then, in his temporal dimension, by the necessity of a nonrecover-
able past and an irreversible time; he needs time as total achievement.

But the return behind time is what escapes the possible; it is an impossibility that here takes on the highest meaning: it signifies the check, the
defeat of the Overman as Will to Power. The Overman will never be able to

do the extreme. Eternal Return is not on the order of power. The experience of the Eternal Return involves a reversal of all these perspectives. The will that wills nothingness becomes the will that wills eternity—and in that process, eternity, with neither will nor end, would turn back on itself. Personal and subjective omnipotence is transformed into the impersonal necessity of "being." Transvaluation does not give us a new scale of values on the basis of negating every absolute value; it makes us attain an order for which the notion of value ceases to apply.

Having thus recovered the idea of eternity and the idea of "being"— and love of the eternal and knowledge of the depths of "being"—does it not seem that we are definitively sheltered from Nihilism? In fact, we are at the heart of Nihilism. With his own incisive simplicity (which, according to Lukàs, leads him to discuss what is inhuman), Nietzsche has expressed it well: "Let us think this thought in its most terrible form: existence as it is, without meaning or aim, yet recurring inevitably without any finale of nothingness: 'the eternal recurrence.' This is the most extreme form of nihilism" [*The Will to Power*]. What does this remark tell us? Until now we thought Nihilism was tied to nothingness. How rash that was: Nihilism is tied to being. Nihilism is the impossibility of coming to an end and finding an outcome in this end. It tells of the impotence of nothingness, the false renown of its victories; it tells us that when we think nothingness, we are still thinking being. Nothing ends; all begins again, the other is still the same, midnight is only a covered-over noon, and the highest noon is the abyss of light from which we can never escape—even through death and that glorious suicide Nietzsche recommends. Nihilism here tells us its final and rather grim truth: it tells of the impossibility of Nihilism.

This has the air of a joke. But if, indeed, we want to admit that all modern humanism, the work of science, and planetary development have as their object a dissatisfaction with what is, and hence the desire to transform being itself, to deny it in order to derive its power, and to use this power to deny the infinite movement of human mastery—then it will appear that this kind of negative weakness, and the way that nothingness is undeniably unmasked as being, lay waste at one stroke to our attempts to dominate the earth and to free ourselves from nature by giving it a meaning—i.e., by denaturalizing or perverting it. But this is only a first way of translating the strange account of the abyss, one that partly explains Zarathustra's distress in understanding that he will never definitively go beyond man's inadequacies, or that he will only be able to do this, paradoxically, by willing his return. But what does this return mean? It affirms that the extreme point of Nihilism is precisely where it is reversed, that Nihilism is reversal itself: it is the affirmation that, in passing from the *no* to the *yes,* refutes Nihilism—even though it does nothing other than affirm it, at which point Nihilism is extended to all possible affirmations. From this we conclude that Nihilism would be identical with the will to overcome Nihilism *absolutely.*

PIERRE KLOSSOWSKI

Nietzsche's Experience of the Eternal Return

To Peter Gast

Sils-Maria, 14 August 1881

The August sun is overhead, the year is slipping away, the mountains and forests are becoming more hushed and more peaceful. Thoughts have emerged on my horizon the likes of which I've never seen—I won't even hint at what they are, but shall maintain my own unshakable calm. I suppose now I'll have to live a few years longer! Ah, my friend, I sometimes think that I lead a highly dangerous life, since I'm *one of those machines that can burst apart!* The intensity of my feelings makes me shudder and laugh. Several times I have been unable to leave my room, for the ridiculous reason that my eyes were inflamed. Why? Because I'd cried too much on my wanderings the day before. Not sentimental tears, mind you, but tears of joy, to the accompaniment of which I sang and talked nonsense, filled with a *new vision* far superior to that of other men.

If I couldn't derive my strength from myself, if I had to depend on the outside world for encouragement, comfort, and good cheer, where would I be! What would I be! There really were moments and even whole periods in my life (e.g., the year 1878) when a word of encouragement, a friendly squeeze of the hand would have been the ideal medicine—and precisely then I was left in the lurch by all those I'd supposed I could rely on, and

From *The New Nietzsche: Contemporary Styles of Interpretation,* edited by David B. Allison. © 1977 by David B. Allison. Delta (Dell Publishing Company), 1977.

who could have done me such kindness. Now I no longer expect it, and feel only a certain dim and dreary astonishment when, for example, I think of the letters I get: it's all so meaningless. Nothing's happened to anyone because of me; no one's given me any thought. It's all very decent and well-intended, what they write me, but distant, distant, distant. Even our dear Jacob Burckhardt wrote such a meek and timorous little letter.

FORGETTING AND ANAMNESIS IN THE EXPERIENCE
OF THE ETERNAL RETURN OF THE SAME

The idea of the Eternal Return came to Nietzsche as a sudden *awakening,* thanks to a *feeling,* a certain state or tonality of mind. Initially confused with this feeling, the idea itself emerges as a specific doctrine; nonetheless, it preserves the character of a revelation—a sudden unveiling. Here the ecstatic character of this experience must be distinguished from the notion of the universal ring, a notion that obsessed Nietzsche in his youth, in his Hellenistic period.

But how does forgetting function in this revelation? More specifically, isn't forgetting the source and indispensable condition not only for the appearance of the Eternal Return but *for transforming the very identity* of the person to whom it appears? Forgetting thus raises eternal becoming and the absorption of all identity to the level of being.

Isn't there a tension implicit in Nietzsche's own experience between the revealed content and didactic message of this content—at least (as an ethical doctrine) when it is formulated in the following way: act as though you had to relive your life innumerable times and wish to relive it innumerable times—for, in one way or another, you must recommence and relive it.

The imperative proposition serves to supplement (the necessary) forgetting by invoking the will (to power); the second proposition foresees the necessity that was undiscerned in the act of forgetting.

Anamnesis coincides with the revelation of the return. But how can the return fail to bring back forgetfulness? Not only do I learn that I (Nietzsche) am brought back to the crucial moment in which the eternity of the circle culminates—at the very point when the truth of its necessary return is revealed to me—but, by the same token, I learn that I was *other* than I am *now* for having forgotten this truth, and thus I have become another by learning it. Will I change and forget once more that I will necessarily change throughout eternity, until I relearn this revelation anew?

The accent must be placed on the loss of a given identity. The "death of God" (of the God who guarantees the identity of the accountable self) opens the soul to all its possible identities, already apprehended through the diverse feelings of the Nietzschean soul. The revelation of the Eternal Return necessarily brings on the successive realizations of all possible identities: "All the names of history, finally, are me"—in the end, "Dionysus and the Crucified." The "death of God," then, corresponds to a feeling in Nietzsche in the same way as the ecstatic moment of the Eternal Return does.

DIGRESSION

The Eternal Return is a necessity that must be willed: only he who I am now can will the necessity of my return and all the events that have resulted in what I am—i.e., inasmuch as the will here supposes a subject. Now this subject can no longer will itself as it has been up to now, but must will all its previous possibilities; for, in adopting the necessity of the return as universal law at the outset, I deactualize my present self to will myself in *all the other selves,* whose entire series must be gone through so that, following the circular movement, I can again become *what I am at the moment in which I discover* the law of the Eternal Return.

The moment the Eternal Return is revealed to me, I cease being my own self, *here and now.* I am capable of becoming innumerable others, and I know that I shall forget this revelation once I am outside my own memory. This forgetting forms the object of my own limits. Likewise, my present consciousness will be established only in the forgetting of my other possible identities.

What is this memory? It is the necessary circular movement to which I yield myself, to which I deliver myself over from myself. Now, if I proclaim the will—and, willing it necessarily, I shall have rewilled it—I shall forcibly have extended my consciousness to this circular movement. And, in the meantime, even though I were to identify myself with the circle, I would never reemerge from this image as myself. In fact, at the moment when I am struck by the sudden revelation of the Eternal Return, *I no longer am.* In order for this revelation to have any meaning, it is necessary that I lose consciousness of myself, and that the circular movement of the return be merged with my unconsciousness until such time as it leads me back to the point where the necessity of living through the entire series of my possibilities is revealed to me. All that remains, then, is for me to rewill myself, no longer as the outcome of these previous possibilities, no longer as one realization among thousands, but as a fortuitous moment the very fortuity of which entails the necessary and integral return of the whole series.

But to rewill myself as a fortuitous moment is to renounce being myself *once and for all;* it is not the other way around—i.e., it is not once and for all that I have renounced being myself. Also, the renunciation must in any case be willed. Moreover, I am not even this fortuitous moment *once and for all* if, indeed, I must rewill this very moment; *one more time!* For nothing? For myself. And here, nothing serves as the circle *once and for all.* It is a valid sign for all that has happened, for all that happens, for all that will *ever* happen in the world.

HOW CAN THE WILL INTERVENE WITHOUT FORGETTING WHAT MUST BE WILLED AGAIN?

Indeed, at the very moment when the circular movement was revealed to me as necessary, this experience appeared to my life as never having taken place before! The high feeling, the elevated state of soul, was required in order for me to know and feel the necessity that all things return. If I meditate upon the elevated state in which the circle is suddenly revealed to me, I conclude that it is not possible that it has not already appeared to me innumerable times, perhaps in other forms. But this conclusion is possible *only* if I admit that this heightened state is not my own obsession; that on the contrary it is the only valid apprehension of being, of reality itself. But I had forgotten all about this, because it is inscribed in the very essence of the circular movement that the movement itself be forgotten from one state to the next (in order that one move on to another state and thus be cast outside of oneself; the alternative being that everything would come to a halt). And even if I didn't forget what I had been in this life, I would still have forgotten that I was cast outside myself into another life in no way differing from the present one!

At the risk of everything coming to a halt? Is this to say that at the time of this sudden revelation the movement was arrested? Far from it. For I myself, Nietzsche, was not able to escape it. This revelation did not occur to me as a reminiscence, nor as an experience of *déjà vu.* All would stop *for me* if I *remembered* a previous identical revelation that—even though I were to continually proclaim this necessary return—would serve to keep me within myself and, thus, outside the truth that I teach. It was therefore necessary that I forget this revelation in order for it to be *true!* For the series that I suddenly glimpse, the series that I must live through in order to be brought back to the same point, this revelation of the Eternal Return of the same implies that *the same revelation* could just as well have occurred *at any other moment* of the circular movement. It must be thus: in order to receive this revelation, I am *nothing* other than the capacity to receive this revelation *at all other moments* of the circular movement: nowhere in particular for me alone, but always in the movement as a whole.

Nietzsche speaks of the Eternal Return of the same as the supreme thought and also as the supreme feeling, as the loftiest feeling. Thus, in unpublished material written at the same time as *The Gay Science,* he states:

> My doctrine teaches: live in such a way that you must desire to live again, this is your duty—you will live again in any case. He to whom effort procures the loftiest feeling, let him make the effort; he to whom repose brings the loftiest feeling, let him rest; he to whom the act of joining, of following and of obeying procures the loftiest feeling, let him obey. Providing that he becomes aware of what procures the loftiest feeling and that he draws back before nothing. Eternity depends upon it.

And he had noted earlier that, unlike natures endowed with an eternal soul fit for an eternal becoming and a future amelioration, present human nature no longer knows how to *wait.* The accent here is less on the will than on desire and necessity, and this desire and this necessity are themselves tied to eternity: whence the reference to the loftiest feeling, or, in Nietzschean terms, to the high feeling—to the elevated state of the soul.

It is such a high state of the soul, in such a feeling, that Nietzsche lived in the moment during which the Eternal Return appeared. But how can a state of soul, a feeling, become a thought, and how can the loftiest feeling—the highest feeling, the Eternal Return—become supreme thought?

1. The state of the soul is a fluctuation of intensity.

2. In order that it be communicable, the intensity must take itself as an object and thus return upon itself.

3. In returning upon itself, the intensity interprets itself. But how can it interpret itself? By becoming a counterweight to itself. For this the intensity must divide, separate, and rejoin: now, this is what happens to it in what could be called moments of rise and fall. However, this is always a matter of the same fluctuation, of the wave in the concrete sense (and let us simply note, in passing, the important place that the spectacle of sea waves holds for Nietzsche's reflection).

4. But does an interpretation presuppose the search for signification? Rise and fall: these are designations, nothing else. Is there any signification beyond this ascertainment of a rise and fall? The intensity never has any sense other than that of being an intensity. It seems that of itself the intensity has no meaning. What is a meaning, and how can it be constituted? Also, what is the agent of meaning?

5. It seems that the agent of meaning, and therefore of signification, is once again the intensity, and this according to its diverse fluctuations. If by itself the intensity has no meaning (other than that of being an intensity), how can it be the agent of signification, or be signified as this or that state of the soul? A little earlier we asked how it could interpret itself, and we answered that it must act as a counterweight to itself in its rise and fall, but this did not go beyond a simple assertion. How, then, can it acquire a meaning, and how can meaning be constituted within the intensity? Precisely in returning upon itself—indeed, through a new fluctuation in which, by repeating itself and imitating itself, it would become a sign.

6. But first of all, a sign traces the fluctuation of an intensity. If a sign keeps its meaning, it is because the degree of intensity coincides with it. It signifies only by a new afflux of intensity, as it were, which rejoins its first trace.

7. But a sign is not only the trace of a fluctuation. It can just as well mark an *absence* of intensity. Here, too, what is peculiar is that a new afflux is necessary, if only to signify this absence.

Whether we name this afflux attention, will, memory, or whether we call this reflux indifference, relaxation, or forgetfulness, it is always a question of the same intensity, in no way differing from the movement of the waves of the same swell: "You and I," Nietzsche used to say, "we are of the same origin! of the same race!"

This flux and this reflux become intermingled, fluctuation within fluctuation, and, just like the shapes that float at the crest of the waves only to leave froth, are the designations left by intensity. And this is what we call thought. But nonetheless, there is something sufficiently open in us—we other, apparently limited and closed natures—for Nietzsche to invoke the movement of waves. This is because signification exists by afflux; notwithstanding the sign in which the fluctuation of intensity culminates, signification is *never absolutely disengaged* from the moving chasms that it masks. Every signification, then, remains a function of the chaos out of which meaning is generated.

INTENSITY AS SUBJECT TO A MOVING CHAOS WITHOUT BEGINNING OR END

An intensity is at work in everyone, its flux and reflux forming the significant or insignificant fluctuations of thought. And while each appears to be in possession of this, in point of fact it belongs to no one, and has neither beginning nor end.

But, contrary to this undulating element, if each of us forms a closed and apparently limited whole, it is precisely by virtue of these traces of signifying fluctuations; i.e., by a system of signs that I will here name the everyday code of signs. So far as the beginning or end of our own fluctuations is concerned—on which basis these signs permit us to signify, to speak to ourselves as well as to others—we know nothing, except that for this code *a* sign always corresponds to the degree of intensity, sometimes the highest, sometimes to the lowest: even if this sign be the *me*, the *I*, the *subject of all our propositions*. It is thanks to this sign, however, which is nothing but an ever variable trace of fluctuation, that we constitute ourselves as *thinking*, that a thought as such occurs to us, even though we are never quite sure that it is not others who think and continue to think in us. But what is this other who forms the *outside* in relation to the *inside* that we hold ourselves to be? Everything leads back to a single discourse, to fluctuations of intensity that correspond to the thought of everyone and no one.

The sign "me" in the everyday code of communication, so far as it verifies our various internal and external degrees of presence and absence, thus assures a variable state of coherence in ourselves and with our surroundings. Thus the thought of no one, this intensity in itself, without determinable beginning or end, finds a necessity in him who appropriates it, and comes to know a destiny in the very vicissitudes of memory and forgetfulness; and this for the subject or the world at large. For a designation to occur, for a meaning to be constituted, *my will* must intervene—but, again, it is no more than this appropriated intensity.

Now, in a feeling, in a state that I will term the loftiest feeling and that I will aspire *to maintain* as the highest thought—what has happened? Have I not exceeded my limits, and by the same token depreciated the everyday code of signs, either because thought abandons me or because I no longer discern the difference between the fluctuations from without and from within?

Up to now, in the everyday sense, thought could always rely on the use of the term "myself." But what becomes of my own coherence at such a degree of intensity where thought ceases to include me in the term "myself" and invents a sign by which it would designate its own self coherency? If this is no longer my own thought, doesn't it signify my exclusion from all possible coherence? If it is still mine, how is it conceivable that it should designate an absence of intensity at the highest degree of intensity?

Let us suppose that the image of the circle is formed when the soul attains the highest state: something happens to my thought so that, by this sign, it dies—so that my thought is no longer really my own. Or, perhaps, my thought is so closely identified with this sign that even to invent this sign, this circle, signifies the power of all thought. Does this mean that the thinking subject would lose his own identity because a coherent thought would itself exclude that identity? Nothing here distinguishes the designating intensity from the designated intensity—i.e., nothing serves to reestablish the ordinary coherency between self and world as constituted by ordinary usage. The same circuit brings me back to the everyday code of signs, and leaves me once again at the mercy of signs as soon as I try to explain the events they represent.

If, in this ineffable moment, I hear it said: "You will return to this moment—you have already returned to it—you will return to it innumerable times," as coherent as this proposition seems according to the sign of the circle from which it flows, all the while remaining this selfsame proposition, so far as this is really me in the context of everyday signs, I fall into incoherency. Incoherency here assumes two forms: in relation to the very coherence of this thought itself, as well as in relation to the everyday code of signs. According to the latter, I can only will *myself once and for all*; it is on this basis that all my designations together with their sense are communicable. But *to will myself again, once more,* implies that nothing ever gets constituted in a *single sense, once and for all.* The circle opens me to inanity and encloses me within the following alternative: *either* all returns because nothing has ever made any sense whatever, *or else* things never made any sense except by the return of all things, without beginning or end.

Here is a sign in which I myself am nothing, that I always return to—for nothing. What is my part in this circular movement in relation to which I am incoherent, or in relation to this thought so perfectly coherent that it excludes me *at the very moment* I think it? What is this emblem of the circle that empties all designation of its content for the sake of this emblem? The soul's elevated state became the *highest thought* only by yielding to its own intensity. In yielding to this state, chaos is restored to the emblem of the circle—i.e., the source of intensity is joined to the product of intensity.

By itself, the circle says nothing, except that existence has sense only in being existence, or that signification is nothing but an intensity. This is why it is revealed in a heightened state of the soul. But how can intensity attain to the actuality of the self that, nevertheless, is exalted by this high state? By freeing the fluctuations that signified it as *me* so that what is willed again once more reechoes its present. What fascinates Nietzsche about this moment is not the fact of *being there,* but the fact of *returning* in what becomes: this necessity to be experienced and relived defies the will for and the creation of sense.

Within the circle, the will exhausts itself by contemplating this return within becoming, and it is revived only in the discordance outside the circle—whence the constraint exercised by *the highest feeling.*

The lofty Nietzschean states found their immediate expression in the aphoristic form: even there, recourse to the everyday code of signs is presented as an exercise in continually maintaining oneself discontinuous with respect to everyday continuity. When these states of feeling blossom forth into fabulous configurations, it seems as if the flux and reflux of contemplative intensity seeks to create points of reference for its own discontinuity. So many elevated states, so many gods, until the universe appears as a dance of the gods: *the universe being only a perpetual flight from and rediscovery of itself through a multitude of gods. . . .*

This dance of the gods pursuing themselves is still only a clarification, in Zarathustra's mythic vision, of this movement of flux and reflux, of the intensity of Nietzschean states, the loftiest of which occurred to him under the sign of the *divine vicious circle.*

The divine vicious circle is only a name for the sign that here takes on a divine countenance, under the aspect of Dionysus: Nietzschean thought breathes more freely in relation to a divine and fabulous countenance than when it struggles against itself, as in the trap of its own thought. Doesn't he say, in fact, that *the true essence of things is an illusion*—an affabulation—by which being represents things, an illusion *without* which being could not be represented at all?

The exalted state of mind in which Nietzsche experienced the vertigo of Eternal Return gave rise to the emblem of the vicious circle; there, the highest intensity of thought (self-enclosed, coherent thought) was instantaneously realized together with a parallel lack of intensity in everyday expression. By the same token, even the term "me" was emptied of all content—the term to which, heretofore, all else had led back.

In effect, so far as the emblem of the *vicious circle* serves to define the *Eternal Return of the same,* a sign occurs to Nietzschean thought *as an event, one that stands for all that can ever happen,* for all that will ever happen, for all that could ever happen in the world, or to thought itself.

THE EXPERIENCE OF ETERNAL RETURN AS
COMMUNICABLE THOUGHT

The very first version Nietzsche gives (in *The Gay Science*) of his Sils-Maria experience—and later, in *Zarathustra*—is expressed essentially as a hallucination: at once, it appears that the moment itself is reflected in a burst of mirrors. Here it is I, the same "I" who awakens to an infinite multiplication of *itself* and of its own life, while a sort of demon (like a genie of the *Thousand and One Nights*) says: You will have to live this life once more and innumerable times more. Subsequent reflection declares: If this thought gained control over you, it would make of you an other.

There is no doubt here that Nietzsche speaks of a *return* of the *identical self*. This is the obscure point that was the stumbling block of his contemporaries and of posterity. Thus, from the outset, this thought of Eternal Return was generally considered to be an absurd fantasy.

Zarathustra considers the will as being bound to the irreversibility of time: this is the first reflective reaction to the obsessional *evidence*. Nietzsche seeks to grasp the hallucination once more at the level of conscious will by means of an "analytical" cure of the will. What is its relation to three-dimensional time (past-present-future)? The will projects its powerlessness on time and thus gives time its irreversible character. The will cannot stem the *flow of time*—the non-willed that time establishes as the order of accomplished fact. The result is the spirit of *vengeance* in the will with respect to what is immovable or unshakable, as well as its belief in the *punitive* aspect of existence.

Zarathustra's remedy is to rewill the *non-willed* insofar as he desires to take the order of accomplished fact upon himself and thus render it *unaccomplished*—i.e., by rewilling it *innumerable times*. This ruse removes the "once and for all," character from all events. Such is the subterfuge that the (in itself unintelligible) Sils-Maria experience first offers to reflection, to the kind of reflection that hinges on the *will*.

Such a ruse, however, is only one way of eluding the temptation inherent in the very reflection upon the Eternal Return: *non-action,* which Zarathustra rejects as a fallacious remedy, is no less subject to the same inversion of time. If all things return according to the law of the vicious circle, then *all voluntary action is equivalent to a real non-action, or all conscious non-action is equivalent to an illusory action.* On the level of conscious decision, not to act corresponds to the *inanity* of the individual will. It would express the soul's intensely elevated state just as much as it would the decision to pursue an action. So how would rewilling the rewilled be creative? To adhere to the return is also to admit that *forgetfulness alone* enabled us to undertake old creations as new creations *ad infinitum*. Formulated at the level of the *conscious, identical self,* the imperative to rewill would remain a tautology: it seems that this imperative (although it demands a decision for eternity) would only concern the behavior of the will for the interval of an individual life—yet what we live through every day is exactly the rewilled, the non-willed, and the enigma of horrifying chance. This tautology is both in the emblem of the circle and in Nietzsche's own thought; and it represents the *return* of all things as well as itself.

The parabola of the two opposite paths, rejoining under the arch of a doorway on whose pediment is inscribed "The Moment" (in *Zarathustra*), only serves to recall the image of the aphorism in *The Gay Science*: the same moonlight, the same spider, will return. The two opposite paths, then, are *one*. An eternity separates them: individuals, things, events, ascending by one, redescending by the other, return alike to the *doorway* of the *moment*, having made *a tour of eternity*. Whoever halts in this "doorway" is *alone* capable of seizing the circular structure of eternal time. But there, as in the aphorism, it is still the individual self who leaves and returns *identical to himself*. Between this parabola and the will's *cure*, by rewilling the rewilled, the connection is certain. Except that it does not carry conviction.

Yet the aphorism claims that in rewilling, the self *changes*, becomes other. Here is precisely where the solution of the enigma resides.

Zarathustra seeks a change not of the *individual*, but of his will: to rewill the rewilled non-willed, this is what the "will to power" would consist in.

But Nietzsche himself dreams of an entirely different sort of change through the change in individual behavior. Rewilling the rewilled, if it is only the will's *assumption of the non-willed* as creative recuperation (in the sense that the enigmatic, the fragmentary, together with a horrifying chance, are all reconstituted into a meaningful unity), nonetheless remains at the level of a "voluntarist" fatalism.

The change of the individual's moral behavior is not determined by the conscious will, but by the economy of the Eternal Return itself. Under the emblem of the *vicious circle*, the very nature of existence (independent of the human will) and, therefore, also of individual acts, is intrinsically modified. Nietzsche says in a note as revealing as it is brief: "*My overcoming of fatalism:* 1. By the Eternal Return and by pre-existence. 2. By the liquidation of the concept of 'will.' "

A fragment from Sils-Maria, dated August 1881, states: "The incessant metamorphosis: in a brief interval of time you must pass through several individual states. Incessant combat is the means."

What is this brief interval? Not just any moment of our existence, but the eternity that separates one existence from another.

This indicates that the object of rewilling is a *multiple alterity* inscribed within the individual. If this is an *incessant* metamorphosis, we can understand why Nietzsche claims that "pre-existence" is a necessary condition for an individual's *being-as-he-is*. Incessant combat would indicate that from now on the follower of the vicious circle must practice this multiple alterity. But this theme will be taken up later on when he envisages a *theory of the fortuitous case.*

These fragments bear so many new elements for developing the thought of the vicious circle: no longer is it only a matter of the will being faced with irreversible time—a will that, when cured of its belief in a punitive existence, would break the chains of its captivity by rewilling the non-willed, thence to recognize itself (within a reversible time) as Will to Power, as creative will.

On the other hand, these fragments give an account of a transfigured existence that—because it is always the circle—wills its own reversibility, to the extent that it relieves the individual of the weight of his own acts *once and for all.* What is at first sight the most crushing pronouncement—namely, *the endless recommencement of the same acts, the same sufferings*—henceforth appears as redemption itself, as soon as the soul knows that it has already lived through other selves and experiences and thus is destined to live through even more. Those other selves and experiences will henceforth deepen and enrich the only life that it knows *here and now.* What has prepared the present life and what now prepares it in turn for still others remains itself totally unsuspected by consciousness.

Rewilling, then, is pure adherence to the vicious circle; to rewill *the entire series one more time*—to rewill every experience, all one's acts, but this time, not as *mine*: it is precisely this *possessiveness* that no longer has any meaning, nor does it represent a goal. Meaning and goal are liquidated by the circle—whence the silence of Zarathustra, the interruption of his message. Unless, of course, a burst of laughter can bear all its own bitterness.

At this point Nietzsche becomes divided in his own interpretation of the Eternal Return. The "Overman" becomes the name for the subject of Will to Power, as well as the *meaning* and the *goal* for the Eternal Return. The Will to Power is only a *humanized* term for the soul of the vicious circle, while the circle itself is pure intensity *without intention.* On the other hand, as Eternal Return the vicious circle is presented as a chain of existence that forms the very individuality of the doctrine's adherents—those who know that they have *already existed* otherwise than they now exist, and that they will yet exist differently, from one "eternity to another."

In this way Nietzsche introduces a renewed version of metempsychosis.

The necessity of a purification, and therefore of a culpability, to be expiated across successive existences before the initiate's soul recovers a pure state of innocence—all this already admits of an immutable eternity (precisely the kind of ancient schema that has been transmitted to gnostic Christianity by the esoteric religions of India and Asia).

But there is nothing of the kind in Nietzsche—neither "expiation" nor "purification" nor "immutable purity." Pre-existence and post-existence are always the surplus of the same present existence, according to the economy of the vicious circle. It supposes that an individual's capacity could never exhaust the full differentiated richness of a single existence, much less its affective potential. Metempsychosis represents the *avatars* of an immortal soul. Nietzsche himself says: "If only we could bear our immortality—that would be the supreme thing." Now, this immortality is not, for Nietzsche, properly individual. The Eternal Return suppresses abiding identities. Nietzsche urges the follower (of the vicious circle) to accept the *dissolution* of his fortuitous soul in order to receive another, equally fortuitous. Having traversed the entire series, this dissolved soul must in turn come back— namely, to the degree of spiritual excitation where the law of the circle appears.

If the law of the vicious circle dictates the individual's metamorphosis, how can it be willed? Suddenly we become aware of the circle's revelation: to remain in this awareness it suffices to live in conformity with the necessity of the circle: to rewill this same experience (the moment when one becomes *him who* is initiated into the secret of the vicious circle) supposes that *all the livable experiences* have been lived through. Therefore, all existence previous to this moment—which privileges one existence among thousands—no less than all that follows, is necessary. To rewill all experiences, all possible acts, all possible happiness and suffering, means that if such an act were accomplished now, if such an experience were now lived, it would have been necessary both for a series to have preceded it and for others to follow; not within the same individual, but in all that belongs to the individual's very potential, so that one day he could find himself *one more time*.

THE DIFFERENCE BETWEEN THE ETERNAL RETURN AND TRADITIONAL FATALISM

Nietzsche completes his thought of fatalism within the image of the circle. Fatalism in itself (the *fatum*) posits a chain of events that is preestablished according to a certain disposition and whose development is realized in an irreversible way. Whatever I do and whatever I decide to do, my decision, contrary to what I think, obeys a *project* that escapes me and of which I am ignorant.

The vicious circle reintegrates the experience of the *fatum* (in the form of a movement without beginning or end) with the play of chance and its thousandfold combinations as so many series forming a chain. As an image of destiny, the circle can only be *rewilled*, for, in any case, it must *recommence*.

Chance is but *one thing* for each of the moments (i.e., for each individual, singular, and therefore fortuitous existence) that compose it. It is by "chance" that the figure of the circle appears to an individual. Henceforth, he will know how to rewill the entire series in order to rewill himself; or, in other words, by virtue of his very existence, he cannot *fail* to rewill the entire series that both leads up to and surpasses his own existence.

The feeling of eternity and the eternalization of desire are merged in a single moment; the representation of an anterior life and of the ulterior life no longer concerns a beyond, or an individual self that would attain this beyond, but, rather, it concerns living the *same life*, experienced across its individual differences. The Eternal Return is only the way it unfolds. The feeling of vertigo results from the *once-and-for-all* when the subject is surprised by the whirl of *innumerable times*. The once-and-for-all disappears: intensity itself issues forth as the vibrations of being—an unending series of vibrations that projects the individual self *outside of itself* as so many dissonances. All resounds until the consonance of the moment is restored—the moment itself in which these dissonances are once again reabsorbed.

At the level of consciousness, meaning and goal are lost. They are *everywhere* and *nowhere* in the vicious circle, since no point of the circle can be both beginning and end at once.

Finally, and from its very inception, the Eternal Return is not a representation, nor is it exactly a postulate. Rather, it is a *lived fact*—as a thought, it is a *sudden* thought. Fantasy or not, the Sils-Maria experience exercises its constraint as an ineluctable necessity. Alternating between dread and delight, the interpretations of Nietzsche will be inspired by this moment, by this felt necessity.

HOW NIETZSCHEAN FATALISM IS CONCLUDED BY ELIMINATING THE CONCEPT OF WILL

Nietzsche does not say that the thought of the Eternal Return and the preexistence it presupposes can itself bring fatalism to a close, for, in the second place, he *does* say that his fatalism is necessary in order to eliminate the concept of will. If the thought of the Eternal Return in its various extensions already abolishes the identity of the self along with the traditional concept of the will, the Nietzsche seems, under the second aspect of his fatalism, to make an allusion to his own physiology. According to this, there is no will but one of *power,* and in this context the will is nothing other than a primordial *impulse.* No moral interpretation grounded on the intellect could ever suspend the innumerable metamorphoses it lives through, the shapes it adopts, or the pretexts that provoke them—whether this be an invoked *goal* or a meaning that is supposedly given within these metamorphoses, within this impulse, or even at the level of consciousness. In this way, fatalism becomes merged with the impulsive force that, precisely, exceeds the initiate's "will" and *already modifies it,* therefore threatening its very continuous identity.

PAUL DE MAN

Rhetoric of Tropes (Nietzsche)

It may seem far-fetched to center a consideration of Nietzsche's relationship to literature on his theory of rhetoric. Why should one choose to consider what, by all evidence, appears to be an eccentric and minor part of Nietzsche's enterprise as a way of access to the complex question of his reflection on literature and on the specifically literary aspects of his own philosophical discourse? An abundance of other, less oblique approaches to the question may appear preferable. The configuration of the earlier literary examples explicitly mentioned by Nietzsche, a constellation that includes a wide variety of writers ranging from Goethe, Schiller, and Hölderlin to Emerson, Montaigne, and Sterne could certainly yield interpretative insights. Or one could consider Nietzsche's literary offspring, which is certainly even more extensive and informative than one suspects. The repertory of the revealed or hidden presence of Nietzsche in the main literary works of the twentieth century still has to be completed. It would reveal many surprises of value to an understanding of our period and literature in general. For Nietzsche is obviously one of those figures like Plato, Augustine, Montaigne, or Rousseau whose work straddles the two activities of the human intellect that are both the closest and the most impenetrable to each other—literature and philosophy.

Nevertheless, the apparently crooked byways of the neglected and inconspicuous corner of the Nietzsche canon dealing with rhetoric will take us quicker to our destination than the usual itinerary that starts out from

From *Allegories of Reading: Figural Language in Rousseau, Nietzsche, Rilke and Proust.* © 1979 by Yale University. Yale University Press, 1979.

studies of individual cases and progresses from there to synthetic generali-
zations. That this area has been neglected or discarded as a possible mainroad
to central problems in the interpretation of Nietzsche is clear from biblio-
graphical evidence: one of the few books dealing with the subject, a recent
German work by Joachim Goth entitled *Nietzsche und die Rhetorik*
(Tübingen, 1970), starting out from a suggestion that goes back to Ernst
Robert Curtius, remains strictly confined to stylistic description and never
pretends to engage wider questions of interpretation. That, on the other
hand, the consideration of Nietzsche's theory of rhetoric, however marginal
it may be, offers at least some promise, is clear from the work of some recent
French commentators such as Philippe Lacoue-Labarthe, Bernard Pautrat,
Sarah Kofman, and others. Writing under the influence of a renewed interest, in France, in the theory of language, their work is oriented towards the
philosophical implications of Nietzsche's concerns with rhetoric rather than
towards the techniques of oratory and persuasion that are obviously present
in his style. I do not plan to deal with these particular contributions which
are still preparatory and tentative at best, but will try instead to indicate, in
too broad and too hasty an outline, how the question of rhetoric can be
brought to bear on some of Nietzsche's texts, early as well as late.

It is well known that Nietzsche's explicit concern with rhetoric is confined to the notes for a semester course taught at the University of Basel
during the winter semester of 1872–73, with no more than two students
present. Parts of these notes have been published in Volume V of the
Kröner-Musarion edition. Only with their complete publication, presumably in the new Colli-Montinari edition, will we be able to judge if the
former editors were justified in their claim that, after the seventh paragraph,
the interest of the notes no longer warranted their publication. It is also well
known that Nietzsche's course on rhetoric was not original and drew abun-
dantly on the textbooks that were current at the time in the academic study
of classical rhetoric, especially Richard Volkmann's [*Die Rhetorik der
Griechen und Römer in systematischer Übersicht,* The Rhetoric of the Greeks
and the Romans: A Systematic Survey (1872)], Gustav Gerber's [*Die Sprache
als Kunst,* Language as Art (1872)] and, on the question of eloquence, the
works of Blass (1868). There is sufficient manipulation of these sources and
sufficient new emphases in Nietzsche's notes to justify their consideration
despite their mixed origins. To claim, however, that they are of more than
local significance takes some more elaboration. At first sight there is little in
these notes to single them out for special attention.

Two main points that can be deducted from the notes deserve to be
stressed. Nietzsche moves the study of rhetoric away from techniques of

eloquence and persuasion [*Beredsamkeit*] by making these dependent on a previous theory of figures of speech or tropes. The notes contain explicit discussion of at least three tropes: metaphor, metonymy, and synecdoche, and announce Nietzsche's intention to follow this up with a taxonomy of tropes that would include catachresis, allegory, irony, metalepsis, etc. Eloquence and style are an applied form derived from the theory of figures. Nietzsche writes: "There is no difference between the correct rules of eloquence [*Rede*] and the so-called rhetorical figures. Actually, all that is generally called eloquence is figural language.

The dependence of eloquence on figure is only a further consequence of a more fundamental observation: tropes are not understood aesthetically, as ornament, nor are they understood semantically as a figurative meaning that derives from literal, proper denomination. Rather, the reverse is the case. The trope is not a derived, marginal, or aberrant form of language but the linguistic paradigm par excellence. The figurative structure is not one linguistic mode among others but it characterizes language as such. A series of successive elaborations show Nietzsche characteristically radicalizing his remarks until they reach this conclusion:

> It is not difficult to demonstrate that what is called "rhetorical," as the devices of a conscious art, is present as a device of unconscious art in language and its development. We can go so far as to say that rhetoric is an extension [*Fortbildung*] of the devices embedded in language at the clear light of reason. No such thing as an unrhetorical, "natural" language exists that could be used as a point of reference: language is itself the result of purely rhetorical tricks and devices. . . . Language is rhetoric, for it only intends to convey a *doxa* (opinion), not an *episteme* (truth). . . . Tropes are not something that can be added or subtracted from language at will; they are its truest nature. There is no such thing as a proper meaning that can be communicated only in certain particular cases. [Musarion, 5:300]

Although it may seem daringly paradoxical, the statement has affinities with similarly oriented formulations in Gerber's *Die Sprache als Kunst*. This is not so surprising if one bears in mind Gerber's own antecedents in German Romanticism, especially in Friedrich Schlegel and Jean Paul Richter; the relationship of Nietzsche to his so-called Romantic predecessors is still largely obscured by our lack of understanding of Romantic linguistic theory. Yet, the straightforward affirmation that the paradigmatic structure of language is rhetorical rather than representational or expressive of a referential, proper meaning is more categorical, in this relatively early Nietzsche text, than in the predecessors from which it stems. It marks a full reversal of the established priorities which traditionally root the authority of the language in its adequation to an extralinguistic referent or meaning, rather than in the intralinguistic resources of figures.

A passage such as this one could still be understood as a belated echo of earlier speculations, long since overcome in the post-Kantian and post-Hegelian syntheses that have put rhetoric back in its proper place, or dismissed it as a form of the aesthetic decadence that Nietzsche will be one of the first to denounce in later, anti-Wagnerian and anti-Schopenhauerian writings. The question remains however whether some of the implications of the early speculations on rhetoric are carried out in later works. At first sight, this hardly seems to be the case. The rhetorical vocabulary, still much in evidence in the *Philosphenbuch* [*Philosopher's Book*] (which dates from the fall of 1872 and thus immediately precedes the course on rhetoric) disappears almost entirely from *Human, All Too Human* on. It seems as if Nietzsche had turned away from the problems of language to questions of the self and to the assertion of a philosophy rooted in the unmediated sense of existential pathos which has been so prevalent in the interpretation of his work.

The validity of this scheme can be put in question by examining one single but typical passage from a later text. It dates from 1888 and is part of the posthumous fragments known as *The Will to Power*. The passage is characteristic of many later Nietzsche texts and is not to be considered as an anomaly. I am not primarily interested in its specific "thesis" but rather in the manner in which the argument is conducted.

The passage has to do with what Nietzsche calls the phenomenalism of consciousness, the tendency to describe mental events such as recollection or emotion in terms derived from the experience of the phenomenal world: sense perception, the interpretation of spatial structures, etc. Under the heading "phenomenalism of the inner world," Nietzsche writes as follows:

> The *chronological reversal* which makes the cause reach consciousness later than the effect.—We have seen how pain is projected in a part of the body without having its origin there; we have seen that the perceptions which one naïvely considers as determined by the outside world are much rather determined from the inside; that the actual impact of the outside world is never a *conscious* one . . . The fragment of outside world of which we are conscious is a correlative of the effect that has

reached us from outside and that is then projected, *a posteriori,* as its "cause."

The argument starts out from a binary polarity of classical banality in the history of metaphysics: the opposition of subject to object based on the spatial model of an "inside" to an "outside" world. As such, there is nothing unusual about the stress on the unreliability, the subjectivity of sense impressions. But the working hypothesis of polarity becomes soon itself the target of the analysis. This occurs, first of all, by showing that the priority status of the two poles can be reversed. The outer, objective event in the world was supposed to determine the inner, conscious event as cause determines effect. It turns out however that what was assumed to be the objective, external cause is itself the result of an internal effect. What had been considered to be a cause, is, in fact, the effect of an effect, and what had been considered to be an effect can in its turn seem to function as the cause of its own cause.

The two sets of polarities, inside/outside and cause/effect, which seemed to make up a closed and coherent system (outside causes producing inside effects) has now been scrambled into an arbitrary, open system in which the attributes of causality and of location can be deceptively exchanged, substituted for each other at will. As a consequence, our confidence in the original, binary model that was used as a starting point is bound to be shaken. The main impact of this deconstruction of the classical cause/effect, subject/object scheme becomes clear in the second part of the passage. It is based, as we saw, on an inversion or reversal of attributes which, in this particular case, is said to be temporal in nature. Logical priority is uncritically deduced from a contingent temporal priority: we pair the polarities outside/inside with cause/effect on the basis of a temporal polarity before/after (or early/late) that remains un-reflected. The result is cumulative error, "the consequence of all previous causal fictions," which as far as the "objective" world is concerned, are forever tied to "the old error of original Cause." This entire process of substitution and reversal is conceived by Nietzsche—and this is the main point for us in this context—as a linguistic event. The passage concludes as follows:

> The whole notion of an "inner experience" enters our consciousness only after it has found a language that the individual *understands*—i.e., a translation of a situation into a *familiar* situation—: "to understand," naïvely put merely means: to be able to express something old and familiar.
>
> [Schlechta, 3:805]

What is here called "language" is the medium within which the play of reversals and substitutions that the passage describes takes place. This medium, or property of language, is therefore the possibility of substituting binary polarities such as before for after, early for late, outside for inside, cause for effect, without regard for the truth-value of these structures. But this is precisely how Nietzsche also defines the rhetorical figure, the paradigm of all language. In the Course on Rhetoric, metonymy is characterized as what rhetoricians also call metalepsis, "the exchange or substitution of cause and effect" and one of the examples given is, revealingly enough, the substitution of "tongue" for language. Later in the same notes metonymy is also defined as hypallagus and characterized as follows:

> The abstract nouns are properties within and outside ourselves that are being torn away from their supports and considered to be autonomous entities. . . . Such concepts, which owe their existence only to our feelings, are posited as if they were the inner essence of things: we attribute to events a cause which in truth is only an effect. The abstractions create the illusion as if *they* were the entity that causes the properties, whereas they receive their objective, iconic existence [*bildliches Dasein*] only from us as a consequence of these very properties.
>
> [Musarion, 5:319]

Practically the same text that, in 1872, explicitly defines metonymy as the prototype of all figural language, describes, in 1888, a metaphysical construct (the phenomenalism of consciousness) as susceptible of being deconstructed as soon as one is made aware of its linguistic, rhetorical structure. We are not here concerned with the consequences of this critique of phenomenalism which is also, in many respects, a prefigurative critique of what will later become known as phenomenology. Readers of *The Will to Power* know that this critique by no means pretends to discard phenomenalism, but puts us on our guard against the tendency to hypostatize consciousness into an authoritative ontological category. And they will also recognize that the pattern of argument here directed against the concept of consciousness is the same pattern that underlies the critique of the main categories that make up traditional metaphysics: the concepts of identity, of causality, of the object and the subject, of truth, etc. We can legitimately assert therefore that the key to Nietzsche's critique of metaphysics—which has, perhaps misleadingly, been described as a mere *reversal* of metaphysics or of Plato—lies in the rhetorical model of the trope or, if one prefers to call it that way, in literature as the language most explicitly grounded in rhetoric.

The idea of a reversal or an exchange of properties (in the previous example, it is the exchange of the attributes of place and causality) is constitutively paired by Nietzsche to the idea of error: the critical deconstruction shows that philosophical models such as the phenomenalism of consciousness are indeed aberrations whose systematic recurrence extends throughout the entirety of classical metaphysics. Would it not follow that, since the aberration turns out to be based on a rhetorical substitution, it would suffice to become aware of this in order to undo the pattern and restore the properties to their "proper" place? If attributes of time and attributes of cause have been improperly associated with each other, one might be able to uncross, so to speak, the polarities that have been exchanged in order to recover a measure of truth. In the example at hand, we could conceivably eliminate the misleading temporal scheme that led to the confusion, and substitute for the derived cause, mistakenly assumed to have an objective existence in the outside world, an authentic cause that could be inferred from the critical deconstruction of the aberrant one. Granted that the misinterpretation of reality that Nietzsche finds systematically repeated throughout the tradition is indeed rooted in the rhetorical structure of language, can we then not hope to escape from it by an equally systematic cleansing of this language from its dangerously seductive figural properties? Is it not possible to progress from the rhetorical language of literature to a language that, like the language of science or mathematics, would be epistemologically more reliable? The ambivalence of Nietzsche's attitude towards science and literature, as it appears, for example, in the use of the term science in the title of "la gaya scienza" or in the later fragments that look back upon *The Birth of Tragedy,* indicates the complexity of his position. One can read these texts as a glorification as well as a denunciation of literature. The general drift of Nietzsche's thought, on this point, can be better understood by taking into account texts that precede the 1873 Course on Rhetoric, especially the never-completed *Philosophenbuch.*

For the very question we are considering, the possibility of escaping from the pitfalls of rhetoric by becoming aware of the rhetoricity of language, is central to the entire *Philosophenbuch* and its only completed unit, the essay *On Truth and Lie in an Extra-Moral Sense* [*Über Wahrheit und Lüge im aussermoralischen Sinn*]. This essay flatly states the necessary subversion of truth by rhetoric as the distinctive feature of all language. "What is truth?" asks Nietzsche, and he answers:

A moving army of metaphors, metonymies and anthropomorphisms, in short a summa of human relationships that are being

> poetically and rhetorically sublimated, transposed, and beauti-
> fied until, after long and repeated use, a people considers them as
> solid, canonical, and unavoidable. Truths are illusions whose
> illusionary nature has been forgotten, metaphores that have been
> used up and have lost their imprint and that now operate as mere
> metal, no longer as coins.

What is being forgotten in this false literalism is precisely the rhetorical, symbolic quality of all language. The degradation of metaphor into literal meaning is not condemned because it the forgetting of a truth but much rather because it forgets the un-truth, the lie that the metaphor was in the first place. It is a naïve belief in the proper meaning of the metaphor without awareness of the problematic nature of its factual, referential foundation.

The first step of the Nietzschean deconstruction therefore reminds us, as in the above quotation, of the figurality of all language. In this text, contrary to what happens in *The Birth of Tragedy*, this insight is openly stated as the main theme of the essay. Does it follow that the text therefore escapes from the kind of error it denounces? And since we can make the possibility of this error distinctive of literature in general, does it then follow that the essay *On Lie and Truth* is no longer literature but something closer to science—as Wittgenstein's *Tractatus* could claim to be scientific rather than literary? Or, if we call a hybrid text like this one "philosophical," can we then define philosophy as the systematic demystification of literary rhetoric?

The text proceeds in its deconstructive enterprise by putting into question some of the concepts that will also be targets of the later critique of metaphysics in *The Will of Power*. It shows, for example, that the idea of individuation, of the human subject as a privileged viewpoint, is a mere metaphor by means of which man protects himself from his insignificance by forcing his own interpretation of the world upon the entire universe, substituting a human-centered set of meanings that is reassuring to his vanity for a set of meanings that reduces him to being a mere transitory accident in the cosmic order. The metaphorical substitution is aberrant but no human self could come into being without this error. Faced with the truth of its nonexistence, the self would be consumed as an insect is consumed by the flame that attracts it. But the text that asserts this annihilation of the self is not consumed, because it still sees itself as the center that produces the affirmation. The attributes of centrality and of selfhood are being exchanged in the medium of the language. Making the language that denies the self into a center rescues the self linguistically at the same time that it asserts its insignificance, its emptiness as a mere figure of speech. It can only persist as self if it is displaced into the text that denies it. The self which was at first the center of the language as its empirical referent now becomes the language of the center as fiction, as metaphor of the self. What was originally a simply referential text now becomes the text of a text, the figure of a figure. The deconstruction of the self as a metaphor does not end in the rigorous separation of the two categories (self and figure) from each other but ends instead in an exchange of properties that allows for their mutual persistence at the expense of literal truth. This process is exactly the same as what Nietzsche describes as the exemplary "lie" of language: "The liar uses the valid designations, words, to make the unreal appear real. . . . He misuses the established linguistic conventions by *arbitrary substitutions or even reversals* of the names." [Schlecta, 3:311] By calling the subject a text, the text calls itself, to some extent, a subject. The lie is raised to a new figural power, but it is nonetheless a lie. By asserting in the mode of truth that the self is a lie, we have not escaped from deception. We have merely reversed the usual scheme which derives truth from the convergence of self and other by showing that the fiction of such a convergence is used to allow for the illusion of selfhood to originate.

The pattern is perhaps clearest in the reversal of the categories of good and evil as they combine with those of truth and lie. The usual scheme derives good from truth and evil from falsehood. But Nietzsche tells the tale of the reversed pattern: in order to survive in society, man began by lying.

> [Then] man forgets that this is the case: his lying then is no longer conscious and is founded on age-old habit—and it is *by this nonawareness,* by this forgetting that he develops a sense of truth. Because he feels obliged to designate a certain thing as "red," another as "cold," a third as "mute," a moral impulse oriented towards truth is awakened: in opposition to the liar, who is trusted by no one and excluded from the group, man discovers the respectability, the reliability and the use of truth.

Thus moral virtue is shown to originate out of lies. But the text cannot go to rest in this deconstruction that would justify, to some extent, the morality of deceit (as we find it, for example, within a political context, in Machiavelli or in Rousseau). For if we believe in the morality of deceit, we also have to believe in the evil of truth, and to the extent that the society is held together by means of deceit, the open assertion of this fact will also destroy the moral order. It could hardly be said, without further qualification, that a text like this one is socially or morally uplifting. Once again, the reversal of polarities

has not led to a restoration of literal truth—in this case, it would be the
assertion that moral education should increase one's skill at lying—but has
driven us further into the complications of rhetorical delusion. We may have
changed the rhetorical mode but we certainly have not escaped from rhetoric. This could hardly have been expected. The original pairing of rhetoric
with error, as we encounter it from the Course on Rhetoric to *The Will to
Power* was based on the cross-shaped reversal of properties that rhetoricians call chiasmus. And it turns out that the very process of deconstruction,
as it functions in this text, is one more such reversal that repeats the selfsame
rhetorical structure. All rhetorical structures whether we call them metaphor, metonymy, chiasmus, metalepsis, hypallagus, or whatever, are based
on substitutive reversals, and it seems unlikely that one more such reversal
over and above the ones that have already taken place would suffice to
restore things to their proper order. One more "turn" or trope added to a
series of earlier reversals will not stop the turn towards error. A text like *On
Truth and Lie,* although it presents itself legitimately as a demystification of
literary rhetoric remains entirely literary, rhetorical, and deceptive itself.
Does this mean that it will end up in a glorification of literature over science
or, as is sometimes claimed of Nietzsche, in a purely literary conception of
philosophy?

Two quotations from the *Philosophenbuch,* closely contemporary to
On Truth and Lie, fully reveal the ambiguity inherent in the question. On
the one hand, the truth-value of literature, albeit a negative one, is recog-
nized and asserted. Art is no longer associated with the Dionysian immediacy of music but is now openly Socratic in its deconstructive function. It
is therefore, of all human activities, the only one that can lay claim to truth:
"Art treats appearance as appearance; its aim is precisely *not* to deceive, it
is therefore *true.*" But the truth of appearance, unlike the truth of being, is
not a threat or a passion that could be described in terms similar to those
used in *The Birth of Tragedy* to evoke the Dionysian pathos of truth. It can
therefore be said that it stands above pleasure and pain, in the ordinary
sense of these terms. The artist, who is truthful in his recognition of illusion
and of lie for what they are, thus gains a special kind of affective freedom,
a euphoria which is that of a *joyful* wisdom or of the Homeric *Heiterkeit*
and that differs entirely from the pleasure principle tied to libido and desire.
"As long as man looks for truth *in the world,* he stands under the domi-
nance of desire [*unter der Herrschaft des Triebes*]: he wants pleasure, not
truth; he wants the belief in truth and the pleasurable effects of this belief."
Only the artist who can conceive of the entire world as appearance is able
to consider it without desire: this leads to the feeling of liberation and

weightlessness that characterizes the man freed from the constraints of referential truth, what Barthes, in more recent times, has referred to as "la
libération du significant." *On Truth and Lie* describes the euphoria of this
type of "truth":

> The intellect, this master of deceit, feels itself freed from its
> habitual servitude when it is allowed to deceive without direct
> harm. Then it celebrates its own saturnalia. It is never so rich, so
> seductive, proud, clever and outrageous: with inventive satisfac-
> tion, it juggles metaphors and tears out [*verrückt*] the border-
> marks of abstractions. For example, he considers the river as if
> it were the moving roadway that carries man to where he would
> otherwise have to walk. . . . It imitates human existence as if it
> were a fine thing and declares itself entirely pleased with it.

This attractive pairing of Heraclites with Stendhal is however not devoid of
warning signals. It has its own pseudo-teleology, the flow of time delighting
in the self-sufficient, innocent spectacle of its own motion. But if this movement is reduced to the mere appearance that it is, it also loses its foundation
and becomes one among the various other metaphors of self-destruction
disseminated throughout this brief text: the insect and the fluttering light,
the conceptual pyramid that turns out to be a tomb, the painter deprived of
his hands, man asleep on the back of a tiger. The implicit threat in all these
images is very similar to the threat implied in mistaking a river for a road.
The critical deconstruction that leads to the discovery of the literary, rhetorical nature of the philosophical claim to truth is genuine enough and
cannot be refuted: literature turns out to be the main topic of philosophy
and the model for the kind of truth to which it aspires. But when literature
seduces us with the freedom of its figural combinations, so much airier and
lighter than the labored constructs of concepts, it is not the less deceitful
because it asserts its own deceitful properties. The conclusion of the essay
shows the artist in a not particularly enviable situation: he is indeed freer
but "he suffers more [than the conceptual philosopher] *when* he suffers; and
he suffers more often, because he does not learn from experience and always
again falls in the same trap in which he fell in the first place. In his suffering,
he is then just as foolish [*unvernünftig*] as in his happiness: he complains
loudly and can find no consolation." An aphorism that dates from exactly
the same period puts it more bluntly and from a less personal point of view:
it may be true that art sets the right norm for truth, but "Truth kills, indeed
kills itself (insofar that it realizes its own foundation in error)." Philosophy

turns out to be an endless reflection on its own destruction at the hands of literature.

This endless reflection is itself a rhetorical mode, since it is unable ever to escape from the rhetorical deceit it denounces. The definition of this mode lies beyond our present scope, though we get some indication from the just-quoted description of the artist's plight in *On Truth and Lie* as well as from the general tonality and structure of this text. First of all, the description is certainly not a tragic one: the suffering described in the passage, as well as the happiness that precedes it, cannot be taken seriously, since both are so clearly the result of foolishness. The same foolishness extends to the text itself, for the artist-author of the text, as artist, is just as vulnerable to it as the artist-figure described in the text. The wisdom of the text is self-destructive (art is true but truth kills itself), but this self-destruction is infinitely displaced in a series of successive rhetorical reversals which, by the endless repetition of the same figure, keep it suspended between truth and the death of this truth. A threat of immediate destruction, stating itself as a figure of speech, thus becomes the permanent repetition of this threat. Since this repetition is a temporal event, it can be narrated sequentially, but what it narrates, the subject matter of the story, is itself a mere figure. A non-referential, repetitive text narrates the story of a literally destructive but nontragic linguistic event. We could call this rhetorical mode, which is that of the "conte philosophique" *On Truth and Lie* and, by extension, of all philosophical discourse, an ironic allegory—but only if we understand "irony" more in the sense of Friedrich Schlegel than of Thomas Mann. The place where we might recover some of this sense is in Nietzsche's own work, not in that of his assumed continuators.

This conclusion as to the fundamentally ironic and allegorical nature of Nietzsche's discourse projects its effect on the works that follow and on those that precede the *Philosophenbuch* as well as on the relationship between the two segments that are thus being more or less arbitrarily isolated. How an ironic reading of an allegorical text such as *Zarathustra* or *The Genealogy of Morals*, or the allegorical reading of ironic aphoristic sequences from *The Gay Science* or *The Will to Power* would have to proceed cannot be outlined here, however sketchily. It may be more productive, in conclusion, to observe how an early text such as *The Birth of Tragedy* fits into this pattern. For one of the most persistent ways in which the illusion that rhetorical blindness can be overcome manifests itself is by the transference of what Nietzsche calls "the old error of original cause" from the *statement* to the *history* of the text. While granting the ambivalence of the later Nietzsche on the subject of truth, one may contrast this wariness with the relative naïveté of the earlier works. Particular texts from, say, *On Truth and Lie* on, can be considered to be epistemologically destructive, but by presenting them as a development moving beyond the assumed mystification of the earlier writings, the "history" of Nietzsche's work as a whole remains that of a narrative moving from false to true, from blindness to insight. But the question remains whether the pattern of this narrative is "historical," i.e., revelatory of a teleological meaning, or "allegorical," i.e., repetitive of a potential confusion between figural and referential statement. Is Nietzsche's work structured as a process, a movement of "becoming"— and Nietzsche's late reference to "the innocence of becoming" is well known—or as a repetition? The importance of the question is apparent from the near-obsessive way in which Nietzsche himself, as well as his interpreters, have been returning to the enigmas of the early *Birth of Tragedy*.

The obvious pathos and exaltations of *The Birth of Tragedy* seems entirely incompatible with irony. It is difficult not to read it as a plea for the unmediated presence of the will, for a truly tragic over an ironic art. If this were indeed the case, then one would have to assume a genuine development, even a conversion within Nietzsche's thought during the years immediately following the writing of *The Birth of Tragedy*. The conversion could have been brought about by his reflections on rhetoric as they appear in the *Philosophenbuch* and in the 1873 course notes, and it would also be apparent in the reaction against Wagner and Schopenhauer in the *Unzeitgemässe Betrachtungen*. The structure of the work as a whole would then be essentially different from that described and acted out in *On Truth and Lie*.

A more rhetorically aware reading of *The Birth of Tragedy* shows that all the authoritative claims that it seems to make can be undermined by means of statements provided by the text itself. And if one also takes into account notes written for *The Birth of Tragedy* but not incorporated in the published text, the ironization implicitly present in the final version becomes quite explicit. Moreover, the forthcoming publication, in the new critical edition of Nietzsche's works, of further lateral material for *The Birth of Tragedy,* shows that the exclusion of these notes was dictated by considerations that disrupt the system of epistemological authority even more deeply. We are told, in these fragments, that the valorization of Dionysos as the primary source of truth is a tactical necessity rather than a substantial affirmation. Nietzsche's auditors have to be spoken to in Dionysian terms because, unlike the Greeks, they are unable to understand the Apollonian language of figure and appearance. In pseudo-historical arguments, reminiscent of Hölderlin's considerations on the dialectical relationship between the Hellenic and the Western world, Nietzsche writes: "The epic fable of the Ancients represented the Dionysian in images. For us, it is the Dionysian that represents (symbolizes) the image. In Antiquity, the Dionysian was explained by the image. Now it is the image that is explained by Dionysos. We have therefore an exactly reversed relationship. . . . For them, the world of representation was clear; for us, it is the Dionysian world that we understand." It follows that the entire system of valorization at work in *The Birth of Tragedy* can be reversed at will. The Dionysian vocabulary is used only to make the Apollonian mode that deconstructs it more intelligible to a mystified audience. This exchange of attributes involving the categories of truth and appearance deprives the two poles of their authority. The binary polarity that structures the narrative of the text turns out to be the same figure we have encountered in all previous examples, the same "reversal of names" that was mentioned in *On Truth and Lie.* If we read Nietzsche with the rhetorical awareness provided by his own theory of rhetoric we find that the general structure of his work resembles the endlessly repeated gesture of the artist "who does not learn from experience and always again falls in the same trap." What seems to be most difficult to admit is that this allegory of errors is the very model of philosophical rigor.

GILLES DELEUZE

Active and Reactive

1. THE BODY

Spinoza suggested a new direction for the sciences and philosophy. He said that we do not even know what a body *can do*, we talk about consciousness and spirit and chatter on about it all, but we do not know what a body is capable of, what forces belong to it or what they are preparing for. Nietzsche knew that the hour had come, "We are in the phase of modesty of consciousness" [*The Will to Power;* hereafter referred to as *WP*]. To remind consciousness of its necessary modesty is to take it for what it is: a symptom; nothing but the symptom of a deeper transformation and of the activities of entirely nonspiritual forces. "Perhaps the body is the only factor in all spiritual development." What is consciousness? Like Freud, Nietzsche thinks that consciousness is the region of the ego affected by the external world [*WP, The Gay Science;* hereafter referred to as *GS*]. However, consciousness is defined less in relation to exteriority (in terms of the real) than in relation to *superiority* (in terms of values). This distinction is essential to a general conception of consciousness and the unconscious. In Nietzsche consciousness is always the consciousness of an inferior in relation to a superior to which he is subordinated or into which he is "incorporated." Consciousness is never self-consciousness, but the consciousness of an ego in relation to a self which is not itself conscious. It is not the master's consciousness but the slave's consciousness in relation to a master who is not himself conscious. "Consciousness usually only appears when a whole wants to subordinate itself to a superior whole . . . Consciousness is born in

From *Nietzsche and Philosophy,* translated by Hugh Tomlinson. © 1983 by the Athlone Press. Columbia University Press, 1983.

relation to a being of which we could be a function." [*La Volonté de Puissance;* hereafter referred to as *VP*. This is not available in English and has not been fully collated with the standard arrangement which is also known as the *Will to Power (WP)* . . . alongside references to . . . (*VP*).] This is the servility of consciousness; it merely testifies to the "formation of a superior body."

What is the body? We do not define it by saying that it is a field of forces, a nutrient medium fought over by a plurality of forces. For in fact there is no "medium," no field of forces or battle. There is no quantity of reality, all reality is already quantity of force. There are nothing but quantities of force in mutual "relations of tension" (*WP*). Every force is related to others and it either obeys or commands. What defines a body is this relation between dominant and dominated forces. Every relationship of forces constitutes a body—whether it is chemical, biological, social or political. Any two forces, being unequal, constitute a body as soon as they enter into a relationship. This is why the body is always the fruit of chance, in the Nietzschean sense, and appears as the most "astonishing" thing, much more astonishing, in fact, than consciousness and spirit. But chance, the relation of force with force, is also the essence of force. The birth of a living body is not therefore surprising since every body is living, being the "arbitrary" product of the forces of which it is composed. Being composed of a plurality of irreducible forces the body is a multiple phenomenon, its unity is that of a multiple phenomenon, a "unity of domination." In a body the superior or dominant forces are known as *active* and the inferior or dominated forces are known as *reactive*. Active and reactive are precisely the original qualities which express the relation of force with force. Because forces which enter into relation do not have quantity without each of them having, at the same time, the quality corresponding to their difference in quantity as such. This difference between forces qualified according to their quantity as active or reactive will be called *hierarchy*.

2. THE DISTINCTION OF FORCES

Inferior forces do not, by obeying, cease to be forces distinct from those which command. Obeying is a quality of force as such and relates to power just as much as commanding does: "individual power is by no means surrendered. In the same way, there is in commanding an admission that the absolute power of the opponent has not been vanquished, incorporated, disintegrated. 'Obedience' and 'commanding' are forms of struggle" (*WP*). Inferior forces are defined as reactive; they lose nothing of their force, of their quantity of force, they exercise it by securing mechanical means and final ends, by fulfilling the conditions of life and the functions and tasks of conversation, adaptation, and utility. This is the point of departure for a concept whose importance in Nietzsche will be seen below, the concept of reaction: the mechanical and utilitarian accommodations, the *regulations* which express all the power of inferior and dominated forces. Here we must note the immoderate taste of modern thought for this reactive aspect of forces. We always think that we have done enough when we understand an organism in terms of reactive forces. The nature of reactive forces and their quivering fascinates us. This is why we oppose mechanical means to final ends in the theory of life; but these two interpretations are only valid for reactive forces themselves. It is true that we do understand the organism in terms of forces. But it is also true that we can only grasp reactive forces for what they are, that is as forces and not as mechanical means or final ends, if we relate them to what dominates them but is not itself reactive. "One overlooks the essential priority of the spontaneous, aggressive, expansive, form-giving forces that give new interpretations and directions, although "adaptation" follows only after this; the dominant role of the highest functionaries within the organism itself . . . is denied" [*On the Genealogy of Morals;* hereafter referred to as *GM*].

It is no doubt more difficult to characterise these active forces for, by nature, they escape consciousness, "The great activity is unconscious" (VP). Consciousness merely expresses the relation of certain reactive forces to the active forces which dominate them. Consciousness is essentially reactive; this is why we do not know what a body can do, or what activity it is capable of (*GS*). And what is said of consciousness must also be said of memory and habit. Furthermore we must also say it of nutrition, reproduction, conservation and adaptation. These are reactive functions, reactive specialisations, expressions of particular reactive forces (*WP*). It is inevitable that consciousness sees the organism from its own point of view and understands it in its own way; that is to say, reactively. What happens is that science follows the paths of consciousness, relying entirely on *other* reactive forces; the organism is always seen from the petty side, from the side of its reactions. The problem of the organism, according to Nietzsche, is not an issue between mechanism and vitalism. What is the value of vitalism as long as it claims to discover the specificity of life in the same reactive forces that mechanism interprets in another way? The real problem is the discovery of active forces without which the reactions themselves would not be forces. What makes the body superior to all reactions, particularly that reaction of the ego that is called consciousness, is the activity of necessarily unconscious forces: "This entire phenomenon of the body is, from the intellectual point of view, as superior to our consciousness, to our spirit to our conscious ways of thinking, feeling and willing, as algebra is superior to the multiplication table" (*VP*). The body's active forces make it a self and define the self as superior and astonishing: "A most powerful being, an unknown sage—he is called Self. He inhabits your body, he is your body" [*Thus Spake Zarathustra;* hereafter referred to as *Z,* "Of the Despisers of the Body"]. The only true science is that of activity, but the science of activity is also the science of what is necessarily unconscious. The idea that science must follow in the footsteps of consciousness, in the same directions, is absurd. We can sense the morality in this idea. In fact there can only be science where there is no consciousness, where there can be no consciousness.

"What is active?—reaching out for power" (*WP*). Appropriating, possessing, subjugating, dominating—these are the characteristics of active force. To appropriate means to impose forms, to create forms by exploiting circumstances [*Beyond Good and Evil;* hereafter referred to as *BGE*]. Nietzsche criticises Darwin for interpreting evolution and chance within evolution in an entirely reactive way. He admires Lamarck because Lamarck foretold the existence of a truly active *plastic force,* primary in relation to adaptations: a force of metamorphosis. For Nietzsche, as for energetics, energy which is capable of transforming itself is called "noble." The power of transformation, the Dionysian power, is the primary definition of activity. But each time we point out the nobility of action and its superiority to reaction in this way we must not forget that reaction also designates a type of force. It is simply that reactions cannot be grasped or scientifically understood as forces if they are not related to superior forces—forces of *another type.* The reactive is a primordial quality of force but one which can only be interpreted as such in relation to and on the basis of the active.

3. QUANTITY AND QUALITY

Forces have quantity, but they also have the quality which corresponds to their difference in quantity: the qualities of force are called "active" and "reactive." We can see that the problem of measuring forces will be delicate because it brings the art of qualitative interpretations into play. The problem is as follows:

1. Nietzsche always believed that forces were quantitative and had to be defined quantitatively. "Our knowledge," he says, "has become scientific to the extent that it is able to employ number and measurement. The attempt should be made to see whether a scientific order of values could be constructed simply on a numerical and quantitative scale of force. All other 'values' are prejudices, naiveties and misunderstandings. They are everywhere reducible to this numerical and quantitative scale" (*WP*).

2. However Nietzsche was no less certain that a purely quantitative determination of forces remained abstract, incomplete and ambiguous. The art of measuring forces raises the whole question of interpreting and evaluating qualities. " 'Mechanistic interpretation': desires nothing but quantities; but force is to be found in quality. Mechanistic theory can therefore only *describe* processes, not explain them" (*WP*). "Might all quantities not be signs of quality? . . . The reduction of all qualities to quantities is nonsense" (*WP*).

Is there a contradiction between these two kinds of texts? If a force is inseparable from its quantity it is no more separable from the other forces which it relates to. *Quantity itself is therefore inseparable from difference in quantity.* Difference in quantity is the essence of force and of the relation of force to force. To dream of two equal forces, even if they are said to be of opposite senses, is a coarse and approximate dream, a statistical dream in which the living is submerged but which chemistry dispels. Each time that Nietzsche criticises the concept of quantity we must take it to mean that quantity as an abstract concept always and essentially tends towards an identification, an equalisation of the unity that forms it and an annulment of difference in this unity. Nietzsche's reproach to every purely quantitative determination of forces is that if annuls, equalises or compensates for differences in quantity. On the other hand, each time he criticises quality we should take it to mean that qualities are nothing but the corresponding difference in quantity between the two forces whose relationship is presupposed. In short, Nietzsche is never interested in the irreducibility of quantity to quality; or rather he is only interested in it secondarily and as a symptom. What interests him primarily, from the standpoint of quantity itself, is the fact that differences in quantity cannot be reduced to equality. Quality is distinct from quantity but only because it is that aspect of quantity that cannot be equalised, that cannot be equalised out in the difference between quantities. Difference in quantity is therefore, in one sense, the irreducible element *of* quantity and in another sense the element which is irreducible *to* quantity itself. Quality is nothing but difference in quantity and corresponds to it each time forces enter into relation. "We cannot help feeling that mere quantitative differences are something fundamentally distinct from quantity, namely that they are *qualities* which can no longer be reduced to one another" (*WP*). The remaining anthropomorphism in this text should be corrected by the Nietzschean principle that there is a subjectivity of the universe which is no longer anthropomorphic but cosmic (*VP*). "To want to reduce all qualities to quantities is madness. . . ."

By affirming chance we affirm the relation of *all* forces. And, of course, we affirm all of chance all at once in the thought of the eternal return. But all forces do not enter into relations all at once on their own account. Their respective power is, in fact, fulfilled by relating to a small number of forces. Chance is the opposite of a *continuum* (on the *continuum*, cf. *VP*). The encounters of forces of various quantities are therefore the concrete parts of chance, the affirmative parts of chance and, as such, alien to every law; the limbs of Dionysus. But, in this encounter, each force receives the quality which corresponds to its quantity, that is to say the attachment which actually fulfills its power. Nietzsche can thus say, in an obscure passage, that the universe presupposes "an absolute genesis of arbitrary qualities," but that the genesis of qualities itself presupposes a (relative) genesis of quantities (*VP*). The fact that the two geneses are inseparable means that we can not abstractly calculate forces. In each case we have to concretely evaluate their respective quality and the nuance of this quality.

4. NIETZSCHE AND SCIENCE

The problem of Nietzsche's relations to science has been badly put. It is claimed that these relations depend on the theory of the eternal return—as if Nietzsche was only interested in science insofar as it favoured the eternal return, and then only vaguely, and insofar as it was opposed to the eternal return took no further interest in it. This is not the case and the origin of Nietzsche's critical position in relation to science must be sought in an entirely different direction, although this direction does open up a new viewpoint on the eternal return.

It is true that Nietzsche had little scientific skill or inclination. But what sets him apart from science is a propensity, a way of thinking. Rightly or wrongly Nietzsche believes that science, in the way it handles quantities always tends to equalise them, to make up for inequalities. Nietzsche, as critic of science, never invokes the rights of quality against quantity; he invokes the rights of difference in quantity against equality, of inequality against equalisation of quantities. Nietzsche imagines a "numerical and quantitative scale," but one in which the divisions are not multiples or factors of one another. What he attacks in science is precisely the scientific mania for seeking balances, the *utilitarianism* and *egalitarianism* proper to science. This is why his whole critique operates on three levels; against logical identity, against mathematical equality and against physical equilibrium. *Against the three forms of the undifferentiated* [these three forms have an essential place in *VP*]. According to Nietzsche science will inevitably fall short of and endanger the true theory of force.

What is the significance of this tendency to reduce quantitative differences? In the first place, it expresses the way in which science is part of the *nihilism* of modern thought. The attempt to deny differences is a part of the more general enterprise of denying life, depreciating existence and promising it a death ("heat" or otherwise) where the universe sinks into the undifferentiated. Nietzsche accuses the physical concepts of matter, weight and heat of being, in the final analysis, agents of an equalisation of quantities, principles of an *"adiaphoria."* It is in this sense that Nietzsche shows that science is part of the ascetic ideal and serves it in its own way (*GM*). But we must also look for the instrument of nihilistic thought in science. The answer is that science, by inclination, understands phenomena in terms of reactive forces and interprets them from this standpoint. Physics is reactive in the same way as biology; things are always seen from the petty side, from the side of reactions. The instrument of nihilistic thought is the triumph of reactive forces.

This is also the principle behind nihilism's manifestations: reactive physics is a physics of *ressentiment,* reactive biology is a biology of *ressentiment.* But we do not yet know why *this* is the only motive of the reactive forces which aim to deny the difference between forces, or how it serves as the principle of *ressentiment.*

Science either affirms or denies the eternal return depending on its standpoint. But the *mechanist* affirmation of the eternal return and its *thermodynamic* negation have something in common: the conservation of energy which is always interpreted so that quantities of energy not only have a constant sum but also cancel out their differences. In both cases we pass from a principle of finitude (the constancy of a sum) to a "nihilistic" principle (the cancelling out of differences in quantities, the sum of which is constant). The mechanist idea affirms the eternal return but only by assuming that differences in quantity balance or cancel each other out between the initial and final states of a reversible system. The final state is identical to the initial state which is itself assumed to be undifferentiated in relation to intermediate states. The thermodynamic idea denies the eternal return but only because it discovers that differences in quantity only cancel each other out in the final state of the system, as a function of the properties of heat. In this way identity is posited in the final undifferentiated state and opposed to the differentiation of the initial state. The two conceptions agree on one hypothesis, that of a final or terminal state, a terminal state of becoming. Being or nothing, being or non-being, are equally undifferentiated: the two conceptions come together in the idea of becoming having a final state, "In metaphysical terms, if becoming could end in being or nothing . . ." (*VP*).

This is why mechanism does not succeed in establishing the existence of the eternal return, any more than thermodynamics succeeds in denying it. Both pass it by and fall into the undifferentiated, fall back into the identical.

According to Nietzsche the eternal return is in no sense a thought of the identical but rather a thought of synthesis, a thought of the absolutely different which calls for a new principle outside science. This principle is that of the reproduction of diversity as such, of the repetition of difference; the opposite of *"adiaphoria."* (*VP*, "There is no *adiaphoria* although we can imagine it.") And indeed, we fail to understand the eternal return if we make it a consequence or an application of identity. We fail to understand the eternal return if we do not oppose it to identity in a particular way. The eternal return is not the permanence of the same, the equilibrium state or the resting place of the identical. It is not the "same" or the "one" which comes back in the eternal return but return is itself the one which ought to belong to diversity and to that which differs.

5. FIRST ASPECT OF THE ETERNAL RETURN: AS COSMOLOGICAL AND PHYSICAL DOCTRINE

Nietzsche's account of the eternal return presupposes a critique of the terminal or equilibrium state. Nietzsche says that if the universe had an equilibrium position, if becoming had an end or final state, it would already have been attained. But the present moment, as the passing moment, proves that it is not attained and therefore that an equilibrium of forces is not possible (*VP*). But why would equilibrium, the terminal state, have to have been attained if it were possible? By virtue of what Nietzsche calls the infinity of past time. The infinity of past time means that becoming cannot have started to become, that it is not something that has become. But, not being something that has become it cannot be a becoming something. Not having become, it would already be what it is becoming—if it were becoming something. That is to say, past time being infinite, becoming would have attained its final state if it had one. And, indeed, saying that becoming would have attained its final state if it had one is the same as saying that it would not have left its initial state if it had one. If becoming becomes something why has it not finished becoming long ago? If it is something which has become then how could it have started to become? "If the universe were capable of permanence and fixity, and if there were in its entire course a single moment of being in the strict sense it could no longer have anything to do with becoming, thus one could no longer think or observe any becoming whatever" (*WP*). This is the view that Nietzsche claims to have found "in earlier thinkers" (WP). Plato said that if everything that becomes can never avoid the present then, as soon as it is there, it ceases to become and is then what it was in the process of becoming (Plato, *Parmenides*, cf. Second Hypothesis—however Nietzsche is thinking more of Anaximander). "But each time I encountered this thought from antiquity," Nietzsche comments, "it was determined by other, generally theological, ulterior motives." By persisting in demanding how becoming could have started and why it has not yet finished, the philosophers of antiquity are false tragics, invoking hubris, crime, and punishment. With the exception of Heraclitus, they did not face up to the thought of pure becoming, nor the opportunity for this thought. That the present moment is not a moment of being or of present "in the strict sense," that it is the passing moment, *forces* us to think of becoming, but to think of it precisely as what could not have started, and cannot finish, becoming.

How does the thought of pure becoming serve as a foundation for the eternal return? All we need to do to think this thought is to stop believing in being as distinct from and opposed to becoming or to believe in the being of becoming itself. What is the being of that which becomes, of that which neither starts nor finishes becoming? *Returning is the being of that which becomes (Revenir, l'être de ce qui devient)*. "That everything recurs is the closest approximation of a world of becoming to a world of being—high point of the meditation" (WP). This problem for the meditation must be formulated in yet another way; how can the past be constituted in time? How can the present pass? The passing moment could never pass if it were not already past and yet to come—at the same time as being present. If the present did not pass of its own accord, if it had to wait for a new present in order to become past, the past in general would never be constituted in time, and this particular present would not pass. We cannot wait, the moment must be simultaneously present and past, present and yet to come, in order for it to pass (and to pass for the sake of other moments). The present must coexist with itself as past and yet to come. The synthetic relation of the moment to itself as present, past and future grounds its relation to other moments. The eternal return is thus an answer to the problem of *passage* [Z, "Of the Victim and the Riddle"]. And in this sense it must not be interpreted as the return of something that is, that is "one" or the "same." We misinterpret the expression "eternal return" if we understand it as "return of the same." It is not being that returns but rather the returning itself that constitutes being insofar as it is affirmed of becoming and of that which passes. It is not some one thing which returns but rather returning itself is the one thing which is affirmed of diversity or multiplicity. In other words, identity in the eternal return does not describe the nature of that which returns but, on the contrary, the fact of returning for that which differs. This is why the eternal return must be thought of as a synthesis; a synthesis of time and its dimensions, a synthesis of diversity and its reproduction, a synthesis of becoming and the being which is affirmed in becoming, a synthesis of double affirmation. Thus the eternal return itself does not depend on a principle of identity but on one which must, in all respects, fulfill the requirements of a truly sufficient reason.

Why is mechanism such a bad interpretation of the eternal return? Because it does not necessarily or directly imply the eternal return. Because it only entails the false consequence of a final state. This final state is held to be identical to the initial state and, to this extent, it is concluded that the mechanical process passes through the same set of differences again. The cyclical hypothesis, so heavily criticised by Nietzsche (*VP*), arises in this way. Because we cannot understand how this process can possibly leave the initial state, re-emerge from the final state, or pass through the same set of differences again and yet not even have the power to pass once through whatever differences there are. The cyclical hypothesis is incapable of accounting for two things—the diversity of co-existing cycles and, above all, the existence of diversity within the cycle. This is why we can only understand the eternal return as the expression of a principle which serves as an explanation of diversity and its reproduction, of difference and its repetition. Nietzsche presents this principle as one of his most important philosophical discoveries. He calls it *will to power*. By will to power "I express the characteristic that cannot be thought out of the mechanistic order without thinking away this order itself" (*WP*).

6. WHAT IS THE WILL TO POWER?

One of the most important texts which Nietzsche wrote to explain what he understood by will to power is the following: "The *victorious* concept 'force,' by means of which our physicists have created God and the world, still needs to be *completed*: an *inner* will must be *ascribed* to it, which I designate as 'will to power' " (*WP*). The will to power is thus ascribed to force, but in a very special way: it is both a complement of force and something internal to it. It is not ascribed to it as a predicate. Indeed, if we pose the question "which one," we cannot say that force is *the one that* wills. The will to power alone is the one that wills, it does not let itself be delegated or alienated to another subject, even to force (*VP*; "Who therefore will power? An absurd question, if being is by itself will to power . . ."). But how then can it be "ascribed"? We must remember that every force has an essential relation to other forces, that the essence of force is its quantitative difference from other forces and that this difference is expressed as the force's quality. Now, difference in quantity, understood in this way, necessarily reflects a differential element of related forces—which is also the genetic element of the qualities of these forces. This is what the will to power is; the genealogical element of force, both differential and genetic. *The will to power is the element from which derive both the quantitative difference of related forces and the quality that devolves into each force in this relation.* The will to power here reveals its nature as the principle of the synthesis of forces. In this synthesis—which relates to time—forces pass through the same differences again or diversity is reproduced. The synthesis is one of forces, of their difference and their reproduction; the eternal return is the synthesis which has as its principle the will to power. We should not be surprised by the word "will"; *which one* apart from the will is capable of serving as the principle of a synthesis of forces by determining the relation of force with forces? But how should the term "principle" be understood? Nietzsche always attacks principles for being too general in relation to what they condition, for always having too broad a mesh in relation to what they claim to capture or regulate. He likes to oppose the will to power to the Schopenhauerian will to live, if only because of the extreme generality of the latter. If, on the contrary, the will to power is a good principle, if it reconciles empiricism with principles, if it constitutes a superior empiricism, this is because it is an essentially *plastic* principle that is no wider than what it conditions, that changes itself with the conditioned and determines itself in each case along with what it determines. The will to power is, indeed, never separable from particular determined forces, from their quantities, qualities, and directions. It is never superior to the ways that it determines a relation between forces, it is always plastic and changing.

Inseparable does not mean identical. The will to power cannot be separated from force without falling into metaphysical abstraction. But to confuse force and will is even more risky. Force is no longer understood as force and one falls back into mechanism—forgetting the difference between forces which constitutes their being and remaining ignorant of the element from which their reciprocal genesis derives. Force is what can, will to power is what wills (*La force est ce qui peut, la volonté de puissance est ce qui veut*). What does this distinction mean? The passage quoted above invites comment on every word. The concept of force is, by nature, *victorious* because the relation of force to force, understood conceptually, is one of domination: when two forces are related one is dominant and the other is dominated. (Even God and the universe are caught in a relation of domination, however debatable the interpretation of such a relation may be in this case.) Nevertheless, this victorious concept of force needs a *complement* and this complement is *internal*, an internal will. It would not be victorious without such an addition. This is because relations of forces remain indeterminate unless an element which is capable of determining them from a double point of view is added to force itself. Forces in relation reflect a simultaneous double genesis: the reciprocal genesis of their difference in quantity and the absolute genesis of their respective qualities. The will to power is thus added to force, but as the differential and genetic element, as the internal element of its production. It is in no way anthropomorphic. More precisely, it is added to force as the internal principle of the determination of its quality in a relation ($x + dx$) and as the internal principle of the quantitative determination of this relation itself (dy/dx). The will to power must be described as the genealogical element of force *and* of forces. Thus it is always through the will to power that one force prevails over others and dominates or commands them. Moreover it is also the will to power (dy) which makes a force obey within a relation; it is through will to power that it obeys.

We have already encountered the relationship between the eternal return and the will to power, but we have neither elucidated nor analysed it. The will to power is both the genetic element of force and the principle of synthesis of forces. But we are not yet able to understand how this synthesis forms the eternal return, how the forces in it necessarily reproduce themselves in conformity with its principle. On the other hand, the existence of this problem reveals a historically important aspect of Nietzsche's philosophy; its complex relations with Kantianism. Kantianism centres on the concept of synthesis which it discovered. Now, we know that the post-Kantians reproached Kant, from two points of view, for having endangered this discovery: from the point of view of the principle which governs the synthesis and from the point of view of the reproduction of objects in the synthesis itself. They demanded a principle which was not merely conditioning in relation to objects but which was also truly genetic and productive (a principle of eternal difference or determination). They also condemned the survival, in Kant, of miraculous harmonies between terms that remain external to one another. With regard to such a principle of internal difference or determination they demanded grounds not only for the synthesis but for the reproduction of diversity in the synthesis as such. [*Translator's note:* The word *divers* which is translated here as "diversity" could also be translated by the word used by Kant's English translators—"manifold"—in

"Kantian" contexts such as the present one. I have retained "diversity" which is more appropriate in most contexts but the Kantian connotation should be borne in mind.] If Nietzsche belongs to the history of Kantianism it is because of the original way in which he deals with these post-Kantian demands. He turned synthesis into a synthesis of forces—for, if we fail to see synthesis in this way, we fail to recognise its sense, nature and content. He understood the synthesis of forces as the eternal return and thus found the reproduction of diversity at the heart of synthesis. He established the principle of synthesis, the will to power and determined this as the differential and genetic element of forces which directly confront one another. Although this supposition must be verified later we believe that there is, in Nietzsche, not only a Kantian heritage, but a half-avowed, half-hidden rivalry. Nietzsche does not have the same position in relation to Kant as Schopenhauer did for, unlike Schopenhauer, he does not attempt an interpretation which would separate Kantianism from its dialectical avatars and present it with new openings. This is because, for Nietzsche, these dialectical avatars do not come from the outside but are primarily caused by the deficiencies of the critical philosophy. Nietzsche seems to have sought (and to have found in the "eternal return" and the "will to power") a radical transformation of Kantianism, a reinvention of the critique which Kant betrayed at the same time as he conceived it, a resumption of the critical project on a new basis and with new concepts.

7. NIETZSCHE'S TERMINOLOGY

We must now fix certain points in Nietzsche's terminology even if this anticipates analyses which remain to be done. All the rigour of his philosophy, whose systematic precision is wrongly suspected, depends on it. This suspicion is wrong in any case, whether this is cause for rejoicing or regret. In fact Nietzsche uses very precise new terms for very precise new concepts:

1. Nietzsche calls the genealogical element of force the will to power. Genealogical means differential and genetic. The will to power is the differential element of forces, that is to say the element that produces the differences in quantity between two or more forces whose relation is presupposed. The will to power is the genetic element of force, that is to say the element that produces the quality due to each force in this relation. The will to power as a principle does not suppress chance but, on the contrary, implies it, because without chance it would be neither plastic nor changing. Chance is the bringing of forces into relation, the will to power is the determining principle of this relation. The will to power is a necessary

addition to force but can only be added to forces brought into relation by chance. The will to power has chance at its heart for only the will to power is capable of affirming all chance.

2. The difference in quantity and the respective qualities of forces in relation both derive from the will to power as genealogical element. Forces are said to be dominant or dominated depending on their difference in quantity. Forces are said to be active or reactive depending on their quality. There is will to power in the reactive or dominated force as well as in the active or dominant force. Now, as the difference in quantity is irreducible in every case, it is pointless to want to measure it without interpreting the qualities of the forces which are present. Forces are essentially differentiated and qualified. They express their difference in quantity by the quality which is due to them. This is the problem of interpretation: to estimate the quality of force that gives meaning to a given phenomenon, or event, and from that to measure the relation of the forces which are present. We must not forget that, in every case, interpretation comes up against all kinds of delicate problems and difficulties; and "extremely fine" perception is necessary here, of the kind found in chemistry.

3. The principle of the qualities of force is the will to power. And if we ask: "which one interprets?", we reply *the will to power;* it is the will to power that interprets (*WP*). But, in order to be the source of the qualities of force in this way, the will to power must itself have qualities, particularly fluent ones, even more subtle than those of force. "What rules is the entirely momentary quality of the will to power" (*VP*). These qualities of the will to power which are immediately related to the genetic or genealogical element, these fluent, primordial and seminal qualitative elements, must not be confused with the qualities of force. It is therefore essential to insist on the terms used by Nietzsche; *active* and *reactive* designate the original qualities of force but *affirmative* and *negative* designate the primordial qualities of the will to power. Affirming and denying, appreciating and depreciating, express the will to power just as acting and reacting express force. (And just as reactive forces are still forces, the will to deny, nihilism, is still will to power: ". . . a *will to nothingness,* an aversion to life, a rebellion against the most fundamental presuppositions of life; but it is and remains a will!" [GM].) This distinction between two kinds of quality is of the greatest importance and it is always found at the centre of Nietzsche's philosophy. There is a deep affinity, a complicity, but never a confusion, between action and affirmation, between reaction and negation. Moreover, the determination of these affinities brings the whole art of philosophy into play. On the one hand, it is clear that there is affirmation in every action and negation in

every reaction. But, on the other hand, action and reaction are more like means, means or instruments of the will to power which affirms and denies, just as reactive forces are instruments of nihilism. And again, action and reaction need affirmation and negation as something which goes beyond them but is necessary for them to achieve their own ends. Finally, and more profoundly, affirmation and negation extend beyond action and reaction because they are the immediate qualities of becoming itself. Affirmation is not action but the power of becoming active, *becoming active* personified. Negation is not simple reaction but a *becoming reactive*. It is as if affirmation and negation were both immanent and transcendent in relation to action and reaction; out of the web of forces they make up the chain of becoming. Affirmation takes us into the glorious world of Dionysus, the being of becoming and negation hurls us down into the disquieting depths from which reactive forces emerge.

4. For all these reasons Nietzsche can say that the will to power is not only the one that interprets but the one that evaluates (*VP:* "Every will implies an evaluation"). To interpret is to determine the force which gives sense to a thing. To evaluate is to determine the will to power which gives value to a thing. We can no more abstract values from the standpoint from which they draw their value than we can abstract meaning from the standpoint from which it draws its signification. The will to power as genealogical element is that from which senses derive their significance and values their value. . . . The signification of a sense consists in the quality of the force which is expressed in a thing: is this force active or reactive and of what nuance? The value of a value consists in the quality of the will to power expressed in the corresponding thing; is the will to power affirmative or negative and of what nuance? The art of philosophy becomes even more complicated as these problems of interpretation and evaluation refer back to and extend one another. What Nietzsche calls *noble, high,* and *master* is sometimes active force, sometimes affirmative will. What he calls *base, vile,* and *slave* is sometimes reactive force and sometimes negative will. Later we will understand why he uses these terms. But a value always has a genealogy on which the nobility or baseness of what it invites us to believe, feel, and think depends. Only a genealogist is able to discover what sort of baseness can find its expression in one value, what sort of nobility in another, because only he knows how to handle the differential element: he is the master of the critique of values. The notion of value loses all meaning if values are not seen as receptacles to be pierced, statues to be broken open to find what they contain, whether it is the most notable or the most base. Like the scattered limbs of Dionysus only the statues of nobility come back together. Talk of

the nobility of values in general shows a type of thought which has too much at stake to hide its own baseness—as if whole domains of values did not derive their sense and their value from serving as refuge and manifestation for all that is vile and slavish. Nietzsche, the creator of the philosophy of values, would have seen, if he had lived longer, his most critical notion serving and turning into the most insipid and base ideological conformism; the hammer strokes of the philosophy of values becoming strokes of flattery; polemic and aggression replaced by *ressentiment*, carping guardian of the established order, watchdog of current values. This is genealogy taken up by slaves—the forgetting of qualities, the forgetting of origins.

8. ORIGIN AND INVERTED IMAGE

In the beginning, at the origin, there is the difference between active and reactive forces. Action and reaction are not in a relation of succession but in one of coexistence in the origin itself. Moreover, the complicity of active forces and affirmation and that of reactive forces and negation is revealed by the principle that the negative is already wholly on the side of reaction. Conversely, only active force asserts itself, it affirms its difference and makes its difference an object of enjoyment and affirmation. Reactive force, even when it obeys, limits active force, imposes limitations and partial restrictions on it and is already controlled by the spirit of the negative (*GM*). This is why the origin itself, in one sense, includes an inverted self-image; seen from the side of reactive forces the differential and genealogical element appears upside down, difference has become negation, affirmation has become contradiction. An inverted image of the origin accompanies the origin; "yes" from the point of view of active forces becomes "no" from the point of view of reactive forces and affirmation of the self becomes negation of the other. This is what Nietzsche calls the "inversion of the value-positing eye" (*GM*). Active forces are noble but they find themselves before a plebeian image, reflected in reactive forces. Genealogy is the art of difference or distinction, the art of nobility; but it sees itself upside down in the mirror of reactive forces. Its image then appears as that of an "evolution." —Sometimes this evolution is understood in the German manner, as a dialectical and Hegelian evolution, as the development of contradiction. Sometimes it is understood in the English manner, as a utilitarian derivation, as the development of profit and interest. But true genealogy is always caricatured in the essentially reactive image that evolution presents of it. Whether it is English or German, evolutionism is the reactive image of genealogy. Thus it is characteristic of reactive forces to deny, from the start, the difference which constitutes them at the start, to invert the differential element from which they derive and to give a deformed image of it. "Difference breeds hatred" (*BGE*). This is why they do not see themselves as forces and prefer to turn against themselves rather than seeing themselves in this way and accepting difference. The "mediocrity" of thought which Nietzsche attacks always reflects a mania for interpreting or evaluating phenomena in terms of reactive forces—every nation chooses its own. But this mania has its origins at the beginning, in the inverted image. Consciousness and consciences are simply enlargements of this reactive image. . . .

Going one step further, let us suppose that, with the help of favourable external or internal circumstances, reactive forces get the better of and neutralise active force. We have now left the origin: it is no longer a question of an inverted image but of a development of this image, an inversion of values themselves (*GM*) so that the low is placed on high and reactive forces have triumphed. If they do triumph it is through the negative will, through the will to nothingness which develops the image; but their triumph itself is not imaginary. The question is: how do reactive forces triumph? That is to say: when they get the better of active forces do reactive forces themselves also become dominant, aggressive and subjugating? Do they, by getting together, form a greater force that would then be active? Nietzsche's answer is that even by getting together reactive forces do not form a greater force , one that would be active. They proceed in an entirely different way— they decompose; *they separate active force from what it can do;* they take away a part or almost all of its power. In this way reactive forces do not become active but, on the contrary, they make active forces join them and become reactive in a new sense. We can see that, from its beginning and in developing itself, the concept of reaction changes in signification: an active force *becomes reactive* (in a new sense) when reactive forces (in the first sense) separate it from what it can do. Nietzsche will analyse how such a separation is possible in detail. But it is important to notice that, even at this stage, he is careful never to present the triumph of reactive forces as the putting together of a force superior to active force but, rather, as a subtraction or division. Nietzsche devotes a whole book to the analysis of the figures of reactive triumph in the human world—*ressentiment,* bad conscience, and the ascetic ideal. In each case he shows that reactive forces do not triumph by forming a superior force but by "separating" active force (cf. the three essays of the *GM*). In each case this separation rests on a fiction, on a mystification or a falsification. It is the will to nothingness which develops the negative and inverted image and makes the subtraction. Now, there is always something imaginary in the operation of subtraction—

as the negative utilisation of number shows. Thus if we want to give a numerical transcription of the victory of reactive forces we must not appeal to an addition by which reactive forces would, by getting together, become stronger than active force, but rather to a subtraction which separates active force from what it can do and denies its difference in order to make it a reactive force. Thus getting the better of action is not enough to stop reaction being reaction; on the contrary. Active force is separated from what it can do by a fiction but is not therefore any less "really" reactive, in fact, this is the way in which it becomes really reactive. This is where Nietzsche's use of the words "vile," "ignoble," and "slave" comes from—these words designate the state of reactive forces that place themselves on high and entice active force into a trap, replacing masters with slaves who do not stop being slaves.

9. THE PROBLEM OF THE MEASURE OF FORCES

This is why we cannot measure forces in terms of an abstract unity, or determine their respective quality and quantity by using the real state of forces in a system as a criterion. We have said that active forces are the superior, dominant and strongest forces. But inferior forces can prevail without ceasing to be inferior in quantity and reactive in quality, without ceasing to be slaves in this sense. One of the finest remarks in *The Will to Power* is: "The strong always have to be defended against the weak" (*VP*). We cannot use the state of a system of forces as it in fact is, or the result of the struggle between forces, in order to decide which are active and which are reactive. Nietzsche remarks, against Darwin and evolutionism, "Supposing, however, that this struggle exists—and it does indeed occur—its outcome is the reverse of that desired by the school of Darwin, of that which one *ought* perhaps to desire with them: namely, the defeat of the stronger, the more privileged, the fortunate exceptions" [*The Twilight of the Idols*; hereafter referred to as *TI*, "Expeditions of an Untimely Man"]. It is primarily in this sense that interpretation is such a difficult art—we must judge whether the forces which prevail are inferior or superior, reactive or active; whether they prevail as *dominated* or *dominant*. In this area there are no facts, only interpretations. The measurement of forces must not be conceived of as a procedure of abstract physics but rather as the fundamental act of a concrete physics, not as an indifferent technique but as the art of interpreting difference and quality independently of fact. (Nietzsche sometimes says: "Outside of the existing social order" *VP*).

This problem reopens an old argument, a famous debate between

Callicles and Socrates (*Gorgias;* discussion on "nature and convention"). The resemblance is so striking that it seems to us that Nietzsche is close to Callicles and that Callicles is immediately completed by Nietzsche. Callicles strives to distinguish nature and law. Everything that separates a force from what it can do he calls law. Law, in this sense, expresses the triumph of the weak over the strong. Nietzsche adds: the triumph of reaction over action. Indeed, everything which separates a force is reactive as is the state of a force separated from what it can do. Every force which goes to the limit of its power is, on the contrary, active. It is not a law that every force goes to the limit, it is even the opposite of law. —Socrates replies to Callicles that there is no way of distinguishing nature and law; for the weak can only prevail if, by banding together, they can form a stronger force than the strong. Law triumphs from the point of view of nature itself. Callicles does not complain of not having been understood, he begins again. The slave does not stop being a slave by being triumphant; when the weak triumph it is not by forming a greater force but by separating force from what it can do. Forces must not be compared abstractly; from the point of view of nature concrete force is that which goes to its ultimate consequences, to the limit of power or desire. Socrates objects a second time; "what matters for you Callicles is pleasure . . . You define all good in terms of pleasure."

We can see here what happens between the sophist and the dialectician, on which side the good faith and the rigorous reasoning is. Callicles is aggressive but has no *ressentiment*. He prefers to give up talking because it is clear that Socrates does not understand the first time and the second time speaks of something else. How can he explain to Socrates that "desire" is not the association of a pleasure and a pain, the pain of experiencing it and the pleasure of satisfying it? How can he explain that pleasure and pain are reactions, properties of reactive forces, the proof of adaptation or lack of it? And how can Socrates be made to understand that the weak do not form a stronger force? Socrates has partially misunderstood and partially mis-heard—he is too full of dialectical *ressentiment* and the spirit of revenge. He who is so exacting towards others, so fastidious when they reply to him. . . .

10. HIERARCHY

Nietzsche also encounters his own Socrates. These are the free thinkers. They say: "What are you complaining about? How could the weak have triumphed if they did not form superior force?" "Let us bow down before accomplished fact" (*GM*). This is modern positivism. They claim to carry out the critique of values, they claim to refuse all appeals to transcendent values, they declare them unfashionable, but only in order to rediscover them as the forces which run the world of today. The value of Church, morality, State etc. is only discussed so that their human force and content can be admired. The free thinker has the strange craze for recovering every content, everything positive, but without ever questioning the nature of these self-styled positives or the origin or quality of the corresponding human forces. This is what Nietzsche calls "fatalism" (GM). The free thinker wants to recover the content of religion but never considers that religion might in fact contain man's basest forces, forces which he might want to leave behind. This is why we can have no confidence in the free thinker's atheism, even when he's a democrat and a socialist: "It is the church, and not its poison that repels us" (GM). The essential characteristics of the free thinker's positivism and humanism are fatalism, interpretative impotence and ignorance of the qualities of force. As soon as something appears as a human force or fact the free thinker applauds it without wondering whether this force is of base extraction, whether this fact is the opposite of a high fact: "Human all-too human." Because it does not take the qualities of forces into account free thought is, by vocation, at the service of reactive forces and expresses their triumph. For the fact is always something used by the weak against the strong; "the fact is always stupid, having at all times resembled a calf rather than a god" [Untimely Meditations; hereafter referred to as UM, "Use and Abuse of History"]. Nietzsche opposes the free spirit to the free thinker, the spirit of interpretation itself which judges force from the standpoint of their origin and quality: "There are no facts, nothing but interpretations" (VP). The critique of the free thinker is a fundamental theme in Nietzsche's work—because this critique discloses a perspective from which many different ideologies can be attacked at once; positivism, humanism, the dialectic—positivism's taste for facts, humanism's exaltation of the human fact and the dialectic's mania for recovering human contents.

In Nietzsche the word hierarchy has two senses. It signifies, firstly, the difference between active and reactive forces, the superiority of active to reactive forces. Nietzsche can thus speak of an "unalterable and innate order of rank in hierarchy" (BGE); and the problem of hierarchy is itself the problem of free spirits [Human, All Too Human; hereafter referred to as HH, Preface 7). But hierarchy also designates the triumph of reactive forces, the contagion of reactive forces and the complex organisation which results—where the weak have conquered, where the strong are contaminated, where the slave who has not stopped being a slave prevails over the master who has stopped being one: the reign of law and of virtue. In this second sense morality and religion are still theories of hierarchy (VP). If we compare the two senses we see that the second is like the reverse of the first. We make Church, morality, and State the masters or keepers of all hierarchy. We have the hierarchy that we deserve, we who are essentially reactive, we who take the triumphs of reaction for a transformation of action and slaves for new masters—we who only recognise hierarchy back to front.

What Nietzsche calls weak or slavish is not the least strong but that which, whatever its strength, is separated from what it can do. The least strong is as strong as the strong if he goes to the limit, because the cunning, the subtlety, the wit and even the charm by which he makes up for his lesser strength are part of this strength so that it is no longer the least. (Zarathustra's two animals are the eagle and the serpent. The eagle is strong and proud but the serpent being crafty and charming is no less strong.) The measure of forces and their qualification does *not* depend on absolute quantity but rather on relative accomplishment. Strength or weakness cannot be judged by taking the result and success of struggle as a criterion. For, once again, it is a fact that the weak triumph: it is even the essence of fact. Forces can only be judged if one takes into account in the first place their active or reactive quality, in the second place the affinity of this quality for the corresponding pole of the will to power (affirmative or negative) and in the third place the nuance of quality that the force presents at a particular moment of its development, in relation to its affinity. Thus reactive force is: 1) utilitarian force of adaptation and partial limitation; 2) force which separates active force from what it can do, which denies active force (triumph of the weak or the slaves); 3) force separated from what it can do, which denies or turns against itself (reign of the weak or of slaves). And, analogously, active force is: 1) plastic, dominant, and subjugating force; 2) force which goes to the limit of what it can do; 3) force which affirms its difference, which makes its difference an object of enjoyment and affirmation. Forces are only concretely and completely determined if these three pairs of characteristics are taken into account simultaneously.

11. WILL TO POWER AND FEELING OF POWER

We know that the will to power is the differential element, the genealogical element which determines the relation of force with force and produces their quality. The will to power must therefore *manifest itself* in force as such. The manifestations of the will to power must be studied very carefully because the dynamism of forces is completely dependent on it. But what does "the will to power manifests itself" mean? The relationship between forces in each case is determined to the extent that each force is *affected* by other, inferior or superior, forces. It follows that will to power is manifested as a capacity for being affected. This capacity is not an abstract possibility, it is necessarily fulfilled and actualised at each moment by the other forces to which a given force relates. We should not be surprised by the double aspect of the will to power: from the standpoint of the genesis or production of forces it determines the relation between forces but, from the standpoint of its own manifestations, it is determined by relating forces. This is why the will to power is always determined at the same time as it determines, qualified at the same time as it qualifies. In the first place, therefore, the will to power is manifested as the capacity for being affected, as the determinate capacity of force for being affected. —It is difficult to deny a Spinozist inspiration here. Spinoza, in an extremely profound theory, wanted a capacity for being affected to correspond to every quantity of force. The more ways a body could be affected the more force it had. This capacity measures the force of a body or expresses its power. And, on the one hand, this power is not a simple logical possibility for it is actualised at every moment by the bodies to which a given body is related. On the other hand, this capacity is not a physical passivity, the only passive affects are those not adequately caused by the given body.

Similarly, for Nietzsche, the capacity for being affected is not necessarily a passivity but an *affectivity,* a sensibility, a sensation. It is in this sense that Nietzsche, even before elaborating the concept of the will to power and giving it its full significance, was already speaking of a *feeling of power.* Before treating power as a matter of will he treated it as a matter of feeling and sensibility. But when he had elaborated the full concept of the will to power this first characteristic did not appear—it became the manifestation of the will to power. This is why Nietzsche always says that the will to power is "the primitive affective form" from which all other feelings derive (*VP*). Or better still: "The will to power is not a being not a becoming, but a *pathos*" (*WP*). That is to say: the will to power manifests itself as the sensibility of force; the differential element of forces manifests itself as their differential sensibility. "The fact is that the will to power rules even in the inorganic world, or rather that there is no inorganic world. Action at a distance cannot be eliminated, for one thing attracts another and a thing feels itself attracted. This is the fundamental fact . . . *In order for the will to power to be able to manifest itself it needs to perceive the things it sees and feel the approach of what is assimilable to it*" (*VP*). The affects of force are active insofar as the force appropriates anything that resists it and compels the obedience of inferior forces. When force is affected by superior forces which it obeys its affects are made to submit, or rather, they are acted (*agies*). Again, obeying is a manifestation of the will to power. But an inferior force can bring about the disintegration or splitting of superior forces, the explosion of energy which they have accumulated. Nietzsche likes to compare the phenomena of atomic disintegration, the division of protoplasm and the reproduction of organic life (*VP*). And not only do disintegration, division and separation always express will to power but so do being disintegrated, being separated and being divided: "Division appears as the consequence of the will to power (*VP*). Given two forces, one superior and the other inferior, we can see how each one's capacity for being affected is fulfilled necessarily. But this capacity for being affected is not fulfilled unless the corresponding force enters into a history or a process of sensible becoming: 1. active force, power of acting or commanding; 2. reactive force, power of obeying or of being acted; 3. developed reactive force, power of splitting up, dividing and separating; 4. active force become reactive, power of being separated, of turning against itself (*WP*).

All sensibility is only a becoming of forces. There is a cycle of force in the course of which force "becomes" (for example, active force becomes reactive). There are even several becomings of forces that can struggle against one another (*WP*). Thus it is not sufficient to parallel or oppose the respective characteristics of active and reactive force. The active and the reactive are qualities of force that derive from the will to power. But the will to power itself has qualities, *sensibilia,* which are like the becomings of forces. The will to power manifests itself, in the first place, as the sensibility of forces and, in the second place, as the becoming sensible of forces: pathos is the most elementary fact from which a becoming arises (*WP*). In general, the becoming of forces must not be confused with the qualities of force: it is the becoming of these qualities themselves, the quality of the will to power itself. The qualities of force can no more be abstracted from their becoming than force itself can be abstracted from the will to power. The concrete study of forces necessarily implies a dynamic.

12. THE BECOMING-REACTIVE OF FORCES

But, the dynamic of forces in fact leads us to a distressing conclusion. When reactive force separates active force from what it can do, the latter also becomes reactive. *Active forces become reactive.* And the word "becoming" must be taken in the strongest sense: the becoming of forces appears as a becoming-reactive. Are there no other ways of becoming? The fact remains that we do not feel, experience or know any becoming but becoming-reactive. We are not merely noting the existence of reactive forces, we are noting the fact that everywhere they are triumphant. How do they triumph? Through the will to nothingness, thanks to the affinity between reaction and negation. What is negation? It is a quality of the will to power, the one which qualifies it as nihilism or will to nothingness, the one which constitutes the becoming-reactive of forces. It must not be said that active force becomes reactive because reactive forces triumph; on the contrary, they triumph because, by separating active force from what it can do, they betray it to the will to nothingness, to a becoming-reactive deeper than themselves. This is why the figures of triumph of reactive forces (*ressentiment,* bad conscience, and the ascetic ideal) are primarily forms of nihilism. The becoming-reactive, the becoming nihilistic, of force seem to be essential components of the relation of force with force. —Is there another becoming? Everything tempts us to think that perhaps there is. But, as Nietzsche often says, we would need another sensibility, another way of feeling. We can not yet reply to this question, we can hardly even contemplate its possibility. But we *can* ask why we only feel and know a becoming-reactive. Is it not because man is essentially reactive? Because becoming-reactive is constitutive of man? *Ressentiment,* bad conscience, and nihilism are not psychological traits but the foundation of the humanity in man. They are the principle of human being as such. Man, "skin disease" of the Earth, reaction of the Earth . . . (Z, "Of Great Events"). It is in this sense that Zarathustra speaks of his "great contempt" for man and of his "great disgust." Another sensibility, another becoming—would they still be man's?

This condition of man is of the greatest importance for the eternal return. It seems to compromise or contaminate it so gravely that it becomes an object of anguish, repulsion and disgust. Even if active forces return they will again become reactive, eternally reactive. The eternal return of reactive forces and furthermore the return of the becoming-reactive of forces. Zarathustra not only presents the thought of the eternal return as mysterious and secret but as nauseating and difficult to bear (cf. also *VP*). The first exposition of the eternal return is followed by a strange vision of a shepherd "writhing, choking, convulsed, his face distorted," a heavy black snake hanging out of his mouth (Z, "Of the Vision and the Riddle"). Later, Zarathustra himself explains the vision: "The great disgust at man—*it* choked me and had crept into my throat . . . The man of whom you are weary, the little man recurs eternally . . . Alas man recurs eternally! . . . And eternal return, even for the smallest—that was my disgust at all existence! Ah, disgust! Disgust! Disgust!" (Z, "The Convalescent"). The eternal return of the mean, small, reactive man not only makes the thought of the eternal return unbearable, it also makes the eternal return itself impossible; it puts contradiction into the eternal return. The snake is an animal of the eternal return; but, insofar as the eternal return is that of reactive forces, the snake uncoils, becomes a "heavy black snake" and hangs out of the mouth which is preparing to speak. For how could the eternal return, the being of becoming, be affirmed of a becoming nihilistic?—In order to affirm the eternal return it is necessary to bite off and spit out the snake's head. Then the shepherd is no longer either man or shepherd, "he was transformed, surrounded with light, he was laughing! Never yet on earth had any man laughed as he laughed" (Z, "Of the Vision and the Riddle"). Another becoming, another sensibility: the Overman.

13. AMBIVALENCE OF SENSE AND OF VALUES

A becoming-active of forces, a becoming-active of reactive forces, would be a different becoming from the one that we know now. The evaluation of such a becoming raises several questions and must be the final test of the systematic coherence of Nietzschean concepts in the theory of force.—Let us consider an initial hypothesis. What Nietzsche calls an active force is one which goes to the limit of its consequences. An active force separated from what it can do by reactive force thus becomes reactive. But does not this reactive force, in its own way, go to the limit of what it can do? If active force, being separated, becomes reactive, does not, conversely, reactive force, as that which separates, become active? Is this not its own way of being active? Concretely, is there not a kind of baseness, meanness, stupidity etc. which becomes active through going to the limit of what it can do? "Rigorous and grandiose stupidity. . . ." Nietzsche writes (BGE). This hypothesis recalls the Socratic objection but is, in fact, distinct from it. One no longer says, like Socrates, that inferior forces only triumph by forming a greater force but rather that reactive forces only triumph by going to the limit of their consequences, that is, by forming an active force.

A reactive force can certainly be considered from different points of view. Illness, for example, separates me from what I can do, as reactive force it makes me reactive, it narrows my possibilities and condemns me to a diminished milieu to which I can do no more than adapt myself. But, in another way, it reveals to me a new capacity, it endows me with a new will that I can make my own, going to the limit of a strange power. (This extreme power brings many things into play, for example: "Looking from the perspective of the sick toward *healthier* concepts and values . . ." *Ecce Homo;* hereafter referred to as *EH*). Here we can recognise an ambivalence important to Nietzsche: all the forces whose reactive character he exposes are, a few lines or pages later, admitted to fascinate him, to be sublime because of the perspective they open up for us and because of the disturbing will to power to which they bear witness. They separate us from our power but at the same time they give us another power, "dangerous"' and "interesting." They bring us new feelings and teach us new ways of being affected. There is something admirable in the becoming-reactive of forces, admirable and dangerous. Not only the sick man, but even the religious man present this double aspect: reactive on the one hand, possessing a new power on the other (GM). "Human history would be altogether too stupid a thing without the spirit that the impotent have introduced into it" (GM). Every time Nietzsche speaks of Socrates, Christ, Judaism, Christianity or any form of decadence or degeneration he discovers this same ambivalence of things, beings, and forces.

Is it, however, exactly the same force that both separates me from what I can do and endows me with a new power? Is it the same illness, is it the same invalid who is the slave of his illness and who uses it as a means of exploring, dominating and being powerful. Is the religion of the faithful who are like bleating lambs and that of certain priests who are like new "birds of prey" the same? In fact the reactive forces are not the same and they change nuance depending on the extent to which they develop their affinity for the will to nothingness. One reactive force both obeys and resists, another separates active force from what it can do; a third contaminates active force, carries it along to the limit of becoming-reactive, into the will to nothingness; a fourth type of reactive force was originally active but became reactive and separated from its power, it was then dragged into the abyss and turned against itself—these are the different nuances, affects and types that the genealogist must interpret, that no one else knows how to interpret. "Need I say after all this that in questions of decadence I am *experienced*? I have spelled them forward and backward. That filigree art of grasping and comprehending in general, those fingers for *nuances*, that psychology of 'looking round the corner,' and whatever else is characteristic of me . . ." (EH). The problem of interpretation is to interpret the state of reactive forces in each case—that is the degree of development that they have reached in relation to negation and the will to nothingness.—The same problem of interpretation would arise on the side of active forces; to interpret their nuance or state in each case, that is, to interpret the degree of development of the relation between action and affirmation. There are reactive forces that become grandiose and fascinating by following the will to nothingness and there are active forces that subside because they do not know how to follow the powers of affirmation (we will see that this problem of what Nietzsche calls "culture" or "the higher man"). Finally, evaluation presents ambivalences which are even more profound than those of interpretation. To judge affirmation itself from the standpoint of negation itself and negation from the standpoint of affirmation; to judge affirmative will from the standpoint of nihilistic will and nihilistic will from the standpoint of affirmative will—this is the genealogist's art and the genealogist is a physician. "Looking from the perspective of the sick toward *healthier* concepts and values and, conversely, looking again from the fullness and self-assurance of a *rich* life down into the secret work of the instinct of decadence" (*EH*). But whatever the ambivalence of sense and values we cannot conclude that a reactive force becomes active by going to the limit of what it can do. For, to go "to the limit," "to the ultimate consequences," has two senses depending on whether one affirms or denies, whether one affirms one's own difference or denies that which differs. When a reactive force develops to its ultimate consequences it does this in relation to negation, to the will to nothingness which serves as its motive force. Becoming active, on the contrary, presupposes the affinity of action and affirmation; in order to become active it is not sufficient for a force to go to the limit of what it can do, it must make what it can do an object of affirmation. Becoming-active is affirming and affirmative, just as becoming-reactive is negating and nihilistic.

14. SECOND ASPECT OF THE ETERNAL RETURN: AS ETHICAL AND SELECTIVE THOUGHT

Because it is neither felt nor known, a becoming-active can only be thought as the product of a *selection*. A simultaneous double selection by the activity of force and the affirmation of the will. But what can perform the selection? What serves as the selective principle? Nietzsche replies: the eternal return. Formerly the object of disgust, the eternal return overcomes disgust and turns Zarathustra into a "convalescent," someone consoled (*Z*, "The Convalescent"). But in what sense is the eternal return selective? Firstly because, as a thought, it gives the will a practical rule (*WP*, "The great selective *thought*"). The eternal return gives the will a rule as rigorous as the Kantian one. We have noted that the eternal return, as a physical doctrine, was the new formulation of the speculative synthesis. As an ethical thought the eternal return is the new formulation of the practical synthesis: *whatever you will, will it in such a way that you also will its eternal return.* "If, in all that you will you begin by asking yourself: is it certain that I will do it an infinite number of times? This should be your most solid centre of gravity" (*VP*). One thing in the world disheartens Nietzsche: the little compensations, the little pleasures, the little joys and everything that one is granted once, only once. Everything that can be done again the next day only on the condition that it be said the day before: tomorrow I will give it up—the whole ceremonial of the obsessed. And we are like those old women who permit themselves an excess only once, we act and think like them. "Oh, that you would put from you all *half*-willing, and decide upon lethargy as you do upon action. Oh that you understood my saying: 'Always do what you will—but first be such as *can* will!'" [*Z*, "Of the Virtue that Makes Small"]. Laziness, stupidity, baseness, cowardice or spitefulness that would will its own eternal return would no longer be the same laziness, stupidity etc. How does the eternal return perform the selection here? It is the *thought* of the eternal return that selects. It makes willing something whole. The thought of the eternal return eliminates from willing everything which falls outside the eternal return, it makes willing a creation, it brings about the equation "willing = creating."

It is clear that such a selection falls short of Zarathustra's ambitions. It is content to eliminate certain reactive states, certain states of reactive forces which are among the least developed. But reactive forces which go to the limit of what they can do in their own way, and which find a powerful motor in the nihilistic will, resist the first selection. Far from falling outside the eternal return they enter into it and seem to return with it. We must therefore expect a second selection, very different from the first. But this second selection involves the most obscure parts of Nietzsche's philosophy and forms an almost esoteric element on the doctrine of the eternal return. We can therefore only summarise these Nietzschean themes, leaving a detailed conceptual explanation until later:

1. Why is the eternal return called "the most extreme form of nihilism" (*WP*)? And if the eternal return is the most extreme form of nihilism, nihilism itself (separated or abstracted from the eternal return) is always an "incomplete nihilism" (*WP*): however far it goes, powerful as it is. Only the eternal return makes the nihilistic will whole and complete.

2. The will to nothingness, as we have investigated it up to now, has always appeared in an alliance with reactive forces. Its essence was to deny active force and to lead it to deny and turn against itself. But, at the same time, it laid in this way the foundation for the conservation, triumph and contagion of reactive forces. The will to nothingness was universal becoming-reactive, the becoming-reactive of forces. This is the sense in which nihilism is always incomplete on its own. Even the ascetic ideal is the opposite of

what we might think, "it is an expedient of the art of conserving life."
Nihilism is the principle of conservation of a weak, diminished, reactive life.
The depreciation and negation of life form the principle in whose shadow
the reactive life conserves itself, survives, triumphs and becomes contagious
[GM].

3. What happens when the will to nothingness is related to the eternal
return? This is the only place where it breaks its alliance with reactive
forces. Only the eternal return can complete nihilism *because it makes
negation a negation of reactive forces themselves.* By and in the eternal
return nihilism no longer expresses itself as the conservation and victory of
the weak but as their destruction, their *self-destruction.* "This perishing
takes the form of a self-destruction—the instinctive selection of that which
must destroy. . . . The will to destruction as the will of a still deeper instinct,
the instinct of self-destruction, the will to nothingness " (*WP*). This is why
Zarathustra, as early as the Prologue, sings of the "one who wills his own
downfall," "for he does not want to preserve himself," "for he will cross the
bridge without hesitation" (*Z*, Prologue). The Prologue to *Zarathustra* contains the premature secret of the eternal return.

4. Turning against oneself should not be confused with this destruction of self, this self-destruction. In the reactive process of turning against
oneself active force becomes reactive. In self-destruction reactive forces are
themselves denied and led to nothingness. This is why self-destruction is
said to be an active operation an *"active destruction"* (*VP, EH*). It and it
alone expresses the becoming-active of forces: forces become active insofar
as reactive forces deny and suppress themselves in the name of a principle
which, a short time ago, was still assuring their conservation and triumph.
Active negation or active destruction is the state of strong spirits which
destroy the reactive in themselves, submitting it to the test even if it entails
willing their own decline; "it is the condition of strong spirits and wills, and
these do not find it possible to stop with the negative of 'judgement'; their
nature demands *active negation*" (*WP*). This is the only way in which
reactive forces *become active.* Furthermore this is why negation, by making
itself the negation of reactive forces themselves, is not only active but is, as
it were, *transmuted.* It expresses affirmation and becoming-active as the
power of affirming. Nietzsche then speaks of the "eternal joy of becoming
. . . that joy which includes even joy in destroying," "The affirmation of
passing away and *destroying,* which is the decisive feature of a Dionysian
philosophy" (*EH,* "The Birth of Tragedy").

5. The second selection in the eternal return is thus the following: the
eternal return produces becoming-active. It is sufficient to relate the will to

nothingness to the eternal return in order to realise that reactive forces do not return. However far they go, however deep the becoming-reactive of forces, reactive forces will not return. The small, petty, reactive man will not return. In and through the eternal return negation as a quality of the will to power transmutes itself into affirmation, it becomes an affirmation of negation itself, it becomes a power of affirming, an affirmative power. This is what Nietzsche presents as Zarathustra's cure and Dionysus's secret. "Nihilism vanquished by itself" thanks to the eternal return (*VP*). This second selection is very different from the first. It is no longer a question of the simple thought of the eternal return eliminating from willing everything that falls outside this thought but rather, of the eternal return making something come into being which cannot do so without changing nature. It is no longer a question of selective thought but of selective being; for the eternal return is being and being is selection. (Selection = Hierarchy)

15. THE PROBLEM OF THE ETERNAL RETURN

All this must be taken as a simple summary of texts. These texts will only be elucidated in terms of the following points: the relation of the two qualities of the will to power (negation and affirmation), the relation of the will to power itself with the eternal return, and the possibility of transmutation as a new way of feeling, thinking and above all being (the Overman). In Nietzsche's terminology the reversal of values means the active in place of the reactive (strictly speaking it is the reversal of a reversal, since the reactive began by taking the place of action). But *transmutation* of values, or *transvaluation*, means affirmation instead of negation—negation transformed into a power of affirmation, the supreme Dionysian metamorphosis. All these as yet unanalysed points form the summit of the doctrine of the eternal return.

From afar we can hardly see this summit. The eternal return is the being of becoming. But becoming is double: becoming-active and becoming-reactive, becoming-active of reactive forces and becoming-reactive of active forces. But only becoming-active has being; it would be contradictory for the being of becoming to be affirmed of a becoming-reactive, of a becoming that is itself nihilistic. The eternal return would become contradictory if it were the return of reactive forces. The eternal return teaches us that becoming-reactive has no being. Indeed, it also teaches us of the existence of a becoming-active. It necessarily produces becoming-active by reproducing becoming. This is why affirmation is twofold: the being of becoming cannot be fully affirmed without also affirming the existence of becoming-active.

The eternal return thus has a double aspect: it is the universal being of becoming, but the universal being of becoming ought to belong to a single becoming. Only becoming-active has a being which is the being of the whole of becoming. Returning is everything but everything is affirmed in a single moment. Insofar as the eternal return is affirmed as the universal being of becoming, insofar as becoming-active is also affirmed as the symptom and product of the universal eternal return, affirmation changes nuance and becomes more and more profound. Eternal return, as a physical doctrine, affirms the being of becoming. But, as selective ontology, it affirms this being of becoming as the "self-affirming" of becoming-active. We see that, at the heart of the complicity which joins Zarathustra and his animals, a misunderstanding arises, a problem the animals neither understand nor recognise, the problem of Zarathustra's disgust and cure. "O you buffoons and barrel organs! answered Zarathustra and smiled again . . . you—have already made an old song of it" (Z, "The Convalescent"). The old song is the cycle and the whole, universal being. But the complete formula of affirmation is: the whole, yes, universal being, yes, but universal being ought to belong to a single becoming, the whole ought to belong to a single moment.

JACQUES DERRIDA

Otobiographies: The Teaching of Nietzsche and the Politics of the Proper Name

1. LOGIC OF THE LIVING FEMININE

"For there are human beings who lack everything, except one thing of which they have too much—human beings who are nothing but a big eye or a big mouth or a big belly or anything at all that is big. Inverse cripples [*umgekehrte Krüppel*] I call them.

"And when I came out of my solitude and crossed over this bridge for the first time I did not trust my eyes and looked and looked again, and said at last, 'An ear! An ear as big as a man!' I looked still more closely—and indeed, underneath the ear something was moving, something pitifully small and wretched and slender. And, no doubt of it, the tremendous ear was attached to a small, thin stalk—but this stalk was a human being! If one used a magnifying glass one could even recognize a tiny envious face; also, that a bloated little soul was dangling from the stalk. The people, however, told me that this great ear was not only a human being, but a great one, a genius. But I never believed the people when they spoke of great men; and I maintained my belief that it was an inverse cripple who had too little of everything and too much of one thing."

When Zarathustra had spoken thus to the hunchback and to those whose mouthpiece and advocate [*Mundstück und Fürsprecher*] the hunchback was, he turned to his disciples in profound dismay and said: "Verily, my friends, I walk among

From *The Ear of the Other: Otobiography, Transference, Translation*, edited by Christie V. McDonald. © 1985 by Schocken Books, Inc.

men as among the fragments and limbs of men [*Bruchstücken and Gliedmassen*]. This is what is terrible for my eyes, that I find man in ruins [*zerstrümmert*] and scattered [*zerstreut*] as over a battlefield or a butcher-field [*Schlachtund Schlächterfeld*].

("On Redemption," *Thus Spake Zarathustra*)

I would like to spare you the tedium, the waste of time, and the subservience that always accompany the classic pedagogical procedures of forging links, referring back to prior premises or arguments, justifying one's own trajectory, method, system, and more or less skillful transitions, reestablishing continuity, and so on. These are but some of the imperatives of classical pedagogy with which, to be sure, one can never break once and for all. Yet, if you were to submit to them rigorously, they would very soon reduce you to silence, tautology, and tiresome repetition.

I therefore propose my compromise to you. And, as everyone knows, by the terms of *academic freedom*—I repeat: a-ca-dem-ic free-dom—you can take it or leave it. Considering the time I have at my disposal, the tedium I also want to spare myself, the freedom of which I am capable and which I want to preserve, I shall proceed in a manner that some will find aphoristic or inadmissible, that others will accept as law, and that still others will judge to be not quite aphoristic enough. All will be listening·to me with one or the other sort of ear (everything comes down to the ear you are able to hear me with) to which the coherence and continuity of my trajectory will have seemed evident from my first words, even from my title. In any case, let us agree to hear and understand one another on this point: whoever no longer wishes to follow may do so. I do not teach truth as such; I do not transform myself into a diaphanous mouthpiece of eternal pedagogy. I settle accounts, however I can, on a certain number of problems: with you and with me or me, and through you, me, and me, with a certain number of authorities represented here. I understand that the place I am now occupying will not be left out of the exhibit or withdrawn from the scene. Nor do I intend to withhold even that which I shall call, to save time, an *autobiographical* demonstration, although I must ask you to shift its sense a little and to listen to it with another ear. I wish to take a certain pleasure in this, so that *you may learn this pleasure from me.*

The said "academic freedom," the ear, and autobiography are my objects—for this afternoon.

A discourse on life/death must occupy a certain space between *logos* and *gramme,* analogy and program, as well as between the differing senses of program and reproduction. And since life is on the line, the trait that relates the logical to the graphical must also be working between the biological and biographical, the thanatological and thantographical.

As you know, all these matters are currently undergoing a reevaluation—all these matters, that is to say, the biographical and the *autos* of the autobiographical.

We no longer consider the biography of a "philosopher" as a corpus of empirical accidents that leaves both a name and a signature outside a system which would itself be offered up to an immanent philosophical reading—the only kind of reading held to be philosophically legitimate. This academic notion utterly ignores the demands of a text which it tries to control with the most traditional determinations of what constitutes the limits of the written, or even of "publication." In return for having accepted these limits, one can then and on the other hand proceed to write "lives of philosophers," those biographical novels (complete with style flourishes and character development) to which great historians of philosophy occasionally resign themselves. Such biographical novels or psychobiographies claim that, by following empirical procedures of the psychologistic—at times even psychoanalystic—historicist, or sociologistic type, one can give an account of the genesis of the philosophical system. We say no to this because a new problematic of the biographical in general and of the biography of philosophers in particular must mobilize other resources, including, at the very least, a new analysis of the proper name and the signature. Neither "immanent" readings of philosophical systems (whether such readings be structural or not) nor external, empirical-genetic readings have ever in themselves questioned the *dynamis* of that borderline between the "work" and the "life," the system and the subject of the system. This borderline—I call it · *dynamis* because of its force, its power, as well as its virtual and mobile potency—is neither active nor passive, neither outside nor inside. It is most especially not a thin line, an invisible or *indivisible* trait lying between the enclosure of philosophemes, on the one hand, and the life of an author already identifiable behind the name, on the other. This divisible borderline traverses two "bodies," the corpus and the body, in accordance with laws that we are only beginning to catch sight of.

What one calls life—the thing or object of biology and biography—does not stand face to face with something that would be its opposable ob-ject: death, the thanatological or thanatographical. This is the first complication. Also, it is *painfully difficult* for life to become an object of science, in the sense that philosophy and science have always given to the word "science" and to the legal status of scientificity. All of this—the difficulty, the delays it entails—is particularly bound up with the fact that the science of life always accommodates a philosophy of life, which is not the case for all other sciences, the sciences of nonlife—in other words, the sciences of the dead. This might lead one to say that all sciences that win their claim to scientificity without delay or residue are sciences of the dead; and, further, that there is, between the dead and the status of the scientific object, a co-implication which *interests* us, and which concerns the desire to know. If such is the case, then the so-called living subject of biological discourse is a part—an interested party or a partial interest—of the whole field of investment that includes the enormous philosophical, ideological, and political tradition, with all the forces that are at work in that tradition as well as everything that has its potential in the subjectivity of a biologist or a community of biologists. All these evaluations leave their mark on the scholarly signature and inscribe the bio-graphical within the bio-logical.

The name of Nietzsche is perhaps today, for us in the West, the name of someone who (with the possible exceptions of Freud and, in a different way, Kierkegaard) was alone in treating both philosophy and life, the science and the philosophy of life *with his name and in his name.* He has perhaps been alone in putting his name—his names—and his biographies on the line, running thus most of the risks this entails: for "him," for "them," for his lives, his names and their future, and particularly for the political future of what he left to be signed.

How can one avoid taking all this into account when reading these texts? One reads only by taking it into account.

To put one's name on the line (with everything a name involves and which cannot be summed up in a *self*), to stage signatures, to make an immense bio-graphical paraph out of all that one has written on life or death—this is perhaps what he has done and what we have to put on active record. Not so as to guarantee him a return, a profit. In the first place, *he* is dead—a trivial piece of evidence, but incredible enough when you get right down to it and when the name's genius or genie is still there to make us forget the fact of his death. At the very least, to be dead means that no profit or deficit, no good or evil, whether calculated or not, can *ever return again* to the bearer of the name. Only the name can inherit, and this is why the name, to be distinguished from the bearer, is always and a priori a dead man's name, a name of death. What returns to the name never returns to the living. Nothing ever comes back to the living. Moreover, we shall not assign him the profit because what he has willed in his name resembles—as do all legacies or, in French, *legs* (understand this word with whichever ear, in whatever tongue you will)—poisoned milk which has, as we shall see in a moment, gotten mixed up in advance with the worst of our times. And it did not get mixed up in this by accident.

Before turning to any of his writings, let it be said that I shall not read Nietzsche as a philosopher (of being, of life, or of death) or as a scholar or scientist, if these three types can be said to share the abstraction of the bio-graphical and the claim to leave their lives and names out of their writings. For the moment, I shall read Nietzsche beginning with the scene from *Ecce Homo* where he puts his body and his name out front even though he advances behind masks or pseudonyms without proper names. He advances behind a plurality of masks or names that, like any mask and even any theory of the simulacrum, can propose and produce themselves only by returning a constant yield of protection, a surplus value in which one may still recognize the ruse of life. However, the ruse starts incurring losses as soon as the surplus value does not return again to the living, but to and in the name of names, the community of masks.

The point of departure for my reading will be what says *"Ecce Homo"* or what says *"Ecce Homo"* of itself, as well as *"Wie man wird, was man ist,"* how one becomes what one is. I shall start with the preface to *Ecce Homo* which is, you could say, coextensive with Nietzsche's entire oeuvre, so much so that the entire oeuvre also prefaces *Ecce Homo* and finds itself repeated in the few pages of what one calls, in the strict sense, the Preface to the work entitled *Ecce Homo*. You may know these first lines by heart:

> Seeing that before long I must confront humanity with the most difficult demand that has ever been made of it, it seems indispensable to me to say *who I am* [*wer ich bin* is italicized]. Really, one should know it, for I have not left myself "without testimony." But the disproportion between the greatness of my task and the *smallness* of my contemporaries has found expression in the fact that one has neither heard nor even seen me. I live on my own credit [I go along living on my own credit, the credit I establish and give myself: *Ich lebe auf meinen eigenen Kredit hin*]: it is perhaps a mere prejudice that I live [*vielleicht bloss ein Vorurteil dass ich lebe*].

His own identity—the one he means to declare and which, being so out of proportion with his contemporaries, has nothing to do with what they know by this name, behind his name or rather his homonym, Friedrich Nietzsche—the identity he lays claim to here is not his by right of some contract drawn up with his contemporaries. It has passed to him through the unheard-of contract he has drawn up with himself. He has taken out a loan with himself and *has implicated us in this transaction through what, on the force of a signature, remains of his text. "Auf meinen eigenen Kredit."* It is also our business, this unlimited credit that cannot be measured against the credit his contemporaries extended or refused him under the name of F. N. Already a false name, a pseudonym and homonym, F. N. dissimulates, perhaps, behind the imposter, the other Friedrich Nietzsche. Tied up with this shady business of contracts, debt, and credit, the pseudonym induces us to be immeasurably wary whenever we think we are reading Nietzsche's signature or "autograph," and whenever he *declares*: I, the undersigned, F. N.

He never knows in the present, with present knowledge or even in the present of *Ecce Homo*, whether anyone will ever honor the inordinate credit that he extends to *himself* in his name, but also necessarily in the name of another. The consequences of this are not difficult to foresee: if the life that he lives and tells to himself ("autobiography," they call it) cannot be *his* life in the first place except as the effect of a secret contract, a credit account which has been both opened and encrypted, an indebtedness, an alliance or annulus, then as long as the contract has not been honored—and it cannot be honored except by another, for example, by you—Nietzsche can write that his life is perhaps a mere prejudice, *"es ist vielleicht bloss ein Vorurteil dass ich lebe."* A prejudice: life. Or perhaps not so much life in general, but *my* life, this "that I live," the "I-live" in the present. It is a prejudgment, a sentence, a hasty arrest, a risky prediction. This life will be verified only at the moment the bearer of the name, the one whom we, in our prejudice, call living, will have died. It will be verified only at some moment after or during death's arrest. [*Arrêt de mort:* both death sentence and reprieve from death.—Tr.] And if life returns, it will return to the name but not to the living, in the name of the living *as* a name of the dead.

"He" has proof of the fact that the "I live" is a prejudgment (and thus, due to the effect of murder which a priori follows, a harmful prejudice) linked to the bearing of the name and to the structure of all proper names. He says that he has proof every time he questions one of the ranking "educated" men who come to the Upper Engadine. As Nietzsche's name is unknown to any of them, he who calls himself "Nietzsche" then holds proof of the fact that he does not live presently: "I live on my own credit; it is perhaps a mere prejudice that I live. I need only speak with one of the 'educated' who come to the Upper Engadine . . . and I am convinced that I do *not* live [*das ich lebe nicht*]. Under these circumstances I have a duty against which my habits, even more the pride of my instincts, revolt at bottom—namely, to say: *Hear me! For I am such and such a person* [literally: I am he and he, *ich bin der und der*]. *Above all, do not mistake me for someone else.*" All of this is emphasized.

He says this unwillingly, but he has a "duty" to say so in order to acquit himself of a debt. To whom?

Forcing himself to say who he is, he goes against his natural *habitus* that prompts him to dissimulate behind masks. You know, of course, that Nietzsche constantly affirms the value of dissimulation. Life is dissimulation. In saying "*ich bin der und der,*" he seems to be going against the instinct of dissimulation. This might lead us to believe that, *on the one hand,* his contract goes against his nature: it is by doing violence to himself that he promises to honor a pledge in the name of the name, in his name and in the name of the other. *On the other hand,* however, this auto-presentative exhibition of the "*ich bin der und der*" could well be still a ruse of dissimulation. We would again be mistaken if we understood it as a simple presentation of identity, assuming that we already know what is involved in self-presentation and a statement of identity ("Me, such a person," male or female, an individual or collective subject, "Me, psychoanalysis," "Me, metaphysics").

Everything that will subsequently be said about truth will have to be reevaluated on the basis of this question and this anxiety. As if it were not already enough to unsettle our theoretical certainties about identity and what we think we know about a proper name, very rapidly, on the following page, Nietzsche appeals to his "experience" and his "wanderings in forbidden realms." They have taught him to consider the causes of idealization and moralization in an entirely different light. He has seen the dawning of a "*hidden* history" of philosophers—*he does not say of philosophy*—and the "psychology of their great names."

Let us assume, in the first place, that the "I live" is guaranteed by a nominal contract which falls due only upon the death of the one who says "I live" in the present; further, let us assume that the relationship of a philosopher to his "great name"—that is, to what borders a system of his signature—is a matter of psychology, but a psychology so novel that it would no longer be legible within the system of philosophy as one of its parts, nor within psychology considered as a region of the philosophical encyclopedia. Assuming, then, that all this is stated in the Preface signed "Friedrich Nietzsche" to a book entitled *Ecce Homo*—a book whose final words are "Have I been understood? *Dionysus versus the Crucified*" [*gegen den Gekreuzigten*], Nietzsche, Ecce Homo, Christ but not Christ, nor even Dionysus, but rather the name of the *versus*, the adverse or countername, the combat called between the two names—this would suffice, would it not, to pluralize in a singular fashion the proper name and the homonymic mask? It would suffice, that is, to lead all the affiliated threads of the name astray in a labyrinth which is, of course, the labyrinth of the ear. Proceed, then, by seeking out the edges, the inner walls, the passages.

Between the Preface signed F. N., which comes after the title, and the first chapter, "Why I Am So Wise," there is a single page. It is an outwork, an *hors d'oeuvre*, an exergue or a flysheet whose *topos*, like (its) temporality, strangely dislocates the very thing that we, with our untroubled assurance, would like to think of as the time of life and the time of life's *récit*, [Rather than attempt to translate this word as "account" or "story" or "narration," it has been left in french throughout.—Tr.] of the writing of life by the living—in short, the time of autobiography.

The page is dated. To date is to sign. And to "date from" is also to indicate the place of the signature. This page is in a certain way dated because it says "today" and today "my birthday," the anniversary of my birth. The anniversary is the moment when the year turns back on itself, forms a ring or annulus with itself, annuls itself and begins anew. It is here: my forty-fifth year, the day of the year when I am forty-five years old, something like the midday of life. The noon of life, even midlife crisis ["Le démon de midi"; literally, the midday demon.—Tr.], is commonly situated at about this age, at the shadowless midpoint of a great day.

Here is how the exergue begins: "*An diesem vollkommhen Tage, wo Alles reift,*" "On this perfect day when everything is ripening, and not only the grape turns brown, the eye of the sun just fell upon my life [has fallen due as if by chance: *fiel mir eben ein Sonnenblick auf meinen Leben*]."

It is a shadowless moment consonant with all the "middays" of Zarathustra. It comes as a moment of affirmation, returning like the anniversary from which one can look forward and backward at one and the same time. The shadow of all negativity has disappeared: "I looked back, I looked forward, and never saw so many and such good things at once."

Yet, this midday tolls the hour of a burial. Playing on everyday language, he buries his past forty-four years. But what he actually buries is death, and in burying death he has saved life—and immortality. "It was not for nothing that I buried [*begrub*] my forty-fourth year today; I had the *right* to bury it; whatever was life in it has been saved, is immortal. The first book of the *Revaluation of All Values,* the *Songs of Zarathustra,* the *Twilight of the Idols,* my attempt to philosophize with a hammer—all presents [*Geschenke*] of this year, indeed of its last quarter. *How could I fail to be grateful to my whole life?*—and so I tell my life to myself" ["*Und so erzähle ich mir mein Leben*"].

He indeed says: I tell my life *to myself*; I recite and recount it thus *for me*. We have come to the end of the exergue on the flysheet between the Preface and the beginning of *Ecce Homo*.

To receive one's life as a gift, or rather, to be grateful to life for what she gives, for giving after all what is *my* life; more precisely, to recognize one's gratitude to life for such a gift—the gift being what has managed to get written and signed with this name for which I have established my own credit and which will be what it has become only on the basis of what this year has given me (the three works mentioned in the passage), in the course of the event dated by an annual course of the sun, and even by a part of its course or recourse, its returning—to reaffirm what has occurred during these forty-four years as having been good and as bound to return eternally, immortally: this is what *constitutes*, gathers, adjoins, and holds the strange present of this auto-biographical *récit* in place. "*Und so erzähle ich mir mein Leben.*" This *récit* that buries the dead and saves the saved or exceptional as immortal is not *auto*-biographical for the reason one commonly understands, that is, because the signatory tells the story of his life or the return of his past life as life and not death. Rather, it is because he tells *himself* this life and he is the narration's first, if not its only, addressee and destination—within the text. And since the "I" of this *récit* only constitutes itself through the credit of the eternal return, he does not exist. He does not sign prior to the *récit qua* eternal return. Until then, *until now*, that I am living may be a mere prejudice. It is the eternal return that signs or seals.

Thus, you cannot think the name or names of Friedrich Nietzsche, you cannot *hear* them before the reaffirmation of the hymen, before the alliance or wedding ring of the eternal return. You will not understand anything of his life, nor of his life and works, until you hear the thought of the "yes, yes" given to this shadowless gift at the ripening high noon, beneath that division whose borders are inundated by sunlight: the overflowing cup of the sun. Listen again to the overture of *Zarathustra*.

This is why it is so difficult to determine the *date* of such an event. How can one situate the advent of an auto-biographical *récit* which, as the thought of the eternal return, requires that we let the advent of all events come about in another way? This difficulty crops up wherever one seeks to make a *determination*: in order to date an event, of course, but also in order to identify the beginning of a text, the origin of life, or the first movement of a signature. These are all problems of the borderline.

Without fail, the structure of the exergue on the borderline or of the borderline in the exergue will be reprinted wherever the question of life, of "my-life," arises. Between a title or a preface on the one hand, and the book to come on the other, between the title *Ecce Homo* and *Ecce Homo* "itself," the structure of the exergue situates the place from which life will be *recited*, that is to say, reaffirmed—*yes, yes, amen, amen*. It is life that has to return eternally (selectively, as the living feminine and not as the dead that resides within her and must be buried), as life allied to herself by the nuptial annulus, the wedding ring. This *place* is to be found neither in the work (it is an exergue) nor in the life of the author. At least it is not there in a simple fashion, but neither is it simply exterior to them. It is in this place that affirmation is repeated; yes, yes, I approve, I sign, I subscribe to this acknowledgment of the debt incurred toward "myself," "my-life"—and I want it to return. Here, at noon, the least shadow of all negativity is buried. The design of the exergue reappears later, in the chapter "Why I Write Such Good Books," where Nietzsche's preparations for the "great noon" are made into a commitment, a debt, a "duty," "my duty of preparing a moment of the highest self-examination for humanity, a *great* noon when it looks back and far forward [*wo sie zurückschaut und hinausschaut*]" ("Dawn").

But the noon of life is not a place and it does not take place. For that very reason, it is not a moment but only an instantly vanishing limit. What is more, it returns every day, always, each day, with every turn of the annulus. Always before noon, after noon. If one has the right to read F. N.'s signature only at this instant—the instant in which he signs "noon, yes, yes, I and I who recite my life to myself"—well, you can see what an impossible protocol this implies for reading and especially for teaching, as well as what ridiculous naiveté, what sly, obscure, and shady business are behind declarations of the type: Friedrich Nietzsche said this or that, he thought this or that about this or that subject—about life, for example, in the sense of human or biological existence—Friedrich Nietzsche or whoever after noon, such-and-such a person. Me, for example.

I shall not read *Ecce Homo* with you. I leave you with this forewarning or foreword about the place of the exergue and the fold that it forms along the lines of an inconspicuous limit: There is no more shadow, and all statements, before and after, left and right, are at once possible (Nietzsche said it all, more or less) and necessarily contradictory (he said the most mutually incompatible things, and he said that he said them). Yet, before leaving *Ecce Homo*, let us pick up just one hint of this contradicting duplicity.

What happens right after this sort of exergue, after this date? (It is, after all, a date: [From "*data littera*," "letter given," the first words of a medieval formula indicating the time and place of a legal act.—Tr.] signature, anniversary reminder, celebration of gifts or givens, acknowledgment of debt.) After this "date," the first chapter ("Why I Am So Wise") begins, as you know, with the origins of "my" life: my father and my mother. In other words, once again, the principle of contradiction in my life which falls between the principles of death and life, the end and the beginning, the high and the low, degeneracy and ascendancy, et cetera. This contradiction is my fatality. And my fatality derives from my very genealogy, from my father and mother, from the fact that I decline, in the form of a riddle, as my parents' identity. In a word, my dead father, my living mother, my father the dead man or death, my mother the living feminine or life. As for me, I am between the two: this lot has fallen to me, it is a "chance," a throw of the dice; and at this place my truth, my double truth, takes after both of them. These lines are well known:

> The good fortune of my existence [*Das Glück meines Daseins*], its uniqueness perhaps [he says "perhaps," and thereby he re- serves the possibility that this chancy situation may have an exemplary or paradigmatic character], lies in its fatality: I am, to express it in the form of a riddle [*Rätselform*], already dead as my father [*als mein Vater bereits gestorben*], while as my mother, I am still living and becoming old [*als meine Mutter lebe ich noch und werde alt*].

Inasmuch as *I am and follow after* my father, I am the dead man and I am death. Inasmuch as *I am and follow after* my mother, I am life that perseveres, I am the living and the living feminine. I am my father, my mother, and me, and me who is my father my mother and me, my son and me, death and life, the dead man and the living feminine, and so on.

There, this is who I am, a certain masculine and a certain feminine. *Ich bin der und der*, a phrase which means all these things. You will not be able to hear and understand my name unless you hear it with an ear attuned to the name of the dead man and the living feminine—the double and divided name of the father who is dead and the mother who is living on, who will moreover outlive me long enough to bury me. The mother is living on, and this living on is the name of the mother. This survival is my life whose shores she overflows. And my father's name, in other words, my patronym? That is the name of my death, of my dead life.

Must one not take this unrepresentable scene into account each time one claims to identify any utterance signed by F. N.? The utterances I have just read or translated do not belong to the genre of autobiography in the strict sense of the term. To be sure, it is not wrong to say that Nietzsche speaks of his "real" (as one says) father and mother. But he speaks of them "*in Rätselform*," symbolically, by way of a riddle; in other words, in the form of a proverbial legend, and as a story that has a lot to teach.

What, then, are the consequences of this double origin? The birth of Nietzsche, in the double sense of the word "birth" (the act of being born and family lineage), is itself double. It brings something into the world and the light of day out of a singular couple: death and life, the dead man and the living feminine, the father and the mother. The double birth explains who I am and how I determine my identity: as double and neutral.

> This double descent [*Diese doppelte Herkunft*], as it were, from both the highest and lowest rungs on the ladder of life, at the same time *décadent* and a *beginning*—this, if anything, explains that neutrality, that freedom from all partiality in relation to the total problem of life, that perhaps distinguishes me. I have a subtler sense of smell [pay attention to what he repeatedly says about hunting, trails, and his nostrils] for the signs of ascent and decline [literally of rising and setting, as one says of the sun: *für die Zeichen von Aufgang und Niedergang*; of that which climbs and declines, of the high and the low] than any other human being before. I am the master *par excellence* for this—I know both, I am both [*ich kenne beides, ich bin beides*].

I am a master, I am the master, the teacher [*Lehrer*] "*par excellence*" (the latter words in French, as is *décadent* earlier in the passage). I know and I am the both of them (one would have to read "the both" as being in the singular), the dual or the double, I know what I am, the both, the two, life the dead [*la vie le mort*]. Two, and from them one gets life the dead. When I say "Do not mistake me for someone else, I am *der und der*," this is what I mean: the dead the living, the dead man the living feminine.

The alliance that Nietzsche follows in turning his signature into riddles links the logic of the dead to that of the living feminine. It is an alliance in which he seals or forges his signatures—and he also simulates them: the demonic neutrality of midday delivered from the negative and from dialectic.

"I know both, I am both.—My father died at the age of thirty-six. He was delicate, kind and morbid, as a being that is destined merely to pass by [*wie ein nur zum Vorübergehn bestimmtes Wesen*]—more a gracious memory of life rather than life itself." It is not only that the son does not survive his father *after* the latter's death, but the father was *already* dead; he will have died during his own life. As a "living" father, he was already only the memory of life, of an already prior life. Elsewhere, I have related this elementary kinship structure (of a dead or rather absent father, already absent to himself, and of the mother living above and after all, living on long enough to bury the one she has brought into the world, an ageless virgin inaccessible to all ages) to a logic of the death knell [*glas*] and of *obsequence*. There are examples of this logic in some of the best families, for example, the family of Christ (with whom Dionysus stands face to face, but as his specular double). There is also Nietzsche's family, if one considers that the mother survived the "breakdown." In sum and in general, if one "sets aside all the facts," the logic can be found in all families.

Before the cure or resurrection which he also recounts in *Ecce Homo*, this only son will have first of all repeated his father's death: "In the same year in which his life went downward, mine, too, went downward: at thirty-six I reached the lowest pint of my vitality—I still lived, but without being able to see three steps ahead. Then—it was 1879—I retired from my professorship at Basel, spent the summer in St. Moritz like a shadow and the next winter, the most sunless of my life, in Naumberg as a shadow. This was my minimum. The *Wanderer and His Shadow* was born at this time. Doubtless I then knew about shadows." A little further, we read: "My readers know perhaps in what way I consider dialectic as a symptom of decadence; for example in the most famous case, the case of Socrates." *Im Fall des Sokrates:* one might also say in his *casus*, his expiration date and his decadence. He is a Socrates, that *décadent par excellence*, but he is also the reverse. This is what he makes clear at the beginning of the next section: "Taking into account that I am a *décadent,* I am also the opposite." The double provenance, already mentioned at the beginning of section 1, then reaffirmed and explained in section 2, may also be heard at the opening of section 3: "This *dual* series of experiences, this access to apparently separate worlds, is repeated in my nature in every respect: I am a *Doppelgänger*, I have a 'second' sight in addition to the first. And perhaps also a third." Second and third sight. Not only, as he says elsewhere, a third ear. Only a moment ago, he has explained to us that in tracing the portrait of the "well-turned-out person" [*wohlgerathner Mensch*] he has just described himself: "Well, then, I am the *opposite* of a *décadent,* for I have just described myself."

The contradiction of the "double" thus goes beyond whatever declining negativity might accompany a dialectical opposition. What counts in the final accounting and beyond what can be counted is a certain step beyond [*"Pas au-delà."* both "step(s) beyond" and "not beyond."—Tr.]. I am thinking here of Maurice Blanchot's syntaxless syntax in his *Pas au-delà* ["The Step Beyond"]. There, he approaches death in what I would call a step-by-step procedure of overstepping or of impossible transgression. *Ecce Homo*: "In order to understand anything at all of my *Zarathustra*, one must perhaps be similarly conditioned as I am—with one foot *beyond* life." A foot (The death of the father, blindness, the foot: one may be wondering why I am not speaking here of oedipus or Oedipus. This was intentionally held in reserve for another reading directly concerned with the Nietzschean thematic of oedipus and the name of Oedipus.), and going beyond the opposition between life and/or death, a single step.

2. THE OTOGRAPH SIGN OF STATE

The autobiography's signature is written in this step. It remains a line of credit opened onto eternity and refers back to one of the two *I*'s, the nameless parties to the contract, only according to the annulus of the eternal return.

This does not prevent—on the contrary, it allows—the person who says "I am noon in the fullness of summer" ("Why I Am So Wise") also to say "I am double. Therefore, I do not mistake myself, at least not yet for my works."

There is here a difference of autobiography, an allo- and thanatography. Within this differance, it is precisely the question of the institution—the teaching institution—that gives a new account of itself. It is to this question, to this institution that I wished to make an introduction.

The good news of the eternal return is a message and a teaching, the address or the destination of a doctrine. By definition, it cannot let itself be heard or understood in the present; it is untimely, differant, and anachronistic. Yet, since this news repeats an affirmation (yes, yes), since it affirms the return, the rebeginning, and a certain kind of reproduction that preserves whatever comes back, then its very logic must give rise to a magisterial institution. Zarathustra is a master [*Lehrer*], and as such he dispenses a doctrine and intends to found new institutions.

Institutions of the "yes," which have need of ears. But how so?

He says, "*Das eine bin ich, das andre sind meine Schriften.*"

> I am one thing, my writings are another matter. Before I discuss them one by one, let me touch upon the question of their being understood or *not* understood. I'll do it as casually as decency permits; for the time for this question certainly hasn't come yet. The time for me hasn't come yet: some of my writings will be born only posthumously. Some day institutions [*Institutionen*] will be needed in which men live and teach as I conceive of living

and teaching; it might even happen that a few chairs will then be set aside [*eigene:* appropriated to] for the interpretation of *Zarathustra*. But it would contradict my character entirely if I expected ears *and hands* for *my* truths today: that today one doesn't hear me and doesn't accept my ideas is not only comprehensible, it even seems right to me. I don't want to be confounded with others—this requires that I do not confuse myself.

The ear, then, is also at stake in teaching and in its new institutions. As you know, everything gets wound up in Nietzsche's ear, in the motifs of his labyrinth. Without getting in any deeper here, I simply note the frequent reappearance of this motif in the same chapter ["Why I Write Such Good Books"] of *Ecce Homo* (One example among many: "All of us know, even know from experience, what a long-eared beast the ass is [*was ein Langohr ist*]. Well then, I dare assert that I have the smallest ears. This is of no small interest to the little ladies [*Weiblein*]—it seems to me that they may feel I understand them better. I am the *anti-ass par excellence* and thus a world-historical monster—I am, in Greek and not only in Greek, the *Anti-Christ*."), and I right away step back, through another effect of the labyrinth, toward a text altogether at the other end, entitled *On the Future of Our Educational Institutions* (1872).

I have, I am, and I demand a keen ear, I am (the) both, (the) double, I sign double, my writings and I make two, I am the (masculine) dead the living (feminine) and I am destined to them, I come from the two of them, I address myself to them, and so on. How does the knot of all these considerations tie up with the tangled politics and policies in *The Future* . . .?

Today's teaching establishment perpetrates a crime against life understood as the living feminine: disfiguration disfigures the maternal tongue, profanation profanes its body.

By nature, everyone nowadays writes and speaks the German tongue as poorly and vulgarly as is possible in the era of journalistic German: that is why the nobly gifted youth should be taken by force and placed under a bell-jar [*Glasglocke*] of good taste and severe linguistic discipline. If this proves impossible, I would prefer a return to spoken Latin because I am ashamed of a language so disfigured and so profaned. . . . Instead of that purely practical method of instruction by which the teacher must accustom his pupils to severe self-discipline in the language, we find everywhere the rudiments of a historico-scholastic method of teaching the mother-tongue: that is to say, people treat it as if it were a dead language and as if one had no obligation to the present or the future of this language.

("Second Lecture")

There is thus a law that creates obligations with regard to language, and particularly with regard to the language in which the law is stated: the mother tongue. This is the living language (as opposed to Latin, a dead, paternal language, the language of another law where a secondary repression has set in—the law of death). There has to be a pact or alliance with the living language and language of the living feminine against death, against the dead. The repeated affirmation—like the contract, hymen, and alliance—always belongs to language: it comes down and comes back to the signature of the maternal, nondegenerate, noble tongue. The detour through *Ecce Homo* will have given us this to think about: History or historical science which puts to death or treats the dead, which deals or negotiates with the dead, is the science of the father. It occupies the place of the dead and the place of the father. To be sure, the master, even the good master, is also a father, as is the master who prefers Latin to bad German or to the mistreated mother. Yet the good master trains for the service of the mother whose subject he is; he commands obedience by obeying the law of the mother tongue and by respecting the living integrity of its body.

> The historical method has become so universal in our time, that even the living body of language [*der lebendige Leib der Sprache*] is sacrificed to its anatomical study. But this is precisely where culture [*Bildung*] begins—namely, in understanding how to treat the living as living [*das Lebendige als lebendig*], and it is here too that the mission of the master of culture begins: in suppressing "historical interest" which tries to impose itself there where one must above all else act [*handeln*: to treat or handle] correctly rather than know correctly [*richtig*]. Our mother tongue is a domain in which the pupil must learn to act correctly.

The law of the mother, as language, is a "domain" [*Gebiet*], a living body not to be "sacrificed" or given up [*preisgeben*] dirt-cheap. The expression "*sich preisgeben*" can also mean to give or abandon oneself for a nominal fee, even to prostitute oneself. The master must suppress the movement of this mistreatment inflicted on the body of the mother tongue, this letting go at any price. He must learn to treat the living feminine correctly.

These considerations will guide my approach to this "youthful work" (as they say) on the *Future of Our Educational Institutions*. In this place of a very dense crisscrossing of questions, we must approach selectively, moving between the issue of the pedagogical institution, on the one hand, and, on the other, those concerning life—death, the-dead-the-living, the language contract, the signature of credit, the biological, and the biographical. The detour taken through *Ecce Homo* will serve, in both a paradoxical and a prudent manner, as our protocol. I shall not invoke the notion of an "already," nor will I attempt to illuminate the "youthful" with a teleological insight in the form of a "lesson." Yet, without giving such a retro-perspective the sense that it has acquired in the Aristotelian-Hegelian tradition, we may be able to fall back on what Nietzsche himself teaches about the line of "credit" extended to a signature, about delaying the date of expiration, about the posthumous differance between him and his work, et cetera. This of course complicates the protocols of reading with respect to *The Future*. . . .

I give notice at the onset that I shall not multiply these protocols in order to dissimulate whatever embarrassment might arise from this text. That is, I do not aim to "clear" its "author" and neutralize or defuse either what might be troublesome in it for democratic pedagogy or "leftist" politics, or what served as "language" for the most sinister rallying cries of National Socialism. On the contrary, the greatest indecency is *de rigueur* in this place. One may even wonder why it is not enough to say: "Nietzsche did not think that," "he did not want that," or "he would have surely vomited this" that there is falsification of the legacy and an interpretive mystification going on here. [I say "vomit deliberately. Nietzsche constantly draws our attention to the value of learning to vomit, forming in this way one's taste, distaste, and disgust, knowing how to use one's mouth and palate moving one's tongue and lips, having good teeth or being hardtoothed, understanding how to speak and to eat (but not just anything!). All of this we know, as well as the fact that the word "*Ekel*" (disgust, nausea, wanting to vomit) comes back again and again to set the stage for evaluation. These are so many questions of styles. It should now be possible for an analysis of the word "*Ekel*," as well as of everything that it carries down with it, to make way for a hand-to-hand combat between Nietzsche and Hegel within that space so admirably marked out by Werner Hamacher (*Pleroma*, 1978) between *Ekel* and *Hegel* in Hegel's *Der Geist des Christentums*. In the lectures *On the Future of Our Educational Institutions*, it is disgust that controls everything—and first of all, in democracy, journalism, the State and its University. For example, following only the lexical occurrences of *Ekel*: "Only by means of such discipline can the young man acquire that physical loathing (*Ekel*) for the elegance of style which is so appreciated and valued by those who work in journalism factories and who scribble novels; by it alone is he irrevocably elevated at a stroke above a whole host of absurd questions and scruples, such, for instance, as whether (Berthold) Auerbach and (Karl) Gutzkow are really poets, for his disgust (*Ekel*) at both will be so great that he will be unable to read them any longer, and thus the problem will be solved for him. Let no one imagine that it is an easy matter to develop this feeling to the extent necessary in order to have this physical loathing; but let no one hope to reach sound aesthetic judgments along any other road than the thorny one of language, and by this I do not mean philological research, but self-discipline in one's mother-tongue" ("Second Lecture").

Without wishing to exploit the German word "*Signatur*," one could say that Nietzsche's historical disgust is aroused first of all by the signature of his era—that by which his era distinguishes, signifies, characterizes, and identifies itself: namely, the democratic signature. To this signature, Nietzsche opposes another one that is untimely, yet to come, and still anachronistic. One could reread the "First Lecture" from this point of view, with particular attention to this passage: "But this belongs to the signature without value (*nichtswürdigen Signatur*) of our present culture. The rights of genius have been democratized so that people may be relieved of the labor by which one forms oneself, and of the personal necessity of culture (*Bildungsarbeit, Bildungsnot*)."] One may wonder how and why what is so naively called a falsification was possible (one can't falsify just anything), how and why the "same" words and the "same" statements—if they are indeed the same—might several times be made to serve certain meanings and certain contexts that are said to be different, even incompatible. One may wonder why the only teaching institution or the only beginning of a teaching institution that ever succeeded in taking as its model the teaching of Nietzsche on teaching will have been a Nazi one.

First protocol: These lectures do not belong simply to the "posthumous" state mentioned by *Ecce Homo*. Had they title to the posthumous, they might have been binding on their author. However, Nietzsche expressly said that he would not want to see the text they constitute published, even after his death. What is more, he interrupted the course of this discourse along the way. I am not saying that he repudiated it entirely or that he repudiated those passages, for instance, that would be most scandalous to any contemporary anti-Nazi democrat. Nevertheless, let's remember that he "swore" not to publish these lectures. On July 25, 1872, after the Fifth Lecture, he writes to Wagner that "in the beginning of the coming winter, I intend to give my Basel audience the sixth and seventh lectures 'on the future of our educational institutions.' I want at least to *have done with it,* even in the diminished and inferior form with which I have treated this theme up until now. To treat it in a *superior* form, I would have to become more 'mature' and try to educate myself." However, he will not deliver these two last lectures and will refuse to publish them. On December 20, he writes to Malvida von Meysenbug: "By now you will have read these lectures and have been startled by the story's abrupt ending after such a long prelude [he is referring to the narrative fiction, the imaginary conversation that opens the first lecture], and see how the thirst for genuinely new thoughts and propositions ended up losing itself in pure negativity and numerous digressions. This reading makes one thirsty and, in the end, there is nothing to drink! Truthfully, what I set out to do in the final lecture—a series of nocturnal illuminations filled with extravagances and colors—was not suitable for my Basel audience, and it was a good thing the words *never left my mouth*" [italics added]. And toward the end of the following February, he writes: "You must believe me . . . in a few years I will be able to do better, and I will want to. In the meantime, these lectures have for me the value of an exhortation: they call me to a duty and a task that are distinctly incumbent upon me. . . . These lectures are summary and, what is more, a bit improvised. . . . Fritsch was prepared to publish them, but I swore not to publish any book that doesn't leave me with a conscience as clear as an angel's."

Other protocol: One must allow for the "genre" whose code is constantly re-marked, for narrative and fictional form and "indirect style." In short, one must allow for all the ways intent ironizes or demarcates itself, demarcating the text by leaving on it the mark of genre. These lectures, given by an academic to academics and students on the subject of studies in the university and secondary school, amount to a theatrical infraction of the laws of genre and academicism. For lack of time, I will not analyze these traits in themselves. However, we should not ignore the invitation extended to us in the Preface to the lectures where we are asked to ready slowly, like anachronistic readers who escape the law of their time by taking time to read—all the time it takes, without saying "for lack of time" as I have just done. These are the terms that will enable one to read between the lines, as he asks us to do, but also to read without trying to preserve "ancient rules" as one usually does. This requires a *meditatio generis futuri*, a practical meditation which goes so far as to give itself time for an effective destruction of the secondary school and university. "What must happen between the time when new legislators, in the service of a totally new culture, will be born and the present time? Perhaps the destruction of the *Gymnasium* [the German secondary school], perhaps even the destruction of the university, or, at the very least, a transformation of these teaching establishments which will be so total that their ancient rules will seem in the eyes of the future to be the remains of a cave-dwellers' civilization." In the meantime, Nietzsche advises us, as he will do in the case of *Zarathustra*, to forget and destroy the text, but to forget and destroy it through action.

Taking into account the present scene, how shall I in turn sift through this text? And what is to be retained of it?

In the first place, a phoenix motif. Once again, the destruction of life is only an appearance; it is the destruction of the appearance of life. One buries or burns what is *already dead* so that life, the living feminine, will be reborn and regenerated from these ashes. The vitalist theme of degeneration/regeneration is active and central throughout the argument. This revitalization, as we have already seen, must first of all pass by way of the tongue, that is, by way of the exercise of the tongue or language, the *treatment* of its body, the mouth and the ear, passing between the natural, living mother tongue and the scientific, formal, dead paternal language. And since it is a question of treatment, this necessarily involves education, training, discipline. The annihilation [*Vernichtung*] of the gymnasium has to prepare the grounds for a renaissance [*Neugeburt*]. (The most recurrent theme in the lectures is that the university, regardless of its opinion in the matter, is nothing but the product or further development of what has been preformed or programmed at the secondary school.) The act of destruction destroys only that which, being already degenerated, offers itself selectively to annihilation. The expression "degeneration" designates both the loss of vital, genetic, or generous forces and the loss of *kind*, either species or genre: the *Entartung*. Its frequent recurrence characterizes culture, notably university culture once it has become state-controlled and journalistic. This concept of degeneration has—*already*, you could say—the structure that it "will" have in later analyses, for example in *The Genealogy of Morals*. Degeneration does not let life dwindle away through a regular and continual decline and according to some homogeneous process. Rather, it is touched off by an inversion of values when a hostile and reactive principle actually becomes the active enemy of life. The degenerate is not a lesser vitality; it is a life principle hostile to life.

The word "degeneration" proliferates particularly in the fifth and last lecture, where the conditions for the regenerative leap are defined. Democratic and equalizing education, would-be academic freedom in the university, the maximal extension of culture—all these must be replaced by constraint, discipline [*Zucht*], and a process of selection under the direction of a guide, a leader or *Führer*, even a *grosse Führer*. It is only on this condition that the German spirit may be saved from its enemies—that spirit which is so "virile" in its "seriousness" [*männlich ernst*], so grave, hard, and hardy; that spirit which has been kept safe and sound since Luther, the "son of a miner," led the Reformation. The German university must be restored as a cultural institution, and to that end one must "renovate and resuscitate the purest ethical forces. And this must always be repeated to the student's credit. He was able to learn on the field of battle [1813] what he could learn least of all in the sphere of 'academic freedom': that one needs a *grosse Führer* and that all formation [*Bildung*] begins with obedience." The whole misfortune of today's students can be explained by the fact that they have not found a *Führer*. They remain *führerlos*, without a leader. "For I repeat it, my friends! All culture [*Bildung*] begins with the very opposite of that which is now so highly esteemed as 'academic freedom': *Bildung* begins with obedience [*Gehorsamkeit*]. subordination [*Unterordnung*], discipline [*Zucht*] and subjection [*Dienstbarkeit*]. Just as great leaders [*die grossen Führer*] need followers, so those who are led need the leaders [*so bedürfen die zu Führenden der Führer*]—a certain reciprocal predisposition prevails in the order [*Ordnung*] of spirits here—yes, a kind of preestablished harmony. This eternal order. . . ."

This preestablished ordinance or ordering of all eternity is precisely what the prevailing culture would attempt today to destroy or invert.

Doubtless it would be naive and crude simply to extract the word "*Führer*" from this passage and to let it resonate all by itself in its Hitlerian consonance, with the echo it received from the Nazi orchestration of the Nietzschean reference, as if this word had no other possible context. But it would be just as peremptory to deny that something is going on here that belongs to the *same* (the same what? the riddle remains), and which passes from the Nietzschean *Führer*, who is not merely a schoolmaster and master of doctrine, to the Hitlerian *Führer*, who also wanted to be taken for a spiritual and intellectual master, a guide in scholastic doctrine and practice, a teacher of regeneration. It would be just as peremptory and politically unaware as saying: Nietzsche never wanted that or thought that, he would have vomited it up, or he didn't intend it in that manner, he didn't hear it with that ear. Even if this were possibly true, one would be justified in finding very little of interest in such a hypothesis (one I am examining here from the angle of a very restricted corpus and whose other complications I set aside). I say this because, first of all, Nietzsche died as always *before* his name and therefore it is not a question of knowing what he would have thought, wanted, or done. Moreover, we have every reason to believe that in any case such things would have been quite complicated—the example of

Heidegger gives us a fair amount to think about in this regard. Next, the effects or structure of a text are not reducible to its "truth," to the intended meaning of its presumed author, or even its supposedly unique and identifiable signatory. And even if Nazism, far from being the regeneration called for by these lectures of 1872, were only a symptom of the accelerated decomposition of European culture and society as diagnosed, it still remains to be explained how reactive degeneration could exploit the same language, the same words, the same utterances, the same rallying cries as the active forces to which it stands opposed. Of course, neither this phenomenon nor this specular ruse eluded Nietzsche.

The question that poses itself for us might take this form: Must there not be some powerful utterance-producing machine that programs the movements of the two opposing forces at once, and which couples, conjugates, or marries them in a given set, as life (does) death? (Here, all the difficulty comes down to the determination of such a set, which can be neither simply linguistic, nor simply historico-political, economic, ideological, psycho-phantasmatic, and so on. That is, no regional agency or tribunal has the power to arrest or set the limits on the set, not even that court of "last resort" belonging to philosophy or theory, which remain subsets of this set.) Neither of the two antagonistic forces can break with this powerful programming machine: it is their *destination*; they draw their points of origin and their resources from it; in it, they exchange utterances that are allowed to pass through the machine and into each other, carried along by family resemblances, however incompatible they may sometimes appear. Obviously, this "machine" is no longer a machine in the classic philosophical sense, because there is "life" in it or "life" takes part in it, and because it plays with the opposition life/death. Nor would it be correct to say that this "program" is a program in the teleological or mechanistic sense of the term. The "programming machine" that interests me here does not call only for decipherment but also for transformation—that is, a practical rewriting according to a theory–practice relationship which, if possible, would no longer be part of the program. It is not enough just to say this. Such a transformative rewriting of the vast program—if it were possible—would not be produced in books (I won't go back over what has so often been said elsewhere about general writing) or through readings, courses, or lectures on Nietzsche's writings, or those of Hitler and the Nazi ideologues of prewar times or today. Beyond all regional considerations (historical, politco-economic, ideological, et cetera), Europe and not only Europe, this century and not only this century are at stake. And the stakes include the "present" in which we are, up to a certain point, and in which we take a position or take sides.

One can imagine the following objection: Careful! Nietzsche's utterances are not the same as those of the Nazi ideologues, and not only because the latter grossly caricaturize the former to the point of apishness. If one does more than extract certain short sequences, if one reconstitutes the entire syntax of the system with the subtle refinement of its articulations and its paradoxical reversals, et cetera, then one will clearly see that what passes elsewhere for the "same" utterance says exactly the opposite and corresponds instead to the inverse, to the reactive inversion of the very thing it mimes. Yet it would still be necessary to account for the possibility of this mimetic inversion and perversion. If one refuses the distinction between unconscious and deliberate programs as an absolute criterion, if one no longer considers only intent—whether conscious or not—when reading a text, then the law that makes the perverting simplification possible must lie in the structure of the text "remaining" (by which we will no longer understand the persisting substance of books, as in the expression *scripta manent*). Even if the intention of one of the signatories or shareholders in the huge "Nietzsche Corporation" had nothing to do with it, it cannot be entirely fortuitous that the discourse bearing his name in society, in accordance with civil laws and editorial norms, has served as a legitimating reference for ideologues. There is nothing absolutely contingent about the fact that the only political regimen to have *effectively* brandished his name as a major and official banner was Nazi.

I do not say this in order to suggest that this kind of "Nietzschean" politics is the only one conceivable for all eternity, nor that it corresponds to the best reading of the legacy, nor even that those who have not picked up this reference have produced a better reading of it. No. The future of the Nietzsche text is not closed. But if, within the still-open contours of an era, the only politics calling itself—proclaiming itself—Nietzschean will have been a Nazi one, then this is necessarily significant and must be questioned in all of its consequences.

I am also not suggesting that we ought to reread "Nietzsche" and his great politics on the basis of what we know or think we know Nazism to be. I do not believe that we as yet know how to think what Nazism is. The task remains before us, and the political reading of the Nietzschean body or corpus is part of it. I would say the same is true for the Heideggerian, Marxian, or Freudian corpus, and for so many others as well.

In a word, has the "great" Nietzschean politics misfired or is it, rather,

still to come in the wake of a seismic convulsion of which National Socialism or fascism will turn out to have been mere episodes?

I have kept a passage from *Ecce Homo* in reserve. It gives us to understand that we shall read the name of Nietzsche only when a great politics
will have effectively entered into play. In the interim, so long as that name
still has not been read, any question as to whether or not a given political
sequence has a Nietzschean character would remain pointless. The name
still has its whole future before it. Here is the passage:

> I know my fate [*Ich kenne mein Los*]. One day my name will be
> associated with the memory of something monstrous
> [*Ungeheures*]—a crisis without equal on earth, the most pro-
> found collision of conscience [*Gewissens-Kollision*], a decision
> [*Entschiedung*] that was conjured up *against* everything that had
> been believed, demanded, hallowed so far. I am no man, I am
> dynamite.—Yet for all that, there is nothing in me of a founder
> of a religion—religions are affairs of the rabble; I find it neces-
> sary to wash my hands after I have come into contact with
> religious people.—I *want* no "believers"; I think I am too mali-
> cious to believe in myself; I never speak to masses—I have a
> terrible fear that one day I will be pronounced *holy*: you will
> guess why I publish this book *before*; it shall prevent people
> from doing mischief with me.
>
> I do not want to be a holy man; sooner even a buffoon.—
> Perhaps I am a buffoon.—Yet in spite of that—or rather *not* in
> spite of it, because so far nobody has been more mendacious
> than holy men—the truth speaks out of me. . . .
>
> The concept of politics will have merged entirely with a war of
> spirits; all power structures of the old society will have been
> exploded—all of them are based on lies: there will be wars the
> like of which have never yet been seen on earth. It is only be-
> ginning with me that the earth knows *great politics* [*grosse
> Politik*].
>
> ("Why I Am a Destiny")

We are not, I believe, bound to decide. An interpretive decision does
not have to draw a line between two intents or two political contents. Our
interpretations will not be readings of a hermeneutic or exegetic sort, but
rather political interventions in the political rewriting of the text and its
destination. This is the way it has always been—and always in a singular
manner—for example, ever since what is called the end of philosophy, and

beginning with the textual indicator named "Hegel." This is no accident. It is an effect of the destinational structure of all so-called post-Hegelian texts. There can always be a Hegelianism of the left and a Hegelianism of the right, a Heideggerianism of the left and a Heideggerianism of the right, a Nietzscheanism of the right and a Nietzscheanism of the left, and even, let us not overlook it, a Marxism of the right and a Marxism of the left. The one can always be the other, the double of the other.

Is there anything "in" the Nietzschean corpus that could help us comprehend the double interpretation and the so-called perversion of the text? The Fifth Lecture tells us that there must be something *unheimlich*—uncanny—about the enforced repression [*Unterdrückung*] of the least degenerate needs. Why "*unheimlich*"? This is another form of the same question.

The ear is uncanny. Uncanny is what it is; double is what it can become; large or small is what it can make or let happen (as in laissez-faire, since the ear is the most tendered and most open organ, the one that, as Freud reminds us, the infant cannot close); large or small as well the manner in which one may offer or lend an ear. It is to her—this ear—that I myself will feign to address myself now in conclusion by speaking still more words in your ear, as promised, about your and my "academic freedom."

When the lectures appear to recommend linguistic discipline as a counter to the kind of "academic freedom" that leaves students and teachers free to their own thoughts or programs, it is not in order to set constraint over against freedom. Behind "academic freedom" one can discern the silhouette of a constraint which is all the more ferocious and implacable because it conceals and disguises itself in the form of laissez-faire. Through the said "academic freedom," it is the State that controls everything. The State: here we have the main defendant indicted in this trial. And Hegel, who is the thinker of the State, is also one of the principal proper names given to this guilty party. In fact, the autonomy of the university, as well as of its student and professor inhabitants, is a ruse of the State, "the most perfect ethical organism" (this is Nietzsche quoting Hegel). The State wants to attract docile and unquestioning functionaries to itself. It does so by means of strict controls and rigorous constraints which these functionaries believe they apply to themselves in an act of total auto-nomy. The lectures can thus be read as a modern critique of the cultural machinery of State and of the educational system that was, even in yesterday's industrial society, a fundamental part of the State apparatus. If today such an apparatus is on its way to being in part replaced by the media and in part associated with them, this only makes Nietzsche's critique of journalism—which he never dissociates from the educational apparatus—all the more striking. No doubt he implements his critique from a point of view that would make any Marxist analysis of this machinery, including the organizing concept of "ideology," appear as yet another symptom of degeneration or a new form of subjection to the Hegelian State. But one would have to look at things more closely: at the *several* Marxist concepts of State, at Nietzsche's opposition to socialism and democracy (in *The Twilight of the Idols*, he writes that "science is part of democracy"), at the opposition science/ideology, and so on. And one would have to look more closely at both sides. Elsewhere we shall pursue the development of this critique of the State in the fragments of the *Nachlass* and in *Zarathustra*, where, in the chapter "On the New Idol," one reads:

> State? What is that? Well, then, open your ears to me. For now I shall speak to you about the death of peoples.
>
> State is the name of the coldest of all cold monsters. Coldly it tells lies too; and this lie crawls out of its mouth: "I, the State, am the people." That is a lie! . . .
>
> Confusion of tongues of good and evil: this sign I give you as the sign of the state. Verily, this sign signifies the will to death! Verily, it beckons to the preachers of death. . . .
>
> "On earth there is nothing greater than I: the ordering finger of God am I"—thus roars the monster. And it is only the long-eared [asses] and shortsighted who sink to their knees! . . .
>
> State I call it where all drink poison, the good and the wicked; state, where all lose themselves, the good and the wicked; state, where the slow suicide of all is called "life."

Not only is the State marked by the sign and the paternal figure of the dead, it also wants to pass itself off for the mother—that is, for life, the people, the womb of things themselves. Elsewhere in *Zarathustra* ("On Great Events"), it is a hypocritical hound, which, like the Church, claims that its voice comes out of the "belly of reality."

The hypocritical hound whispers in your ear through his educational systems, which are actually acoustic or acroamatic devices. Your ears grow larger and you turn into long-eared asses when, instead of listening with small, finely tuned ears and obeying the best master and the best of leaders, you think you are free and autonomous with respect to the State. You open wide the portals [*pavillons*] of your ears to admit the State, not knowing that it has already come under the control of reactive and degenerate forces. Having become all ears for this phonograph dog, you transform yourself into a high-fidelity receiver, and the ear—your ear which is also the ear of the other—begins to occupy in your body the disproportionate place of the "inverted cripple."

Is this our situation? Is it a question of the same ear, a borrowed ear, the one that you are lending me or that I lend myself in speaking? Or rather, do we hear, do we understand each other already with another ear?

The ear does not answer.

Who is listening to whom right here? Who was listening to Nietzsche when, in the Fifth Lecture, he lent his voice to the philosopher of his fiction in order to describe, for example, this situation?

> Permit me, however, to measure this autonomy [*Selbstständigkeit*] of yours by the standard of this culture [*Bildung*], and to consider your university solely as a cultural establishment. If a foreigner desires to know something of our university system, he first of all asks emphatically: "How is the student connected with [*hängt zusammen*] the university?" We answer: "By the ear, as a listener." The foreigner is astonished: "Only by the ear?" he repeats. "Only by the ear," we again reply. The student listens. When he speaks, when he sees, when he walks, when he is in good company, when he takes up some branch of art: in short, when he *lives*, he is autonomous, i.e., not dependent upon the educational institution. Very often the student writes as he listens; and it is only at these moments that he hangs by the umbilical cord of the university [*an der Nabelschnur der Universität hängt*].

Dream this umbilicus: it has you by the ear. It is an ear, however, that dictates to you what you are writing at this moment when you write in the mode of what is called "taking notes." In fact the mother—the bad or false mother whom the teacher, as functionary of the State, can only simulate— dictates to you the very thing that passes through your ear and travels the length of the cord all the way down to your stenography. This writing links you, like a leash in the form of a umbilical cord, to the paternal belly of the State. Your pen is its pen, you hold its teleprinter like one of those Bic ballpoints attached by a little chain in the post office—and all its movements are induced by the body of the father figuring as alma mater. How an umbilical cord can create a link to this cold monster that is a dead father or the State—this is what is uncanny.

You must pay heed to the fact that the *omphalos* that Nietzsche compels you to envision resembles both an ear and a mouth. It has the invaginated folds and the involuted orificiality of both. Its center preserves itself at the bottom of an invisible, restless cavity that is sensitive to all waves which, whether or not they come from the outside, whether they are emitted or received, are always transmitted by this trajectory of obscure circumvolutions.

The person emitting the discourse you are in the process of teleprinting in this situation does not himself produce it; he barely emits it. He reads it. Just as you are ears that transcribe, the master is a mouth that reads, so that what you transcribe is, in sum, what he deciphers of a text that precedes him, and from which he is suspended by a similar umbilical cord. Here is what happens. I read: "It is only at these moments that he hangs by the umbilical cord of the university. He himself may choose what he will listen to; he is not bound to believe what he hears; he may close his ears if he does not care to hear. This is the acroamatic method of teaching." Abstraction itself: the ear can close itself off and contact can be suspended because the *omphalos* of a disjointed body ties it to a dissociated segment of the father. As for the professor, who is he? What does he do? Look, listen:

> As for the professor, he speaks to these listening students. Whatever else he may think or do is cut off from the students' perception by an immense gap. The professor often reads when he is speaking. As a rule he prefers to have as many listeners as possible; in the worst of cases he makes do with just a few, and rarely with just one. One speaking mouth, with many ears, and half as many writing hands—there you have, to all appearances, the external academic apparatus [*äusserliche akademische Apparat*]; there you have the University culture machine [*Bildungsmaschine*] in action. The proprietor of the one mouth is severed from and independent of the owners of the many ears; and this double autonomy is enthusiastically called "academic freedom." What is more, by increasing this freedom a little, the one can speak more or less what he likes and the other may hear more or less what he wants to—except that, behind both of them, at a carefully calculated distance, stands the State, wearing the intent expression of an overseer, to remind the professors and students from time to time that it is the aim, the goal, the be-all and end-all [*Zweck, Ziel und Inbegriff*] of this curious speaking and hearing procedure.

End of quotation. I have just read and you have just heard a fragment of a discourse lent or cited by Nietzsche, placed in the mouth of an ironic philosopher ("the philosopher laughed, not altogether good-naturedly," before holding forth as has just been related). This philosopher is old. He has left the university, hardened and disappointed. He is not speaking at noon but after noon—at midnight. And he has just protested against the unexpected arrival of a flock, a horde, a swarm [*Schwarm*] of students. What do you have against students? they ask him. At first he does not answer; then he says:

> "So, my friend, even at midnight, even on top of a lonely mountain, we shall not be alone; and you yourself are bringing a pack of mischief-making students along with you, although you well know that I am only too glad to put distance between me and *hoc genus omne*. I don't quite understand you, my distant friend . . . in this place where, in a memorable hour, I once came upon you as you sat in majestic solitude, and where we would earnestly deliberate with each other like knights of a new order. Let those who can understand us listen to us; but why should you bring with you a throng of people who don't understand us! I no longer recognize you, my distant friend!"
>
> We did not think it proper to interrupt him during his disheartened lament: and when in melancholy he became silent, we did not dare to tell him how greatly this distrustful repudiation of students vexed us.

OMPHALOS

The temptation is strong for *all* of us to recognize ourselves on the program of this staged scene or in the pieces of this musical score. I would give a better demonstration of this if the academic time of a lecture did not forbid me to do so. Yes, to recognize *ourselves, all* of us, in these premises and within the walls of an institution whose collapse is heralded by the old midnight philosopher. ("Constructed upon clay foundations of the current *Gymnasien*-culture, on a crumbling groundwork, your edifice would prove to be askew and unsteady if a whirlwind were to swirl up.")

Yet, even if we were all to give in to the temptation of recognizing ourselves, and even if we could pursue the demonstration as far as possible, it would still be, a century later, all of us men—not all of us women—who we recognize. For such is the profound complicity that links together the protagonists of this scene and such is the contract that controls everything, even their conflicts: woman, if I have read correctly, never appears at any point along the umbilical cord, either to study or to teach. She is the great "cripple," perhaps. No woman or trace of woman. And I do not make this remark in order to benefit from that supplement of seduction which today enters into all courtships or courtrooms. This vulgar procedure is part of what I propose to call "gynegogy."

No woman or trace of woman, if I have read correctly—save the mother, that's understood. But this is part of the system. The mother is the faceless figure of a *figurant*, an extra. She gives rise to all the figures by losing herself in the background of the scene like an anonymous persona. Everything comes back to her, beginning with life; everything addresses and destines itself to her. She survives on the condition of remaining at bottom.

ALEXANDER NEHAMAS

How One Becomes What One Is

People are always shouting they want to create a better future. It's not true. The future is an apathetic void, of no interest to anyone. The past is full of life, eager to irritate us, provoke and insult us, tempt us to destroy or repaint it. The only reason people want to be masters of the future is to change the past.
—MILAN KUNDERA, *The Book of Laughter and Forgetting*

Being and becoming, according to Nietzsche, are not at all related as we commonly suppose. "Becoming," he writes, "must be explained without recourse to final intentions . . . Becoming does not aim at a final state, does not flow into 'being' " [*The Will To Power*; hereafter referred to as *WP*]. One of his many criticisms of philosophers ("humans have always been philosophers") is that they have turned away from what changes and concentrated instead on what is: "But since nothing *is*, all that was left to the philosophers as their 'world' was the imaginary" (*WP*). His thinking is informed by his opposition to the very idea of a distinction between appearance and reality: "The true world—we have abolished. What world has remained? The apparent one perhaps? But no! *With the true world we have also abolished the apparent one*" [*The Twilight of the Idols*; hereafter referred to as *TI*]. "The 'true world' and the 'apparent world'—that means: the mendaciously invented world and reality" [*Ecce Homo*; hereafter referred to as *EH*, Pref.] He denies that the contrast itself is sensible: "The apparent world and the world invented by a lie—this is the antithesis." And he concludes that the pointlessness of this antithesis implies that "no shadow of a right remains to speak here of appearance" (*WP*).

From *Nietzsche: Life as Literature*. © 1985 by the President and Fellows of Harvard University. Harvard University Press, 1985.

Nietzsche does not simply attack the distinction between appearance and reality. He also offers, as we have seen, a psychological account of its origin. He claims that the distinction is simply a projection onto the external world of our belief that the self is a substance, somehow set over and above its thoughts, desires, and actions. Language, he writes, "everywhere . . . sees a doer and doing; it believes in will as *the* cause; it believes in the ego, in the ego as being, in the ego as substance, and it projects this faith in the ego-substance upon all things—only thereby does it first *create* the concept of a 'thing' . . . the concept of being follows, and is a derivative of, the concept of ego" (*TI*).

We must now take up the close analogy [Nietzsche] finds to hold between things in general and the self in particular. He believes that both concepts are improper in the same way; the idea that "becoming . . . does not flow into 'being' " applies to the self as well as to the world at large. But if this is so, how are we to account for the phrase that stands at the head of this chapter? How are we to interpret that most haunting of his many haunting philosophical aphorisms, the phrase "How one becomes what one is" (*Wie man wird, was man ist*), which constitutes the subtitle of *Ecce Homo*, Nietzsche's intellectual autobiography and, with ironic appropriateness, the last book he ever was to write?

It could be, of course, that this phrase was simply a very clever piece of language that happened to catch (as well it might have) Nietzsche's passing fancy. But this would be too simple, and not true. The idea behind the phrase and the phrase itself occur elsewhere in *Ecce Homo* and can actually be found throughout his writing. Nietzsche first uses a related expression as early as 1874, in *Schopenhauer as Educator*, the third of his *Untimely Meditations* [hereafter referred to as *UM*]: "Those who do not wish to belong to the mass need only to cease taking themselves easily; let them follow their conscience, which calls to them: 'Be your self [*sei du selbst*]! All that you are now doing, thinking, desiring, is not you yourself' " (*UM*). The formulation is simplified in *The Gay Science* [hereafter referred to as *GS*]: "What does your conscience say?—You must become who you are [*du sollst der werden, der du bist*]" (*GS*). Later on in this same work Nietzsche writes that, in contrast to those who worry about "the moral value" of their actions, he and the type of people to which he belongs "want to become those we are" (*GS*). And, in the late writings, we have already found Zarathustra saying that he "once counseled himself, not for nothing: Become who you are!" [*Thus Spake Zarathustra*; hereafter referred to as *Z*]. In short, this phrase leads, if not to the center, at least through the bulk of Nietzsche's thought.

The phrase "Become who you are" is problematic, and not only because Nietzsche denies the distinction between becoming and being. Its interpretation is made even more difficult because he is convinced that the very idea of the self as a subject in its own right, from which he claims this distinction is derived, is itself an unjustified invention: "There is no such substratum; there is no 'being' behind doing, effecting, becoming; 'the doer' is merely a fiction added to the deed—the deed is everything" [*Genealogy of Morals*; hereafter referred to as *GM*]. But if there is no such thing as the self, there seems to be nothing that one can in any way become.

In reducing the agent self to the totality of its actions ("doings"), Nietzsche is once again applying his doctrine of the will to power, part of which consists in the identification of every object in the world with the sum of its effects on every other thing. This view, as we have seen, does away altogether with things as they have traditionally been conceived. And this immediately raises in regard to the self a problem that has already confronted us in general terms: how can we determine which actions to group together as actions of one agent; who is it whose deed is supposed to be "everything"? But even before we can seriously raise this question, the following passage, which goes yet one step further, puts another obstacle in our way: "The 'spirit,' something that thinks—this conception is a second derivative of that false introspection which believes in "thinking': first an act is imagined which simply does not occur, 'thinking,' and secondly a subject-substratum in which every act of thinking, and nothing else, has its origin: that is to say, *both the deed and the doer are fictions*" (*WP*). We must postpone for the moment the discussion of this twist, which seems to leave us with no objects whatsoever. Instead, we must begin by placing Nietzsche's reduction of each subject to a set of actions within the context of his denial of the distinction between appearance and underlying reality: "What is appearance to me now?" he asks in *The Gay Science*. "Certainly not the opposite of some essence: what could I say about any essence except to name the attributes of its appearance!" The connection between these two views immediately blocks what might otherwise seem an obvious interpretation of the phrase that concerns us.

Such an interpretation would proceed along what we might call Freudian lines. It would be an effort to identify the self that one both is and must become with that group of thoughts and desires which, for whatever reason, are repressed, remain hidden, and constitute the reality of which one's current, conscious self is the appearance. This approach naturally allows for the reinterpretation of one's conscious thoughts and desires as a means of realizing who one really is and determining the underlying thoughts and desires of which these are merely signs. To that extent, I think, it would be congenial to Nietzsche, who had once written: "There is no trick which enables us to turn a poor virtue into a rich and overflowing one; but we can reinterpret its poverty into a necessity so that it no longer offends us when we see it and we no longer sulk at fate on its account" (GS). This passage raises crucial questions regarding self-deception, which we shall eventually have to face. But for the moment we must simply note that, despite its emphasis on reinterpretation, this view cannot account for Nietzsche's aphorism. The similarities and connections between Nietzsche and Freud are many and deep. But the vulgar Freudian idea that the core of one's self is always there, formed to a great extent early on in life, and waiting for some sort of liberation is incompatible both with Nietzsche's view that the self is a fiction and with his general denial of the idea of a reality that underlies appearance.

In addition this interpretation depends centrally on the idea that one's fixed or true self is there to be found; it thus contradicts Nietzsche's ambiguous attitude toward the question whether truth is discovered or created: " 'Truth' is . . . not something there, that might be found or discovered—but something that must be created and that gives a name to a process, or rather to a will-to-overcome that has in itself no end—introducing truth as a *processus in infinitum*, an active determining—not a becoming conscious of something that is in itself firm and determined" (WP). Nietzsche actually thinks that there is a close connection between the belief that truth is an object of discovery and the belief that the self is a stable object. It is very important to social groups, he writes at one point, that their members not keep too many secrets from one another. The need for truthfulness, the obligation to show "by clear and constant signs" who one is, he continues, has arisen partly for that reason. But if this is to be a plausible demand at all, "you must consider yourself knowable, you may not be concealed from yourself, you may not believe that you change. Thus, the demand for truthfulness presupposes the knowability and stability of the person. In fact, it is the object of education to create in the herd member a definite faith concerning human nature: it first invents the faith and then demands 'truthfulness' " (WP).

By contrast, Nietzsche writes, he wants to "transform the belief 'it *is* thus and thus' into the will 'it *shall become* thus and thus' " (WP). In general he prefers to think of truth as the product of creation rather than as the object of discovery. His attitude toward the self is similar. The people who "want to become those they are" are precisely "human beings who are new, unique, incomparable, who give themselves laws, who *create them-*

selves" (*GS*; my italics). *Thus Spake Zarathustra* is constructed around the idea of creating one's own self or, what comes to the same thing, the *Übermensch*. Zarathustra and his disciples as well are constantly described as "creators." Nietzsche is paying Goethe, one of his few true heroes, his highest compliment when he writes of him that "he created himself" (*TI*).

Yet once again we must come to terms with the ambiguity which Nietzsche's attitude on this issue too inevitably exhibits. Despite his constant attacks on the notion that there are antecedently existing things and truths waiting to be discovered, despite his almost inordinate emphasis on the idea of creating, Zarathustra at one point enigmatically says, "Some souls one will never discover, unless one invents them first." This same equivocal view comes into play later when he tells his disciples, "You still want to create the world before which you can kneel." And even though Nietzsche writes that "the axioms of logic . . . are . . . a means for us to *create* reality" (*WP*), he still believes that "rational thought is interpretation according to a scheme that we cannot throw off" (*WP*). Making and finding, creating and discovering, imposing laws and being constrained by them are involved in a complicated, almost compromising relationship. Our creations eventually become our truths, and our truths circumscribe our creations.

It seems, then, that the self, even if it is to be at some point discovered, must first be created. We are therefore faced with the difficult problem of seeing how that self can be what one is before it comes into being itself, before it is itself something that is. Conversely, if that self is something that is, if it is what one already is, how is it still possible for one to become that self? How could, and why should, *that* self be what one properly is and not some, or any, other? Why not, in particular, one's current self, which at least has over all others the significant advantage of existing?

Let us stop for a moment to note that, however equivocal, Nietzsche's emphasis on the creation of the self blocks another apparently obvious interpretation of the phrase "Become who you are." This interpretation holds that to become what one is is to actualize all the capacities for which one is inherently suited. It might be inaccurate but not positively misleading to say that such a view follows along Aristotelian lines. By appealing to the distinction between actuality and potentiality, this construction may account for some of the logical peculiarities of Nietzsche's phrase, since one may not (actually) be what one (potentially) is. But despite this advantage, such an interpretation faces two serious difficulties. The first is that, since one's capacities are in principle exhaustible, if one does actualize them, then one *has* in fact become what one is. But in that case becoming has ceased; it has "flowed into being" in the very sense in which we have seen Nietzsche deny that this is possible. The second difficulty is that to construe becoming as the realization of inherent capacities makes the creation of the self appear very much like the uncovering of something that is already there. Yet Nietzsche seems intent on undermining precisely the idea that there are antecedently existing possibilities grounded in the nature of things or of people, even though (as on the view we are considering) we may not know in advance what these are: this is a significant part of his scattered but systematic attack on the very notion of "the nature" of things.

We are therefore still faced with the problem of explaining how a self that truly must be created and that does not in any way appear to exist can be considered that which an individual is. In addition, Nietzsche's view, to which we keep returning, that becoming does not aim at a final state puts yet another obstacle in our way, for Nietzsche holds that constant change and the absence of stability characterize the world at large: "If the motion of the world aimed at a final state, that state would have been reached. The sole fundamental fact, however, is that it does not aim at a final state" (*WP*). He also holds that exactly the same is true of each individual. In *The Gay Science*, for example, he praises "brief habits," which he characterizes as "an inestimable means for getting to know *many* things and states." Later on in the same work he relies on a magnificent simile between the will and a wave in order to express his faith that continual change and renewal are both inevitable and inherently valuable:

> How greedily this wave approaches, as if it were after something! How it crawls with terrifying haste into the inmost nooks of this labyrinthine cliff! It seems that something of value, great value, must be hidden there.—And now it comes back, a little more slowly but still quite white with excitement; is it disappointed? Has it found what it looked for? Does it pretend to be disappointed?—But already another wave is approaching, still more greedily and savagely than the first, and its soul, too, seems to be full of secrets and the last to dig up treasures. Thus live waves—thus live we who will—more I shall not say.

The idea of constant change is also one of the main conceptions around which *Zarathustra* revolves: "All the permanent—that is only a parable. And the poets lie too much . . . It is of time and becoming that the best parables should speak: let them be a praise and a justification of all impermanence . . . there must be much bitter dying in your life, you creators. Thus are you advocates and justifiers of all impermanence. To be the child who is newly born, the creator must also want to be the mother who gives birth."

These passages suggest that Nietzsche is himself an advocate of all impermanence. But if this is so, he cannot think that there is any such thing as being at all: what relation, then, could possibly exist between becoming and being? To answer this question we must examine Nietzsche's own notion of being, which, like all such traditional notions, assumes a double aspect in his writing. Though he denies that being, construed as anything that is not subject to history and change, exists, he still constantly relies on this concept as he himself interprets it. Perhaps, then, his interpretation is unusual enough to escape the contradictions that have stopped us so far without lapsing at the same time into total eccentricity.

A first glimmer of the answer to the questions I have been raising may appear through the final obstacle that is still in our way. We have already seen that Nietzsche is convinced that the ego, construed as a metaphysically abiding subject, is a fiction. But also, as by now we may be prepared to expect, he does not even seem to believe in the most elementary unity of the person as an agent. Paradoxically, however, his shocking and obscure breakdown of what we have assumed to be the essential unity of the human individual may be the key to the solution of our problems. It may also be one of Nietzsche's great contributions to our understanding of the self as well as to our own self-understanding.

Consider the breakdown first. As early as the time when he was writing the second volume of *Human, All-Too-Human*, Nietzsche had written that students of history are "happy, unlike the metaphysicians, to have in themselves not one immortal soul but many mortal ones." In *The Gay Science* he had already denied that consciousness constitutes or underlies "the unity of the organism." We might of course suppose that Nietzsche is here merely denying that we have any grounds for supposing that we know that the self abides over time. This would be a skeptical position common to a number of modern philosophers who wrote under the influence of Hume. But that this is not all what Nietzsche's view amounts to is shown by the following radical and, for our purposes, crucial passage from *Beyond Good and Evil* [hereafter referred to as *BGE*]:

> The belief that regards the soul as something indestructible, eternal, indivisible, as a monad, as an *atomon*: this belief ought to be expelled from science! Between ourselves, it is not at all necessary to get rid of "the soul" at the same time . . . But the way is open for new versions and refinements of the soul-hypothesis; and such conceptions as "mortal soul," and "soul as subjective

multiplicity," and "soul as social structure of the drives and affects" want henceforth to have citizens' rights in science.

The idea of "the subject as multiplicity" constantly emerges in *The Will to Power*, where we find the following characteristic passage: "The assumption of one single subject is perhaps unnecessary; perhaps it is just as permissible to assume a multiplicity of subjects, whose interaction and struggle is the basis of our thought and our consciousness in general? A kind of aristocracy of 'cells' in which dominion resides? To be sure, an aristocracy of equals, used to ruling jointly and understanding how to command?" In the same note Nietzsche includes "the subject as multiplicity" and "the continual transitoriness and fleetingness of the subject: 'Mortal soul' " in a list of his own "hypotheses." I have already discussed in detail his view that all "unity is unity only as organization and cooperation" and his opposition to the belief in the subject, which, he claims, "was only invented as a foundation of the various attributes." As with all social and political entities, unity cannot be presupposed; it is achieved, if it is achieved at all, only when the elements of the system are directed toward a common end and goal.

This political metaphor for the self, which, despite Nietzsche's reputation, is at least more egalitarian than Plato's, can now set us, I think, in the right direction for understanding the phrase that concerns us. Nietzsche believes that we have no good grounds for assuming a priori that a living subject, or anything else for that matter, is already unified, that its unity is something it possesses in itself. He is deeply suspicious of the idea of unity in general: as Zarathustra says, "Evil I call it, and misanthropic—all this teaching of the One and the Plenum and the Unmoved and the Sated and the Permanent." And yet, not at all surprisingly by now, it is also Zarathustra who claims that "this is all my creating and striving, that I create and carry together into One what is fragment and riddle and dreadful accident."

Nietzsche's denial of the unity of the self follows from a view we have already seen in connection with the will to power. This is his view that the "mental acts" of thinking and desiring (to take these as representative of the rest) are indissolubly connected with their contents, which are in turn indissolubly connected with the contents of other thoughts, desires, and, of course, actions (*WP*). He holds, first, that we are not justified in separating such an act from its content; to remove the "aim" from willing is, he writes, to eliminate willing altogether, since there can only be a "willing *something*" (*WP*). And it is this view, as we have said, that allows him, despite his tremendous and ever-present emphasis on willing, to make the shockingly but only apparently incompatible statement that "there is no such thing as will" (*WP*). His position on the nature of thinking is strictly parallel: " 'Thinking,' as epistemologists conceive it, simply does not occur: it is a quite arbitrary fiction, arrived at by selecting one element from the process and eliminating all the rest, an artificial arrangement for the purposes of intelligibility" (*WP*).

The considerations that underlie Nietzsche's approach must be something like the following. We tend first to isolate the content of each thought and desire from that of all the others; we suppose that each mental act intends a distinct mental content, whose nature is independent of the content of all other mental acts. My thought that such-and-such is the case is *there* and remains what it is whatever else I may come to think, want, and do in the future. Though my thought may turn out to have been false, its significance is given and determined once and for all. Having now isolated the contents of our mental acts from one another, we proceed to separate the content of each act from the act that intends it. My thinking is an episode which we take to be distinct from what it concerns (or "intends"). Having performed these two "abstractions," we are now confronted with a set of qualitatively identical entities—thoughts, or thinkings—that we can attribute to a subject which, since it performs all these identical and therefore perfectly compatible and harmonious acts, we can safely assume to be unified.

It seems to me that it is this view that underwrites Nietzsche's conviction that the deed itself is a fiction and the doer "a second derivative." He appears to think that we tend to take the self without further thought as one because when we try to form a conception of the self in the first place, we commonly fail to take the contents of our mental acts into account. The strategy of abstracting from these contents and concentrating on the qualities of the mental states themselves with the purpose of finding out what the true self is can be traced back to Descartes's *Meditations*. Can doubt, understanding, affirming, desiring, being averse, imagining, or perceiving, Descartes asks, "be distinguished from my thought"? Can any of them "be said to be separated from myself?" By these "attributes" Descartes clearly understands only the mental acts themselves, and nothing besides. In particular, he excludes their content: even if what I imagine is false, he argues, "nevertheless this power of imagining does not cease to be really in use, and it forms part of my thought"; even if I am perceiving nothing real, he insists, "still it is at least quite certain that it seems to me that I see light, that I hear noise, and that I feel heat. That cannot be false."

But for Nietzsche each "thing" is nothing more, and nothing less, than the sum of all its effects and features. Since it is nothing *more* than that sum, it is not at all clear that conflicting sets of features are capable of generating a single subject: conflicting features, unless we already have an independent subject whose features we can show them to be, generate distinct things. But since a thing is also nothing *less* than the sum of its features, when we come to the case of the self, what we must attribute to each subject, what we must use in order to generate it, cannot be simply the sum of its mental acts considered in isolation from their content: " 'The subject' is the fiction that many similar states in us are the effect of one substratum: but it is we who first created the 'similarity' of these states; our adjusting them and making them similar is the fact, not their similarity (—which ought rather to be denied—)" (*WP*). What we must therefore attribute to the self is the sum of its acts along with their contents: each subject is constituted not simply by the fact *that* it thinks, wants, and acts but also by precisely *what* it thinks, wants, and does. And once we admit contents, we admit conflicts. What we think, want, and do is seldom if ever a coherent collection. Our thoughts contradict one another and contrast with our desires, which are themselves inconsistent and are in turn belied by our actions. The unity of the self, which Nietzsche identifies with this collection, is thus seriously undermined. This unity, he seems to believe, is to be found, if it is to be found at all, in the very organization and coherence of the many acts that each organism performs. It is the unity of these acts that gives rise to the unity of the self, and not, as we often think, the fact of a single self that unifies our conflicting tendencies.

An immediate difficulty for Nietzsche's view seems to be caused by his apparent failure to distinguish clearly between unity as coherence on the one hand and unity as "numerical identity" on the other. Numerical identity is singleness. And one might argue that even if the self is not organized and coherent in an appropriate manner, this still need not prevent it from being a single thing. In fact, this argument continues, it is only because the self is a single thing in the first place that it is at all sensible to be concerned with its coherence: whose coherence would even be in question otherwise? The idea that we are faced with conflicting groups of thoughts and desires itself depends on the assumption that these are the thoughts and desires of a single person: why else would they be conflicting rather than merely disparate?

We might try to reply that Nietzsche is concerned only with the problem of the coherence of selves that are already unified and not with the grounds of these selves' identity and unity. But in fact his own view that everything is a set of effects results precisely in blurring this distinction and prevents us from giving this easy and uninteresting answer. Since there is nothing above or behind such sets of effects, it is not clear that Nietzsche can consistently hold that there is anything to the identity of each object above the unity of a set of effects established from some particular point of view; it is not clear, that is, that Nietzsche can even envisage the distinction between coherence and numerical identity. But the question, then, is pressing: what is it that enables us to group some multiplicities together so as to form a single self and to distinguish them from others, which belong to distinct subjects?

At this point we can appeal once again to our political metaphor for the self. On a very basic level the unity of the body provides for the identity that is necessary, but not at all sufficient, for the unity of the self. Nietzsche, quite consistently, holds that the unity of the body, like all unity, is itself not an absolute fact: "The evidence of the body reveals a tremendous multiplicity"; the title of note 660 of *The Will to Power* is "The Body as a Political Structure." But in most cases, this multiplicity is, from our own point of view, organized coherently; the needs and goals of the body are usually not in conflict with one another: "The body and physiology the starting point: why?—we gain the correct idea of the nature of our subject-unity, namely as regents at the head of a communality (not as 'souls' or 'life forces'), also of the dependence of these regents upon the ruled and of an order of rank and division of labor as the conditions that make possible the whole and its parts" (*WP*). This too is the point Zarathustra makes when he says that the body is "a plurality with one sense, a war and a peace, a herd and a shepherd" (*Z*).

Because it is organized coherently, the body provides the common ground that allows conflicting thoughts, desires, and actions to be grouped together as features of a single subject. Particular thoughts, desires, or actions move the body in different directions, they place it in different situations and contexts, and can even be said to fight for its control. Exactly the same is true of their patterns—that is, of our character traits. Dominant habits and traits, as long as they are dominant, assume the role of the subject; in terms of our metaphor, they assume the role of the leader. It is such traits that speak with the voice of the self when they are manifested in action. Their own coherence and unity allow them to become the subject that, at least for a while, says "I." In the situation I am discussing, however, the leadership is not stable. Different and even incompatible habits and character traits coexist in the same body, and so different patterns assume the role of "regent" at different times. Thus we identify ourselves differently over time. And though, as is often the case with the voice of the state, the

"I" always seems to refer to the same thing, the content to which it refers and the interests for which it speaks do not remain the same. It is constantly in the process of changing. This process may sometimes tend in the direction of greater unity.

Such unity, however, which is at best something to be hoped for, certainly cannot be presupposed. Phenomena like *akrasia*, or weakness of will, and self-deception, not to mention everyday inconsistency, are constantly posing a threat to it. Wittgenstein once wrote that "our language can be seen as an ancient city: a maze of little streets and squares, of old and new houses, and of houses with additions from various periods; and this surrounded by a multitude of new boroughs with straight regular streets and uniform houses" (*Philosophical Investigations*). In a recent discussion of *akrasia* and self-deception, Amélie Rorty has used this same metaphor for the self. She urges that we think of the self not as a contemporary city built on a regular grid but more as a city of the Middle Ages, with many semi-independent neighborhoods, indirect ways of access from one point to another, and without a strong central municipal administration. She writes, "We can regard the agent self as a loose configuration of habits, habits of thought and perception and motivation and action, acquired at different stages, in the service of different ends" ("Self-Deception, Akrasia, and Irrationality").

The unity of the self, which therefore also constitutes its identity, is not something given but something achieved, not a beginning but a goal. And of such unity, which is at best a matter of degree and which comes close to representing a regulative principle, Nietzsche is not at all suspicious. It lies behind his earlier positive comments on "the One," and he actively wants to promote it. It is precisely its absence that he laments when, addressing his contemporaries, he writes, "With the characters of the past written all over you, and these characters in turn painted over with new characters: thus have you concealed yourselves perfectly from all interpreters of characters" (Z).

Nietzsche's view, it may now appear, is surprisingly similar to Plato's analysis of the soul in the *Republic*. Both divide the subject, both depend on a political metaphor for the self, and both are faced with the problem of relocating the agent once they have accomplished their division. But within the terms provided by this comparison, the differences between the two views are still striking. Nietzsche's breakdown of the individual is much more complicated and much less systematic than Plato's. He rejects Plato's belief that there are only three sources of human motivation. And he fights vehemently against Plato's conviction that reason should be the one that dominates. Having identified a large number of independent motives and character traits, Nietzsche, in contrast to Plato, considers that the question which should govern the self requires a different answer in each particular case. And he insists that this answer cannot be constrained by moral considerations.

The particular traits that dominate on one occasion can sometimes simply disregard their competitors and even refuse to acknowledge their existence: this is the case of self-deception. Or they may acknowledge them, try to bring them into line with their own evaluations, and fail: this is the case of *akrasia*. Or again they can try, and manage, to incorporate them, changing both themselves and their opponents in the process: this is to take a step toward the integration of the self which, in the ideal case, constitutes the unity which we too are pursuing:

> No subject "atoms." The sphere of a subject constantly growing or decreasing, the center of the system constantly shifting: in cases where it cannot organize the appropriate mass, it breaks into two parts. On the other hand, it can transform a weaker subject into its functionary without destroying it, and to a certain extent form a new unity with it. No "substance," rather something that in itself strives after greater strength, and that wants to preserve itself only indirectly (it wants to *surpass* itself—).   (*WP*)

This passage makes it clear that at least in some of the cases in which Nietzsche speaks of mastery and power, he is concerned with mastery and power over oneself, envisaging different habits and character traits competing for the domination of a single person. This is one of the reasons why I think that a primary, though by no means the only, object of the will to power is one's own self. But more important, we find in this passage the suggestion that, as our metaphor has already led us to expect, what says "I" is not the same at all times. And we can also see that the process of dominating, and thus creating, the individual, the unity that concerns us, is a matter of incorporating more and more character traits under a constantly expanding and evolving rubric. This may now suggest that, on Nietzsche's own understanding of these notions, the distinction between becoming and being is not absolute, and that his concept of "being" may indeed avoid the difficulties that earlier appeared to face it. But this suggestion must be elaborated in some detail before we can take it seriously.

Nietzsche often criticizes the educational practices of his time. One of his central objections to education in late nineteenth-century Germany is that it encouraged people to want to develop in all directions instead of showing them how they could fashion themselves into true individuals, sometimes even at the cost of eliminating certain beliefs and desires which they previously valued (*TI*). In *The Will to Power*, for example, he writes, "So far, the Germans . . . are nothing: that means they are all sorts of things. They will become something: that means, they will stop some day being all sorts of things." But the project of "becoming an individual" and of unifying one's own features requires hardness (a favorite term with him) toward oneself. Its opposite, which he finds everywhere around him, is "tolerance toward oneself"; this is an attitude that "permits several convictions, and they all get along with each other: they are careful, like all the rest of the world, not to compromise themselves. How does one compromise oneself today? If one is consistent. If one proceeds in a straight line. If one is not ambiguous enough to permit five conflicting interpretations. If one is genuine" (*TI*). This crucial passage suggests that Nietzsche is not as unqualified a friend of polysemy as it is sometimes claimed today. But the main point on which one must insist in this context is that though he clearly believes that certain character traits may have to be eliminated if unity is to be achieved, he does not in any way consider that such eliminated features are to be disowned.

It is . . . one of Nietzsche's most central views that everything one does is equally essential to who one is. Everything that I have ever done has been instrumental to my being who I am today. And even if today there are actions I would never do again and character traits I am grateful to have left behind forever, I would not have my current preferences had I not had those other preferences earlier on. My thoughts and actions are so intimately involved with one another and with my whole history that it is very difficult to say where one ends and another begins: "The most recent history of an action relates to this action: but further back lies a prehistory which covers a wider field: the individual action is at the same time a part of a much more extensive, later fact. The briefer and the more extensive processes are not separated" (*WP*).

It begins to seem, then, that Nietzsche does not think of unity as a state of being that follows and replaces an earlier process of becoming. Rather, he seems to think of it as a continual process of integrating one's character traits, habits, and patterns of action with one another. This process can also, in a sense, reach backward and integrate even a discarded characteristic into the personality by showing that it was necessary for one's subsequent development. When one shows this, of course, that trait's "nature" is itself altered through a highly complex process:

One thing is needful.—To "give style" to one's character—a great and rare art! It is practiced by those who survey all the strengths and weaknesses of their nature and then fit them into an artistic plan until every one of them appears as art and reason and even weaknesses delight the eye. Here a large mass of second nature has been added; there a piece of original nature has been removed—both times through long practice and daily work at it. Here the ugly that could not be removed is concealed; there it has been reinterpreted and made sublime. Much that is vague and resisted shaping has been saved and exploited for distant views . . . In the end, when the work is finished, it becomes evident how the constraint of a single taste governed and formed everything large and small. Whether this taste was good or bad is less important than one might suppose, if only it was a single taste!   (GS)

This process is as gradual as it is difficult; as Zarathustra says: "Verily, I too have learned to wait—thoroughly—but only to wait for *myself*. And above all I learned to stand and walk and run and jump and climb and dance. This, however, is my doctrine: whoever would learn to fly one day must first learn to stand and walk and run and climb and dance: one cannot fly into flying" (Z). The unity Nietzsche has in mind can become apparent and truly exist only over time. Though if it is ever achieved, it is achieved at some time, what is achieved at that time is the unification of one's past with one's present. The future is, therefore, always a danger to it: any new event may prove impossible to unify, at least without further effort, with the self into which one has developed.

But apart from this problem, the unity Nietzsche is after is also in danger from the constant possibility of self-deception, for one may "give style" to one's character and constrain it by "a single taste" simply by denying the existence, force, or significance of antithetical styles and tastes and by considering only part of oneself as the whole. Nietzsche seems aware of this difficulty. This is shown by his distinction between two sorts of people who have faith in themselves. Some, he writes, have faith because they refuse to look at all: "What would they behold if they could see to the bottom of themselves!" Others must acquire it slowly and are faced with it as a problem themselves: "Everything good, fine, or great they do is first of all an argument against the skeptic inside them" (GS). The possibility that we are deceiving ourselves cannot ever be eliminated; unity can always be achieved by refusing to acknowledge an existing multiplicity.

It would be more accurate to say, however, that only the feeling of unity, and not unity itself, can be secured in this way. One can think that the difficult task described in the passages we are considering has been completed when in fact one has not succeeded at all. The distinction can be made because the notions of style and character are essentially public. Nietzsche, of course, constantly emphasizes the importance of evaluating oneself only by one's own standards. Nevertheless, especially since he does not believe that we have any special access to knowledge of ourselves, such questions are finally decided from the outside. This outside, which includes looking at one's own past, may consist of a very select public, of an audience that perhaps does not yet exist. Still, the distinction between the fact and the feeling of unity must be pressed and maintained. Zarathustra taunts the sun when he asks what its happiness would be were it not for those for whom it shines (Z; GM). Similarly, it takes spectators for unity to be made manifest and therefore for it to be there. To an extent, one is at the mercy of one's audience. Nietzsche in particular, as we shall see at the end of this chapter, may be totally at the mercy of his readers.

Akrasia, the inability to act according to our preferred judgment, is a clear sign that unity is absent. It indicates that competing habits, patterns of valuation, and modes of perception are at work within the same individual—if we can use the term at all at this stage. Nietzsche is a great enemy of the notion of the freedom of will; naturally, however, he is no less opposed to the notion of the compelled or unfree will. Both ideas, he writes, are "mythology": in real life "it is only a matter of strong and weak wills" [BGE; TI]. But strength and weakness are themselves notions that he interprets in his own way, connecting them with the very kind of organization and integration that I have been discussing:

> *Weakness of the will*: that is a metaphor that can prove misleading. For there is no will, and consequently neither a strong nor a weak will. The multitude and disgregation of impulses and the lack of any systematic order among them result in a "weak will"; their coordination under a single predominant impulse results in a "strong will": in the first case it is the oscillation and the lack of gravity; in the latter, the precision and clarity of the direction.
>
> (WP)

But despite denying that both freedom and necessity exist, Nietzsche can also have Zarathustra praise those occasions "where necessity was freedom itself." Similarly, he takes "peace of soul" to signify either a mind becalmed, an empty self-satisfaction, or, on the contrary, "the expression of maturity and mastery in the midst of doing, creating, working, and willing—calm breathing, *attained* 'freedom of the will' " (*TI*; *GM*). Once again, Nietzsche appropriates traditional concepts for his own idiosyncratic, but not totally eccentric or unrelated, purposes.

Freedom of the will so construed is not the absence of casual determination but a harmony among all of a person's preference schemes. It is a state in which desire follows thought, and action follows desire, without tension or struggle, and in which the distinction between choice and constraint may well be thought to disappear. Nietzsche thinks of this state as a limiting case, to be reached, if at all, only with the greatest difficulty. In this we once again see his complex relation to Socrates, who in Plato's early dialogues argues that everyone already is in that condition and that only ignorance of the good prevents us from actually doing it.

Nietzsche is very clear about the extraordinary difficulty with which this state of harmony of thought and action can be reached. Success can in this case too be expressed through his political metaphor: "*L'effet c'est moi*: what happens here is what happens in every well-constructed and happy commonwealth; namely, the governing class identifies itself with the success of the commonwealth" (*BGE*). In more literal terms, success consists in having the minimum level of discord among the maximum possible number of diverse tendencies. This view, which is anticipated by section 290 of *The Gay Science*, is explicit in the following passage: "The highest human being would have the highest multiplicity of drives, in the relatively greatest strength that can be endured. Indeed, where the plant 'human being' shows itself strongest one finds instincts that conflict powerfully (e.g., in Shakespeare) but are controlled" (*WP*). It is just because of his ability to control this multiplicity that Goethe, who tried "to form a totality out of himself, in the faith that only in the totality everything redeems itself and appears justified" (*WP*), and who according to Nietzsche bore all the conflicting tendencies of his age within him, became his great hero: "What he wanted was totality . . . he disciplined himself to wholeness, he *created* himself" (*TI*; *WP*).

An even better example, though unavailable to Nietzsche, is once again Proust's narrator, who creates himself, out of everything that has happened to him, in his own writing—as in what follows we shall see that Nietzsche himself tries to do. In addition, Proust's narrator believes "that in fashioning a work of art we are by no means free, that we do not choose how we shall make it but that it preexists and therefore we are obliged, since it is both necessary and hidden, to do what we should have to do if it were a law of nature, that is to say to discover it" (*Remembrance of Things Past*). Yet this discovery, which he explicitly describes as "the discovery of our true life," can be made only in the very process of creating the work of art which describes and constitutes it. And the ambiguous relation between discovery and creation, which matches exactly Nietzsche's own view, also captures perfectly the tension in the very idea of being able to become who one actually is.

The creation of the self therefore appears to be the creation, or imposition, of a higher-order accord among our lower-level thoughts, desires, and actions. It is the development of the ability, or the willingness, to accept responsibility for everything that we have done and to admit what is in any case true: that everything that we have done actually constitutes who each one of us is.

From one point of view this willingness is a new character trait, a new state of development that is reached at some time and replaces a previous state. From another point of view, however, to reach such a state is not at all like having one specific character trait replace another, as when courage, for example, replaces cowardice, or munificence miserliness. The self-creation Nietzsche has in mind involves accepting everything that we have done and, in the ideal case, blending it into a perfectly coherent whole. Becoming brave is becoming able to avoid all the cowardly actions in which I may have previously engaged and to pursue a new kind of action instead. But I need not alter my behavior just because I realize that all my actions are my own. What, if anything, will change depends on the patterns that have characterized my behavior so far and on the new sorts of actions, if any, in which I may now want to engage.

But Nietzsche's conception of the unified self is still compatible with continued change, and this provides a sharp contrast between his view and a realization many of us make at some point in our life, when we see or decide that our character has developed enough and that we neither need nor want to change any more. Becoming who one is, in Nietzsche's terms, excludes such complacency altogether: "All those who are 'in the process of becoming' must be furious when they perceive some satisfaction in this area, an impertinent 'retiring on one's laurels' or 'self-congratulation' " (WP). The creation of the self is not a static episode, a final goal which, once attained, forecloses the possibility of continuing to change and to develop.

For one thing, it is not at all clear that such an "episode" can actually occur, that it does not constitute, as I have said, a regulative principle. If there were a good sense in which we could count our mental states, then perhaps we might succeed in fitting "all" of them together. Yet how they fit with one another clearly has a bearing on how they are counted—whether, for example, two thoughts separated by time may not after all be parts of one single longer thought. Nietzsche's view that the contents of our acts are indissolubly connected with one another argues for the same point, for to be able to reinterpret a thought or an action and thus to construe it as only part of a longer, "more extensive" process, as only a part of a single mental act, has exactly the same consequence: there is no such thing as the number of our experiences and actions.

More important, however, is the fact that so long as we are alive, we are always finding ourselves in new and unforeseen situations; we constantly have new thoughts and desires, we continue to perform new actions. In their light we may at any point come to face the need to reinterpret, to reorganize, or even to abandon earlier ones. And Nietzsche's exhortation "to revolve around oneself; no desire to become 'better' or in any way other" (WP; Z) is quite compatible with this continual development. To desire to remain who I am in this context is not so much to want any specific character traits to remain constant: the very same passage speaks of "multiplicity of character considered and exploited as an advantage" (cf. GS). Rather, it is to desire to appropriate and to organize as my own all that I have done, or at least that I know I have done, into a coherent whole. It is simply to become able to accept all such things, good and evil, as things I have done. It is not to cultivate stable character traits that make my reactions predictable and unsurprising. It is not simply to age, though aging is certainly connected with it: the young still have "the worst of tastes, the taste for the unconditional" and have not yet learned "to put a little art in their feelings and rather to risk trying even what is artificial—as the real artists of life do" (BGE). Rather, it is to become flexible enough to use whatever I have done, do, or will do as elements within a constantly changing, never finally completed whole.

Because they are continually being reinterpreted, none of the elements of this whole need remain constant. Zarathustra's mistrust of unity—his desire to avoid goals of stability—is his aversion to the permanence of specific character traits, parallel to Nietzsche's praise of ""brief habits" in section 295 of The Gay Science. By contrast, when he proudly describes his own teaching as "carrying into One" fragments, riddles, and accidents, he refers to the never-ending integration and reinterpretation of such brief habits.

The final mark of this integration, its limiting case, is provided by nothing other than the test involved in the thought of the eternal recurrence. This is the desire to do again what I have already done in this life if I were to live again: " 'Was that life?' I want to say to death," Zarathustra exclaims, " 'Well then! Once more!' " (Z). We have seen that the opportunity to live again would necessarily involve the exact repetition of the very same events that constitute my present life. The question therefore is not whether I would or would not do the same things again; in this matter there is no room for choice. The question is only whether I would *want* to do the same things all over again. This is simply the question whether I am glad to have done whatever I have done already, and therefore the question whether I would be willing to acknowledge all my doings as my own.

Becoming and being are therefore related in a way that does not make nonsense of Nietzsche's imperative to "become who you are." To be who one is, we can now see, is to be engaged in a constantly continuing and continually broadening process of appropriation of one's experiences and actions, of enlarging the capacity for assuming responsibility for oneself which Nietzsche calls "freedom" (TI). He writes: "To impose upon becoming the character of being: that is the supreme will to power." But the character of being is not stability and permanence. On the contrary, as this interpretation implies, "that *everything recurs* is the closest *approximation of a world of becoming to a world of being*" (WP).

The eternal recurrence signifies my ability to want my life and the whole world to be repeated just as they are. This is the ability to make "a Dionysian affirmation of the world as it is, without subtraction, exception, or selection—it wants the eternal circulation:—the same things, the same logic and illogic of entanglements. The highest state a philosopher can attain: to stand in a Dionysian relationship to existence—my formula for this is *amor fati*" (WP). In the limiting case this desire presupposes that I have assembled all that I have done and all that has led to it into a whole so unified that nothing can be removed without that whole crumbling down. Being, for Nietzsche, is that which one does not *want* to be otherwise.

What one is, then, is just what one becomes. In counseling himself to become who he is, Zarathustra becomes able to want to become what in fact he does become and not to want anything about it, about himself, to be different. To become what one is, we can see, is not to reach a specific new state and to stop becoming—it is not to reach a state at all. It is to identify oneself with all of one's actions, to see that everything one does (what one becomes) is what one is. In the ideal case it is also to fit all this into a coherent whole and to want to be everything that one is: it is to give style to one's character; to be, we might say, becoming.

The idea of giving style to one's character brings us back to Nietzsche's view that to have a single character or "taste" is more important than the quality of that taste itself (GS). And this idea, in turn, raises the notorious problem of his immoralism, his virulent contempt for traditional moral virtue, and his alleged praise of cruelty and the exploitation of the "weak" by the "strong."

Nietzsche certainly glorifies selfishness, but he is, once again, equally serious in denying a sharp distinction between egoism and altruism. He speaks of "some future, when, owing to continual adaptation, egoism will at the same time be altruism," when love and respect for others will just be love and respect for oneself: "Finally, one grasps that altruistic actions are only a species of egoistic actions—and that the degree to which one loves, spends oneself, proves the degree of individual power and personality" (WP). And though he also believes that mindless cruelty has certainly been practiced by people on one another in the past and that it will continue to be practiced by us in the future, this is not the cruelty he praises. In fact he thinks that its net effect is the opposite of its intent:

> Every living thing reaches out as far from itself with its force as it can, and overwhelms what is weaker: thus it takes pleasure in itself. The increasing "humanizing" of this tendency consists in this, that there is an ever subtler sense of how hard it is really to incorporate another: while a crude injury done others certainly demonstrates our power over them, it at the same time estranges their will from us even more—and thus makes them less easy to subjugate.

We have already seen that such "subjugation" can result in a new alliance, a new unity, even a new self (WP). Since the self is not an abiding substance, it too changes as it incorporates other objects "without destroying" them. In the final analysis, Nietzsche's ominous physical metaphors can be applied even to the behavior of a powerful and influential teacher.

In any case, Nietzsche's view that character is important independently of its moral quality should not be dismissed out of hand. I am not certain of the proper word in this context, and I use this one with misgivings, but I think that there is something admirable in the very fact of having character or style. This does not mean that merely having character overrides all other considerations and justifies any sort of behavior. This is not true, nor does it represent Nietzsche's attitude, which is only that "whether this taste was good or bad is *less important* than one might suppose" (GS; my italics). But Nietzsche believes that the evaluation of people and lives must appeal to a formal factor in addition to the content of our actions, the nature of which itself depends, as Aristotle also argued, on character: "An action is perfectly devoid of value: it all depends on *who* performs it" (WP). He wants to introduce, at least as a major consideration, the question whether a person's actions, whatever their moral quality, together constitute a personality. This is not merely a sensible consideration; it is in fact one on which we often rely in our everyday dealings with one another.

It is not clear to me whether a consistently and irredeemably vicious person does actually have a character; the sort of agent Aristotle describes as "bestial" probably does not (*Nicomachean Ethics*). In some way there is something inherently praiseworthy in having character or style that prevents extreme cases of vice from being praised even in Nietzsche's formal sense. Perhaps the viciousness of such people overwhelms whatever praise we might otherwise be disposed to give them. Probably, however, the matter is more complicated. The existence of character is not quite as independent of the quality of the actions of which it constitutes the pattern: consistency may not in itself be sufficient for its presence. Being *too* consistent, after all, often suggests the absence of character and a mechanical way of acting. Perhaps, to appeal to another Aristotelian idea, some sort of moderation in action may in the long run be necessary for having character. Nietzsche would not, of course, accept Aristotle's view that moderation in every specific area of behavior consists in a mean between excess and defect: these are for him the materials through which a higher synthesis, which he sometimes calls "the grand style," may emerge. In any case, he would attribute character to more types of agent than Aristotle would and would praise them on account of that character even if their actions were, from a moral point of view, seriously objectionable.

Even when we admire immoral people of character, our admiration is bound to be most often mixed. Yet there are many cases in which we feel absolutely free to admire characters who are (or who, in the nature of the case, would be if they existed) dreadful people: we do so constantly in the case of literature. The best argument for Nietzsche's view of the importance of character is provided by the great literary villains, figures like Richard III (in Shakespeare's version), Fagin, Don Giovanni, Fyodor Karamazov, Charlus. In their case we freely place our moral scruples in the background. What concerns us about them is the overall manner of their behavior, the very structure of their minds, and not primarily the content of their actions. Here we can admire without reservations or misgivings.

Once again, literature emerges as the model behind Nietzsche's view of the importance of character and the nature of the self. Because organization is the most crucial feature of literary characters, the quality of their actions is secondary: the significance and nature of a character's action is inseparable from its place in that organization. Ideally, absolutely everything a character does is equally essential to it; characters are supposed to be constructed so that their every feature supports and is supported by every other. These are the features I discussed in connection with the eternal recurrence [elsewhere]. Nietzsche came to see perfect self-sufficiency as a proper test for the perfect life at least partly because his thinking so often concerned literary models.

It might be objected to this view that our admiration for villainous or even inconsistent characters (who are consistently depicted) is directed not at those characters themselves but at the authors who create them. Therefore, this argument concludes, Nietzsche's generalization from literature to life is once again shown to be illegitimate. But we should note that when it comes to life, the "character" and the "author" are one and the same, and admiring the one cannot be distinguished from admiring the other. This is also the reason, I suspect, that though inconsistent characters can be admired in literature, they cannot be admired in life: in life an inconsistent character constitutes a poor author; there is no room for the distinction between creature and creator. The parallel between life and literature may not be perfect, but it is not flawed in the manner this objection envisages.

Nietzsche always depended on literary and artistic models for understanding the world. This accounts for some of his most peculiar thoughts, and it underlies some of his most original ideas. As early as *The Birth of Tragedy* [hereafter referred to as *BT*] he saw Dionysus reborn in the person of Wagner and in the artwork of the future by means of a process that was the symmetrical opposite of what he took to be the process of the dissolution of classical antiquity (*BT*). But, as Paul de Man has written, "passages of this kind are valueless as arguments, since they assume that the actual events in history are founded in formal symmetries easy enough to achieve in pictorial, musical, or poetic fictions, but that can never predict the occurrence of a historical event" (*Allegories of Reading*). We know that Nietzsche, who was a compulsive letter writer, preferred what in his time still was a literary genre in its own right to conversation and personal contact as a means of communication even with his close friends. Often enough he urges that we fashion our lives in the way artists fashion their works: "We should learn from artists while being wiser than they are in other matters. For with them this subtle power [of arranging, of making things beautiful] usually comes to an end where art ends and life begins; but we want to be the poets of our life—first of all in the smallest, most everyday matters" (*GS*). Nietzsche writes that freedom is "facility in self-direction. Every artist will understand me" (*WP*). And it is primarily in artists that he finds the peace of soul we have already seen him call "attained freedom of the will." As he writes, it is artists who "seem to have more sensitive noses in these matters, knowing only too well that precisely when they no longer do something 'voluntarily' but do everything of necessity, the feeling of freedom, subtlety, full power, of creative placing, disposing, and forming reaches its peak—in short, that necessity and 'freedom of will' then become one in them" (*BGE*).

How, then, can one achieve the perfect unity and freedom that are primarily possessed by perfect literary characters? How does one become both a literary character who, unlike either the base Charlus or the noble Brutus, really exists and also that character's very author?

One way of achieving this perhaps impossible goal might be to write a great number of very good books that exhibit great apparent inconsistencies among them but that can be seen to be deeply continuous with one another when they are read carefully and well. Toward the end of this enterprise one can even write a book about these books that shows how they fit together, how a single figure emerges through them, how even the most damaging contradictions may have been necessary for that figure or character or author or person (the word hardly matters here) to emerge fully from them: "*Natura non facit saltum.*—However strongly one may develop upwards and appear to leap from one contradiction to another, a close observation will reveal the dovetails where the new building grows out of the old. This is the biographers' task: they must reflect upon their subject on the principle that nature takes no jumps" [*The Wanderer and His Shadow* (hereafter referred to as *WS*)].

Zarathustra had said, "What returns, what finally comes home to me, is my own self" (*Z*). Now Nietzsche can write of his *Untimely Meditations*, three of which concern important historical figures and one history itself: "At bottom they speak only of me . . . *Wagner in Bayreuth* is a vision of my future, while in *Schopenhauer as Educator* my innermost history, my *becoming*, is inscribed." Earlier Nietzsche had written: "Now something that you formerly loved . . . strikes you as an error . . . But perhaps this error was as necessary for you then, when you were still a different person—you are always a different person—as all your present 'truth' " (*GS*). Now he can look back at *Schopenhauer as Educator* and claim:

> Considering that in those days I practiced the scholar's craft, and perhaps *knew* something about this craft, the harsh psychology of the scholar that suddenly emerges in this essay is of some significance: it expresses the *feeling of distance*, the profound assurance about what could be my task and what could only be

means, *entr'acte* and minor works. It shows my prudence that I
was many things and in many places in order to be able to
become one thing—to be able to attain one thing. I *had* to be a
scholar, too, for some time.   (*EH*)

One way, then, to become one thing, one's own character, what one is, is,
after having written all these other books, to write *Ecce Homo* and even to
give it the subtitle "How One Becomes What One Is." It is to write this
self-referential book in which Nietzsche can be said with equal justice to
invent or to discover himself, and in which the character who speaks to us
is the author who has created him and who is in turn a character created by
or implicit in all the books that were written by the author who is writing
this one.

But the fact that this character emerges out of many works may seem
to present a serious difficulty for this interpretation of unity and, in particular, for the literary model on which I have claimed it depends. Literary
characters often appear in numerous works; Odysseus and Oedipus keep
reemerging in Western literature. And though there is a popular view that
behind each character there is a "myth" or "legend" that dictates that some
of that character's features must remain invariant across different treatments, this view is simply popular—and nothing else. The "myth" consists
of those features which, as a matter of fact, have remained the same so far
in a character's treatment. It is an abstraction from such particular treatments and has no prescriptive powers of its own. No noncircular argument
can show that an Odysseus who did not participate in the siege of Troy, or
an Odysseus who returned to Ithaca immediately after the war, or even an
Odysseus who was slow witted and clumsy could not be the "real" Odysseus.
Euripides, after all, has given us a Helen who never went to Troy. But if no
such myth dictates the essential features of each character, then different
treatments can attribute, without contradiction, inconsistent properties to
any particular character. This may imply that there can be no single literary
character called "Odysseus," or that literary characters in general cannot be
unified in the manner that I have presupposed: perhaps Odysseus is a single
character who is nevertheless, as all characters can be, deeply inconsistent.
If this is so, then it may seem that Nietzsche had too naive an understanding
of literary characters or that it was wrong to attribute this model to him.
Conversely, it may seem that even if Nietzsche intended to create a literary
character out of himself, he still need not have aimed at unity and coherence: literariness and unity, according to this argument, do not go with one
another.

Now it is absolutely true that literary characters have no essence and can well be inconsistent across different works. But who are the characters who, like Odysseus, have offered themselves for the greatest number of different treatments and versions? They are precisely those who, at least at some point in their history, were given a highly unified, coherent, and consistent presentation. It is just this feature, I think, that provokes other authors into creating variants of these characters with the aim of seeing whether they will still be recognizable. Inconsistency can therefore easily arise across different works; it may even be considered a desirable feature for a character in the long run: the most interesting characters are often those who keep reappearing in fiction. But this does not imply that each particular version of a character is itself inconsistent. On the contrary, the great characters are those who receive many treatments which, though perhaps inconsistent with one another, are still internally coherent and highly organized. Since Nietzsche, therefore, is developing only a single treatment of this character, nothing prevents him from aiming at coherence on the basis of the literary model which, we can insist, he accepts.

This misplaced objection, however, inadvertently reveals a new dimension in Nietzsche's project. Apart from creating a unified and coherent version of a character, his project has also given rise to a large number of different interpretations, or versions, of that character. Each one of those versions, the present one included, aims at unity and coherence in its own right. Even interpretations that attribute to Nietzsche inconsistent or polysemous views do so for a reason; the Nietzsche such interpretations produce is still, at least in principle, consistent and seriously motivated. But there are by now many different versions of Nietzsche, many of which (like the different versions of some literary characters) are inconsistent with one another. And this, as I think Nietzsche actually hoped, may make the questions "Who is the real Nietzsche? Which is the correct interpretation of his views?" as easy or as difficult to answer, and perhaps as pointless to pose, as the questions "Who is the real Odysseus? Which is the correct version of his story?" But even though such questions may be pointless, we can still ask and decide whether some specific interpretation of Nietzsche is better than another, just as we can decide that Tennyson's version of Odysseus is a trifle compared to Homer's. We must keep resisting, in this context too, the assumption that Nietzsche's perspectivism itself tries to undermine: even if there is no "ultimate" truth, it does not follow that every view is as good as every other.

Nietzsche's enterprise, however, may still appear to many of his readers to be doomed from its beginning. No one has managed to bring life closer to literature than he did, and yet the two may finally refuse to become one, making his ideal of unity impossible to approach. *Ecce Homo*, one might argue, leaves great parts of Nietzsche's life undiscussed, and, unfortunately for him, his life did not end with it but twelve miserable years later. To make a perfectly unified character out of all that one has done, as Nietzsche wants, may involve us in a vicious effort: we may have to be writing our autobiography as we are living our life, and we would also have to be writing about writing that autobiography, and to be writing in turn about that, and so on, and so on without end. But as Nietzsche had written long before his own end: "Not every end is a goal. A melody's end is not its goal; nevertheless, so long as the melody has not reached its end, it also has not reached its goal. A parable" (*WS*). This parable explicates the phrase that has occupied us and expresses Nietzsche's attitude toward the relationship between the world and art as well as anything he ever wrote. But for some the doubt remains whether any melody, however complicated, could ever be a model that a life (which is not to say a biography) can imitate.

Nietzsche, though, writes: "One does best to separate artists from their work, not taking them as seriously as their work. They are, after all, only the precondition of their work, the womb, the soil, sometimes the dung and manure on which, out of which, it grows—and therefore in most cases something one must forget if one is to enjoy the work itself" (*GM*). What, then, if the work itself, in its totality, results in the construction of a character whose "biography" it turns out to be ? In that case the doubt that was lingering just above may be counterbalanced by the suspicion that only the "biography" that emerges through Nietzsche's works, and not the "life" out of which they grow, is of any importance. In his eyes, at least, it is only such a character who can influence history and thought and who, like the Socrates who emerges out of Plato's dialogues, can manifest the will to power in fashioning values and modes of life. We have seen that characters are usually evaluated without regard for their morality, for the specific content of their actions; they are in this sense situated "beyond good and evil." But what mode of evaluation is appropriate for the character who emerges out of Nietzsche's writing and who is beyond good and evil not only in this generalized sense but also because, in the manner which by now we have found to be essential to him, the very content of his actions is an effort to base all evaluation beyond good and evil, beyond regard for the specific content of our actions?

WERNER HAMACHER

"Disgregation of the Will": Nietzsche on the Individual and Individuality

Individuality: the word is spoken—and not only in the language of philosophy—with a forked tongue.

The concept of individuality, logically determined as mediating between the generality of what it asserts and the specificity of what it means, speaks already of a commonality, of a partaking in the common, that threatens the claim to individuality. The concept of individuality betrays individuality in the very act by which this concept attempts to seize, in mediation, individuality's substance. And the betrayal is double: the concept betrays individuality by sacrificing individuality's claim of immediate singularity to the power of the generalized and generally comprehensible language and language use; and by means of this betrayal, it also indicates the specific structure of individuality both in relation to itself and in relation to generality. The ambiguity of the concept of individuality has left its traces in all systems dedicated to that concept's determination. To enter their history at a relatively arbitrary point: Leibniz insists that each individual is individuated throughout its entire essence ("omne individuum sua tota Entitate individuatur"), and that it before comprises an infinity of determinations that correspond to the infinity of the universe even as they escape all finite knowing. He thus characterizes individuality as the representation of a totality with which it nonetheless does not coincide. According to Leibniz, the only entity capable of a complete knowledge of the individual is the one

From *Reconstructing Individualism: Autonomy, Individuality, and the Self in Western Thought*, edited by Thomas C. Heller, Morton Sosna, & David E. Wellbery. © 1986 by the Board of Trustees of the Leland Stanford Junior University. Stanford University Press, 1986.

that gathers the totality of necessary determinations unto or into itself and that is therefore not subject to the conditions of their representation. The individual is thus a monadic unity of an infinity of determinations, and it can be grasped only by an infinite faculty of knowledge—that of God. Finite individuals are incapable of knowing themselves as individuals. Leibniz grasps individuality with reference to the universality of God; he grasps the representative character of the individual's infinite determination with reference to the presence of an absolutely necessary essence—as with reference to the vanishing point wherein all determinants of the individual are gathered and wherein the individual as such disappears into the universal. Thus conceived, individuality is a fundamentally theological concept destined or determined to redeem finite individuals from their contingency. When Christian Wolff defines the individual, in his *Philosophia prima sive ontologia*, as that "quod omnimode determinatum est," he expresses in the most simple way the consequence of Leibniz's thought about individuality: the individual is thoroughly determined from or by the totality of its logical, historical, social, and psychic conditions; and it is determined toward or for totality, such that no genuine force of determination can be attributed to the individual by which it might autocratically distance itself from the teleological movement dictated to it. Individuality is hence the not merely theological but also teleological concept of a totality of determinations each of which holds itself in a prestabilized harmony with all the others, a harmony whose stability is impregnable. The *compossibilitas* of all single determinations is the securing and totalizing ground of the individuality they unite into a destiny, and it is the ground of the knowledge of this destiny. The individual is the essence or entity established by its universal determination.

Rejecting the fundamental ontological and epistemological assumptions of the Leibniz-Wolff school, Kant made clear in his reflections on the *prototypon transcendentale* that thorough determination can only be attributed to a thoroughly necessary being, that is, to a highest being, an *ens entium*, which can never be considered an objective being, since it is inaccessible to finite understanding. Rather, this being can always only be considered a general form of representation regulatively underlying our constitution of objects. Individuality thus figures as an unknowable and nonpresentable prototype of objects that, being imitations of it, can never attain to its degree of positive determination. Finite reason constitutes the individual—that is, the infinitely determinate—as finite, changes the particular into the nonspecifically general, detypifies the typical and reduces its being in each representation. Since the original (*Urbild*) is no longer given but rather merely given up or projected, objects hover on the brink of forfeiting at once their imitative character and their determinate form. After Kant, the concept of individuality lacks the assured ground of a determination that could render it an object of knowledge, lacks the nonproblematic theo-teleological destiny by means of which the demand for its internal totality could be fulfilled.

The formula "Individuum est ineffabile" from Goethe's letter to Lavater of September 20, 1780, arises, then, not from a sensualist animosity to conceptual rigor, but rather from an insight delivered by the disintegration of the great seventeenth- and eighteenth-century systems: that the individual must remain inaccessible to a finite faculty of representation, that its particularity cannot be grasped using general linguistic conventions, and that, because it is itself finite, even it does not possess the means to express itself in its totality as individual. In expressing itself as individual, it neither expresses itself as a whole nor expresses itself wholly: the whole has become, for knowledge and for language, a merely finite, temporally as well as structurally limited generality. Henceforth, individuality can stand for the capacity to project oneself onto an indeterminable multiplicity of possible forms, each of which is open to further possibilities of determination and none of which can terminate in a paradigmatic form. Individuality is no longer either the representation of a prior or transcendentally guaranteed presence or the forerunner of a universality in which it could realize its determination. Both Schlegel's thoughts on individuality, formulated in his encounter with Fichte, and Kierkegaard's thoughts on individuality, formulated in his encounter with Hegel and Schlegel, are to be read in this context.

For Nietzsche, the historically individual is first of all a form of past greatness whose attempted representation or repetition must deprive it of precisely its individuality. In *On the Use and Disadvantage of History for Life*, the second of the *Untimely Meditations*, he connects the conditions not only of the writing of history but of history itself and of the making of history to the efficacy of authentic individuality:

> In order for [a comparison between the greatness of the past and the greatness of the present] to have a strengthening effect, how much variety must be overlooked, how violently must the individuality of the past be forced into a general form and all its sharp angles and lines smashed to pieces! In principle, that which was once possible could indeed only present itself as possible for the second time if the Pythagoreans were right in believing that, given the same constellation of heavenly bodies, the same would

have to repeat itself also on earth, and down to the smallest details.

The conditions of the representation of the individual demand the generalization—that is to say, the deindividualization, the rape and ruin—of the individual (and even of its possibility) by imposing a universal law. Wherever the individual is repeated, it is already no longer the individual that it is supposed once to have been. The individuality whose images the past holds in store is merely a mythical figure, which can pass as a stereotype through changing times, lending them an aura of lasting glory. The individuality of the historical ideal, whose destiny is to distribute impulses of life in the present, must, by virtue of its character as ideal type, dig life's grave. Such an individuality allows not the individual but only its stiff, typical, and typifying form to be seized. The individual, however, would be precisely that which is consumed in no type, no form, no figure, and no codifiable reference.

Since it is governed by the law of repetition, even the present itself is incapable of offering what the form of representation destroys:

> The individual has withdrawn itself into the interior: outside, one can no longer find its slightest trace; apropos of which, one might doubt that there could be causes at all were there not effects. Or do we need to engender a species of eunuchs to serve as attendants in the great historical world-harem? On them, of course, pure objectivity is beautifully becoming. But it almost seems as if the task were to watch over history to make sure that nothing comes of it but stories, and certainly nothing with the remotest resemblance to an event!

Under the pressure of traditional, representative types or models of individuality, the individual has forfeited the ability to differentiate itself effectively from the historical world to which it alludes in knowledge and action. It has become assimilated to the types in distinction from which it was to have borne witness to its own historical, sexual, and semantic difference. It is an equal among equals, castrated, deprived of precisely what made it individual, unequal—it is a eunuch among women. But in the realm of equality—whether historical equality between past and present, epistemological equality between what thinks and what is thought, juridical equality among the citizens of a society, or physiological equality between different genders or different ages—there is no history. History, as Nietzsche conceives of it, depends upon the inequality, indeed, the incommensurability, of the moments that take part in it. In the individual, this incommensurability stands out, becomes a power that deforms and transforms the uniformity of the historical stances and substances of knowledge; only thus can it become a properly historical power.

Individuality is so fully determined as incommensurability that no individual could correspond to its concept if it were at one with and equal to itself, if it were a thoroughly determined, whole form. *Human, All Too Human* proposes, in the interests of knowledge, that one not uniformize oneself into rigidity of bearing and that one not treat oneself "like a stiff, steadfast, *single* individual." Only the individual's nonidentity with itself can constitute its individuality. Measured against itself as concept, bearing, and function, the individual proves to be other, to be more—or less—than itself. Its individuality is always only what reaches out beyond its empirical appearance, its social and psychological identities, and its logical form. Individuality is unaccountable surplus.

Now if individuality is the irreducibly unequal, and if the individuality of past and present life is betrayed in the typological identifications of idealist, positivist, archaeological, and teleological historiographies, then the ground of the possibility of individuality—and so of any discussion, be it affirmative or critical, of individuality—can only lie in the margin of difference between the uniformity of the hitherto historical and a future as yet uninvested with types, meanings, and values. The term "individuality" properly applies only to what transgresses the series of forms and the form of forms (typological knowledge and its objective correlatives), dissociating itself from the rigor mortis of canonical life forms, eluding the subsumptive compulsion of general categories, advancing toward a future that withdraws from every typology and objectification. Individuality is always still to come. Never already given, it is what gives itself up—projects itself—out of the future as a possibility for the present, what has always not quite yet given itself up, and what, in this way, in its giving, withholds itself. Indeed, there can be no life except where this individuality opens itself onto its future possibility. Hence the importance of the concept of individuality in Nietzsche's thought. "Even we are not yet persuaded . . . that we truly have life within us," he writes in the second of the *Untimely Meditations*. As a "lifeless and yet uncannily mobile concept- and word-factory, I may still have the right to say of myself, 'Cogito, ergo sum,' but never, 'Vivo, ergo cogito.' I am guaranteed the emptiness of 'being,' not the fullness and greenness of 'life'; my original feeling ensures only that I am a thinking being, not that I am a living being; ensures not that I am an *animal*, but only that I am a *cogital*. 'First grant me life' "—thus cries out every individual. "Who will grant you this life? No god and no human: only your own youth."

No power that transcends the individual—neither another human being nor anything above the human nor even this particular human being—is the source of historical life; instead, that source is what, in the individual, reaches out as "youth" beyond the borders of its historical determination into a still-open future. The proposition with which free individuality grants itself existence—not expresses or constates its being, since substantial being is not given to it—reads no longer "Cogito, ergo sum" or, as simple performance, "Ego sum," but rather "Ero sum." With regard to my indetermination by or as totality and my interminable futurity, I grant myself being. Only my futurity gives me life. This life is never something present to hand that could be seized in descriptive speech, never something already there or captured in the statement of the whole of its readiness, but rather it is always what, in all futures, is still to come and what, in language, is merely announced. Its discourse involves not predication but rather predication in the sense of pre-diction and promise, of pro-nunciation. By pro-nouncing in this manner I grant myself being. Individual being is never established in my speech but is rather announced there as a claim, reserving my futurity. Hence never is it stated sufficiently or with a completeness that could be generalized. If the life of historical generalities is subject to laws—and the second of Nietzsche's *Untimely Meditations* attempts to describe certain of these laws—then the futurity of this life and the form of language that corresponds to this futurity in the never-sufficient announcement of its life comprise the law of these laws.

To this notion of the futurity of the life that the language of free individuality inaugurates, one might object that no language could do without conventional rules of meaning. Nietzsche not only never denied the conventionalism of forms of language and life but devoted a large portion of his analytical labors to demonstrating that even the forms of logic, which don't wear the signs of their historicity on their sleeves, have the character of conventions motivated by cognitive economy. Yet these forms gain meaning only because they collectively relate to a future whose possibilities can be thoroughly determined by none of them, to a future that will decide upon their survival or decay. Thus, even the phenomena of the past and the present must be understood not merely within the frame of such conventional rules but rather in terms of what, as the future, alone sanctions the legitimacy of any given rule or threatens to withdraw this sanction. Nietzsche writes: "The judgment of the past is always an oracular judgment: only as master-builders of the future, as the initiated ones of the present will you comprehend it," and "Only he who builds the future [has] a right . . . to pass judgment on the past." Even with the images of great historical individuals and individual epochs, individuality stands out only under a gaze out of the future. And even if language and social life are subject to conventional rules, they still gain eloquence and comprehensibility only in the space open to the future, the realm in which their validity, language, and comprehensibility is not assured but suspended. Understanding the evidence is possible only given the suspension of what is understood to be self-evident; language is possible only given the suspension of its traditional forms and living present. Indeed, the most general appears only on the site of what it cannot seize, namely, where it carries the future signature of the individual. Past and present owe their meaning to what, as individual, surpasses their totality, its rules, and its forms. Life springs forth out of its own future; the whole out of a particularity cut off from itself, whose progressive departure incessantly unsettles the borders of the whole and prevents it from closing itself off. Nietzsche's individuality opens to indeterminacy that which was, for Leibniz and his school, the *omnimode determinatum*, the individual. The individual, as the open ground of the thoroughly determinate, is its determinant indetermination.

The emphatic formulations that introduce *Schopenhauer as Educator*, the third of the *Untimely Meditations*, can only be properly understood when one takes into account the excessive function, in every sense, Nietzsche gives to what is individual and to the idea of the sovereign individual. He writes:

> At bottom, every human knows quite well that he is only in the world one time, uniquely, and that no accident, however strange, will shake together for a second time such an oddly bright sundriness into the sameness that he is. . . . The artists alone hate this negligent hanging about in borrowed mannerisms and drapery of opinions, and they unveil the secret, the bad conscience of everyman, the sentence: Every human is a one-time miracle. . . . The human who does not want to belong to the mass need only cease to be comfortable with himself: let him follow his conscience, which calls out to him: "Be yourself! What you're doing, supposing, desiring now—that's not you at all. . . . Each one carries a productive uniqueness within himself as the core of his being; and when he becomes conscious of this uniqueness, a strange radiance appears about him, that of the unusual."

To all appearances, the Nietzsche of this text and of countless others subordinates productive uniqueness—the engenderment and education of which, despite its debt to chance, is the main concern of *Schopenhauer as Educator*—to an utterly anti-individual purpose, namely, the metaphysical purpose of assisting nature to enlightenment about itself and of thereby consummating its perfection. This purpose is served by the "engenderment of the philosopher, the artist, and the saint within us and without us."

According to "We Philologists," a note composed about the same time, "only in three forms of existence [does] a human [remain] an individual: as philosopher, as saint, and as artist." The *summum* of individuality, which nature achieves in the philosopher, the saint, and the artist, touches what is bare of all individuality. Indeed, the highest destiny and determination of individuality, its telos and its sense, is to lead the natural universe—which, through its spatiotemporal existence, and thus through the effects of the *principium individuationis*, has become foreign to itself—back into unity, to reconcile it with itself, and so to become the organ of its self-knowledge, its self-relation, its self. Individuality is destined to be extinguished, at its climax, in the undifferentiated—at the point "where the I is wholly dissolved and its life of suffering is no longer or nearly no longer experienced as an individual life but as the deepest feeling of the sameness, togetherness, and oneness of all that is alive." Individuality is here, much as in Schopenhauer, essentially a function of the self-totalization of totality, of the systematization of the system. And yet, only—as Nietzsche acknowledges in the *correctio* from "no longer" to "nearly no longer"—nearly. Only a most extreme individuality, namely, individuality opposed to the forms of the general consciousness subject to the *principium individuationis*, can suture the gap between the system of nature and the "feeling of the . . . oneness of all that is alive." And this individuality opposed to individuality can only *nearly* sew up the gap between the oneness and the allness of the living, since it too is subject to the principle of (dis)articulation. Such individuality is the disunity of unity and the possible but never-achieved unity of the differentiated. Individuality, and *a fortiori* that of the philosopher, the artist, or the saint, is the moment in which the totality of the living comes to itself, without ever arriving at itself. Its productive uniqueness is productive difference.

Nietzsche treats the problem of individuality similarly in an earlier work, *The Birth of Tragedy*, where he argues that the Apollonian principle of division and differentiation is already at work in the original unity of the Dionysian. Individuation, "dismemberment, the properly Dionysian affliction," torments the "originally unified, the eternally afflicted and self-contradictory," not as a violence from without, but as the accomplishment of its immanent process. And if the Dionysian finds deliverance from the affliction of individuation, it is only in the fleeting forms of interpretation, appearance, and therefore, yet again, individuation. What inflicted the wound is supposed to heal it, but the wound, individuation, is also the life of the original unity of the whole. Thus Nietzsche tries, in this conception of the tragic process, even if not independently of Schopenhauer, to think the Dionysian process of unification and generalization as a process of its immanent Apollo, of the god of individuation—that is, of dismemberment, deception, and the nonsublatably apparent decay into appearance of what truly is. Schopenhauer, on the other hand, to whom Nietzsche's conception alludes, had placed individuality as a fault in direct opposition to the "indestructibility of our essential being in itself. For at bottom each individuality is only a special mistake, a fault, something that it would be better not to have around, from which it is indeed the actual purpose of life to draw us away."

Nietzsche had, then, in *The Birth of Tragedy* already freed himself, by means of the thought of the mutual implication of his two principles, from Schopenhauer's hypostasis of an indestructible life substance, a substance from which individuality represented merely a regrettable, even sinful, deviation. And soon after his homage to Schopenhauer in *Untimely Meditations*, he could also explicitly turn away from the pessimistic philosophy of his teacher, from the condemnation of individuation as the original sin of humanity, a turn that occurs with increasing emphasis in *Human, All Too Human* and *The Gay Science*. A note from the posthumous papers of the 1880s returns critically to Schopenhauer's theory of individuation and attacks in particular the notion that individuation is fault, error, and aberration:

> The pessimistic condemnation of life in Schopenhauer is a moral condemnation. Translation of the herd's criteria into the language of metaphysics. The "individual" is meaningless, so why not give it an origin in the "in-itself" (and give his being meaning as "aberration")? . . . The failure of science to comprehend the individual becomes the object of due revenge: the individual is *the entire previous life* in *one line* and *not its result*.

The individual is hence not a tangent flying off from the circle of totality, not an error straying into the nothingness of its being from the will's way, the way trodden by only the great individuals, the philosophers, artists, and saints. The individual is also not the result of a process of procreation, for as such it would be a mere example governed by a racial type or lineage. It is the entire life process itself: "Each individual being is in fact *the whole process* in a straight line . . . , and therefore the individual has *monstrously grand significance*."

This historicized Leibnizian thesis—that the individual is the whole process and that no foreign instance could stand opposed to its internal universality—is, as it were, crossed out by the further determination that the individual can lay claim to "*monstrously grand significance*" only as a being capable of autonomy. Only in setting new goals for itself, only in tracing the design of a future into which it projects itself, proving itself free of conventions, customs, and morals, free for its own future self, does the individual become the monstrously significant single being in which the whole process of its becoming places itself under the sign of its own futurity. Only in relation to itself as the still-outstanding debt of a future self can it be a single and unique whole, free of any pregiven totality.

Another sketch intimately related in conception reads: "The *excessive* force in *intellectuality*, setting new goals *for itself*; certainly not merely to command and lead the lower world or for the maintenance of the organism, of the 'individual.' We are *more* than the individual: we are the whole chain, as well, with the tasks of all the chain's futures." This accent upon new goals is reinforced by the following entry, which emphasizes how important the unheard-of is for the theory of exegesis:

> The individual both *is* and *produces* what is wholly *new*; he is absolute, all acts wholly *his own*. The isolated one draws the values that guide his acts ultimately only out of himself: since he must *interpret for himself in a wholly individual manner* even the words he inherits. The *exegesis* of the formula is at least personal; even if he *produces* no formula, as an *exegete* he is still productive.

The innovative character of the individual owes itself, however, to a specific trait of the force that posits values and new interpretations of words. This trait is—beyond the narrow sphere of literary hermeneutics—in every sense decisive for the structures not only of inherited formulas and types of action, but also of individuality.

But the trait would not preserve the organism or its resultant process; it would merely conserve what is already given. Rather, it can be a force for individuation and absolutization only insofar as it is a (self-)excessive force. Only the "feeling of fullness, of power wanting to overflow, . . . the consciousness of a richness wanting to give gifts, deliver up," only this excess of force transgresses the borders of a given inherited context; only this gets beyond the formulas, types, and values of social action, the grammatical rules, words, and codified meanings of a language, undoing their solutions in the act of interpreting them by the new. The individuating force surpasses the individual as determined by the historical totality of his moments. It de-terminates the determined. The individuating force wrests the determined from its determinations and limits, de-limits it and delivers it as a problem or task to a temporal excess that can be contained by no past and no present. The motor of the passage from the conventional formula to its interpretation, from universal type to specific transformation, is neither the individual as an organic unity or a unity of consciousness, nor individuality as an essence of personal identity, but rather individuality as the force that individuates by overabundance and anticipation. Since excess alone individuates, separate beings and their configurations are in debt to this over-abundance of waiting. The individual is therefore neither an aspect of the whole, whether the latter be conceived as *totum* or *compositum*, nor the autonomous gestalt of a self-positing, substantial subject. What arises as individuality out of the excess of force structurally outdoes totality and subjectivity, and since there could be neither totality nor subjectivity without this excess, the outdoing of both is one of the conditions of their possibility. Individuality—or, more strictly, singularity—is, as *transcendens*, the transcendental of subjectivity. If there is an autonomy of the individual, it is only by virtue of what exceeds even this autonomy.

The fact that the life of the individual is inscribed in what goes beyond the sphere of its personal or objective givenness renders problematic the concept of life and the concept of individuality and its Being, as well as the language in which these concepts are articulated. In aphorism 262 of *Beyond Good and Evil*, in the chapter "What Is Noble?," Nietzsche pursues this problem, which does not reduce to the problem of the individual forms of discourse on individuality but concerns the articulation of a transcendental language. In accordance with the fictive history of society that he develops here—a history, one might add, of socialization in general—a species or type "becomes fixed, by the long struggle with essentially the same [unfavorable] conditions . . . into rigidity, monotony, and simplicity of form." If in a "fortunate situation . . . the monstrous pressure" to which the type is subject ever subsides, "the fetters and constraints of old training are suddenly [torn] asunder. The variation, whether as deviation [into the higher, freer, or more strange] or as deterioration and monstrosity, suddenly comes on stage in the greatest fullness and splendor; the separated one dares to be separate, dares to remove himself." Deviation and degeneration, atypicality and monstrosity—in short, individuality—arise not simply from a continuous historical process but from the contingency of the lucky break that allows the fetters and traits of training to be broken and the suddenly old morality to be transgressed, so that the "as it were exploding egoisms, wildly turned against one another . . . no longer know how to curb themselves by means of this morality."

Trace, training, and rein rip apart in the fortunate situation in which the type seems to have blossomed into pure autonomy. Their constraint, the force of sociality become excessive, drives the type beyond itself. "It was this morality itself that had accumulated the monstrous force that bent the bow in such a threatening manner—now it is, now it is becoming 'outlived'!" This morality of the type—of unity, universality, sociability, and form, of the determinant trait or trace and its restraint—has "outlived" itself. The type lives beyond itself, beyond its own life. It outlives its own life, though no longer as itself, no longer as the type and according to the measure of the life it has broken in and holds fixed, but rather as "the greater, more multifarious, more extensive life." The type "outlives" itself as "the individual." Of unity, a structurally illimitable multiplicity remains; of the generality of the communal polis and state, a disorganized anarchy of individuals remains; of logical universality, concepts luxuriating in self-incomprehension remain; of the drawn-out trait that held all within firm, objectifying contours, infinite self-withdrawal remains; and of the life that was coextensive with the reach of form, only "youthful, still undrained, still unexhausted decay" remains. For insofar as it "outlives" itself, life becomes—in accordance with a nuance of meaning in the German as well as the English word—obsolete, useless, extinct. Life is "outlived." It no longer lives.

"Outlived" in this manner, life, although now something other than itself, nonetheless lives on out. Nietzsche writes, "Now it is, now it is becoming 'outlived,' " and, playing out the various potential significations of the word "outlived" in this aphorism, in the next sentence he turns to argue that the "dangerous and uncanny point has been reached where the greater, more multifarious, more extensive life lives on *out away* from the old morality"—and from the forms of life contained within it. "The 'individual' stands there, forced into being his own lawgiver, into conceiving his own arts and stratagems for the preservation, exaltation, and deliverance of the self." It is indeed, then, as another phrase puts it, "the genius of the race, overflowing out of all cornucopias of the good and the bad," that "lives on out away" from itself. But it "outlives" itself only as an overflowing, excessive genius that does not contain itself within the race, and it remains alive only as the atypical monstrosity of the individual, who can no longer have the resources of his race or her type at its disposal.

In the individual, this life's form—the life of the society—and its sense "outlive" themselves. But, far from sublating itself, society's life maintains itself in the individual only in delivering itself up to its own decay. In its individual survival, the society does not preserve the essence of its composition but rather essentially decomposes. The individual composes the decomposition of his society. "Outlived"—this means, in "to be outlived," to be wasted, insubstantial, without force; it means also, in "to become outlived," that something not used up, something not exhausted, endures beyond the outlived; and it means—in accordance with a sense of the German word that had itself been outlived but that Nietzsche reenlivened by his metaphorics of luxuriance—to live too excessively, to overlive an oversized, outsized life. In the sentence "The individual outlives," to which Nietzsche's aphorism can be condensed, all of these threads of meaning knot themselves together; the extinct type—of life, of being—has, in the exuberant splendor of the individual, lived out beyond itself in such a manner that now it merely decays there. The individual is nothing other than the unreined, voluptuous self-outliving of life, the ongoing passing away of an excessive being no longer susceptible of being seized in the unity of a historical, social, or logical form. Individuality "is" outliving. Living without living. "Living."

The individual does not live. It outlives. Its being is being out and being over, an insubstantial remainder and excess beyond every determinable form of human life. Instead of being a social or psychic form of human existence, the individual—the self-surpassing of type, or genius—is the announcement of what, generally translated as "superman" or "overman," is best translated in this context as "outman." But the individual is this announcement only in the mode of an uncanny, dangerous, luxuriating monstrosity, in the form of one who, having outlasted the death of its type, has returned to earth in the form of a living corpse. In the individual, Nietzsche diagnoses a "fateful togetherness of spring and fall," which reminds one of the "sign of ascent and descent" that he reads in himself and of which he enigmatically writes in *Ecce Homo*: "I have . . . already died as my father; as my mother I live on and grow old." Given the fact that in the form of his own maternity he outlives the form of his own paternity—that he outlives himself and, thus living on, doubled, is his own *Doppelgänger*—Nietzsche sees the good fortune of his existence and its "singularity, perhaps." The splitting and doubling of the constitutive trait of the type, and not the type's unity, first give rise to the singularity of a being. Only the dividual is the individual—"perhaps." This "perhaps" signals, beyond all empirical uncertainty, the impossibility of achieving any unambiguously exact knowledge of a being whose singularity lies in its very sundrance.

Although the formulation "something becomes or gets outlived" may leave room for the hope that what outlives it is, by contrast, not yet used up or forceless, that what outlives is opposed to what gets outlived as life is opposed to death, or that the dividing line between both is as distinct as that which defines the type, the comment on the "fateful togetherness of spring and fall" in the epoch of individuality instructs us that there can be an outliving only by virtue of the alliance—the misalliance—between this outliving and degeneration itself. The individual is the incommensurable, insofar as incommensurability is the site where two irreconcilable magnitudes coincide. In the individual resides no undrained or unexhausted positive force, but rather there the "still undrained, still unexhausted decay" lives on and out. The individual is not merely spring and fall together; it is the springtime of the fall. If the type or model was the site of force, life, and being that presented itself within the borders of its form and was supposed to preserve itself there, then the "excessive force" and the "out(size) life" of the individual release that which ruptures the form of the being of self-preserving societal life: the individual's finitude. The being that "outlives" itself in the individual is delivered up to finitude. The individual, the "outliving," does not live on.

Nietzsche takes up again at the end of his aphorism the problem and the word "outliving"—thus underlining its determinant status for this text—and writes about those who alone survive under the conditions of the general breakdown of a society decomposing into individuals: "Only the average ones would have the prospect of carrying on, of propagating themselves—they are the people of the future, the only ones to live on and out." The criterion of the type, lost to individuality, is reproduced for the purposes of self-maintenance in a quantitatively determined criterion of the mean. But since the morality of the mean and of average democratic equality does not serve the intensification but rather serves the mere conservation of forces under the conditions of their decline, the mean and its corresponding doctrine of equality are indebted to the excess of individuality against which they attempt to defend themselves. Sheer living on is an apotropaism against the finitude of the "outliving" from which it arose. Because the constancy outliving grants is merely appearance, discourse on the outliving of the average as its survival can only be ironic, as Nietzsche himself implies. But discourse on the "outliving" of the individual, which only carries itself out in the excess of passing away, is no less inauthentic.

Nietzsche writes in one of his late notations, under the title "Renaissance and Reformation":

What does the Renaissance *prove?* That the reign of the "individual" can only be brief. The prodigality is too extreme; it has not even an outside chance to collect or to capitalize, and exhaustion follows at its heels. There are times when everything is *squandered*, when even the force itself with which one collects, converts into capital, and piles riches upon riches is squandered.

The realm of the "individual"—Nietzsche places the word again and again in quotation marks in order to point out its inauthentic use and its terminological vagueness—is the realm of waste, waste even of the force that could re-collect, summarize, preserve, and increase what has been so lavishly spent. What wastes itself in the individual and its "outliving" cannot—not even under the title "individual"—be converted into capital. The individual is just this wastefulness and incapability to collect and convene itself, either in the temporal unity of the duration of its outliving, in the unity of social life, or in the unity of a concept.

If the title "individuality" in Nietzsche's writings says nearly the exact opposite of what it means in traditional philosophical texts, the manner in which Nietzsche uses the word "outliving" corresponds that much more exactly to the event of individuality his text sketches out. For instead of gathering into one what is not itself a unit, this word—which thus ceases to be a "word"—disperses, in a grammatically and contextually determined manner, in at least four different directions of signification: it means at once *longius vivere, supervivere, defungere,* and *excedere*—"living-out-away-from," "outliving," "out-" or "overliving," and "outlived." The word that is to articulate the over- and out-structure of the individual is itself over- and out-determined in such a way that its individual significative moments can no longer be gathered together into a semantic continuum and thus converted into capital. These individual significative moments, like the "egoisms," are individuals and individuals of individuals "side by side and often mutually entangled and ensnared . . . a monstrous ruination and self-ruin, thanks to the as it were exploding egoisms wildly turned against one another."

In "outliving," the individual significative moments outlive their own lexical senses and those of competing semantic tendencies just as the social type, the principle of sociality, and the continuum of sense that sociality guarantees outlive themselves in individuals. Individuality—like every other word in the epoch of "outliving"—takes on meaning only at the price of being ceaselessly irritated by some other meaning, in such a manner that the meaning taken on or assumed, because it is so loosely associated with its word, can be at any time overwhelmed and suppressed by another meaning. For the diversity of these meanings, there is no commonality other than the disparate commonality of "outliving." The construction of internally con-

tradictory principles, excluded from the classical onto-logic that defined the
individual by the immanence of its predicates in their subject, becomes, in
the case of the structure of "outliving," an event that cannot be brought
back under the domination of a semantic or pragmatic type, no matter what
means of semiological purification might be employed to this end. The type
has "outlived" itself and is "outlived": the individual—"outlived"—does
not survive its outliving; the semantic surplus and the equally large semantic
deficit of these sentences can be brought into the form of a clear and distinct
meaning only by means of an arbitrary reduction.

Nietzsche would not have withheld from such a reduction and its resultant form the attribute of mediocrity. But every semantic restriction depends on the excessive character of "outliving" (the restriction itself having
no other sense than that of conservative survival), and further, every language and every other form of life in society is sketched out in view of the
production of a continuum of sense (the continuum being given to this form
in neither world nor text). For these reasons, the hyposemic exuberance of
the word and thing "outliving" is the abyssal condition for every conventional use of language and for every life that executes itself in the forms of
social exchange and communication. The indetermination, the over- and
out-determination of "outliving," determines every life. The individual—
"outliving"—would hence be the transcendental of the universal. To the
same degree as it offers to universality—to society and concept—the ground
of its possibility, it lets universality internally decompose. The individual—
"outlived"—does not outlive the "over-" of its overlife. It grants neither the
permanence that the type had promised nor the constancy that the mean
ironically proclaims. Language becomes individual—the language of "outliving"—speaks no longer with the certainty of a general, communicable
sense or of a type uninterruptedly producing new universalities; it speaks,
"outlived," in that it breaks down. If its "outliving" is transcendental, it is
so only insofar as it detransendentalizes.

Individuality's structure of dissociation, excess, and remainder affects,
further, the central category of Nietzsche's late work—the category of the
will. Nietzsche points this out, in aphorism 262 of *Beyond Good and Evil*,
with characteristically casual discretion: "Once again, danger is here, the
mother of morality, the great danger, this time located in the individual, in
what touches one most closely, and in one's friend, in the street, in one's
own child, in one's own heart, in all that is most properly and secretly one's
desire and will." Like the individual, the will and even what is most proper
to the will are in danger of wasting themselves, of exhausting and ruining
themselves. Because the will, which has created the type in order to accu-

mulate its own power, can only be the will to itself and the will to unconditioned autonomy of will insofar as it is already "excessive force," it too
must transgress the organizational form of the type and any determined
logical, aesthetic, or social structure; it must "outlive" itself in the disintegration of the forms that fix it. The will itself is and is becoming "outlived."
It is no longer the center of autonomous operations but rather, disintegrated
with itself, it is exposed to a tropical proliferation of its moments become
monstrous or unseemly. This inevitable turning of the will against itself is
for Nietzsche the signature of modernity. He describes it in the positivist
sciences, in the growth of democratic ideals, and in the style of literary and
musical decadence, and he analyzes it with the most vehement sarcasm
throughout *The Case of Wagner*, in the disintegration of organic forms in
Wagner's music.

In a passage that in great part assimilates the convictions of the theo-
retician of decadence Paul Bourget, Nietzsche writes:

> I shall consider here only the problem of *style*. What marks out
> every *literary décadence?* That life is no longer at home in the
> whole. The word becomes sovereign and leaps out of the sen-
> tence, the sentence invades and obscures the sense of the page,
> the page takes on life at the expense of the whole—the whole is
> no longer a whole. But that is a simile for every style of *décadence*:
> in every case, anarchy of the atoms, disgregation of the will,
> "freedom of the individual," to put it in moral terms—and when
> expanded into a political theory, "*equal* rights for all."

As the word leaps out of the sentence, the moment out of the totality, so the
whole leaps away from the whole and becomes its mere suggestion. The
whole exists merely as a theatrical play: it is pieced together, calculated,
synthetic, an artifact. In contrast, the part is larger than the whole, more
lively, organic, and authentic, and the whole merely a part of that part
which has become sovereign over it. Thus, with stylistic decomposition, the
whole disintegrates not simply into a chaos of parts but rather into, on the
one hand, a whole that is essentially appearance, drama, suggestion, rhetoric, hypnosis, and mass-persuasion and, on the other hand, details in which
alone life still survives and in which the truth about life can be said: that it
is over and can now at most be feigned.

There are two sides of decadence, just as there are two Wagners: "Aside
from Wagner the mesmerist and painter of frescoes, there is also a Wagner
who leaves little precious objects aside: our most grandly melancholic mu-
sician. . . . A lexicon of Wagner's most intimate words, mere little things of

five to fifteen beats, mere music, which *no one knows*." Unconcealed decadence of style, disarranged by no totalization, shows itself in the "overliveli-
ness [or "outliveliness"] of the most small," shows itself, that is, where the
individuated moments "outlive" both style and work and give the lie,
through the exuberance of their life, to the mere appearance of life, an
appearance engendered by technical management and propagated by the
whole. The detail that has emancipated itself from the community of the
work does not lie: its mere existence already tells the truth about the lie of
the whole, tells the truth that there is no truth aside from the technical
production of truth, and tells this truth in such a manner that no one—
unless he should be called Nietzsche—apprehends it. The trivialities, the
little things in which Wagner's greatness consists, are of the sort that—and
Nietzsche underlines this—"*no one knows*." What no one knows can confront no one under the shining appearance of the whole. But where it is
acknowledged, as in Nietzsche, it stands under the sign of melancholy, of
the loss of its own fulfilled presence. The "little precious objects," the "most
small," the nuances have, scarcely leaving any sheen of appearance, withdrawn. They are left aside without substantial center. With them, both the
realm of technics and positivity and the realm of aesthetics and phenomenality are abandoned.

Decadence of style corresponds ontologically to the disgregation of the
will. When style as organic form deteriorates, so too does the will: for the
will, as will, is nothing other than style. And when style, because of its
decomposition, can only be feigned, the will is mere theatricality, rhetoric,
and mass hypnosis. The will, "outlived," proves to have been technical
management. It degenerates into the play whose movements it no longer
dictates, and succumbs to disgregation in a passivity that is its conceptual
contrary. "Disgregation" does not mean merely disintegration, dissolution
of a whole form closed upon itself; as a term in the then-contemporary
physics, with which Nietzsche was well enough acquainted, it also means
the separation of the molecules of a body upon increased heat. (It is difficult,
in this context, not to think of his remark that Wagner's music sweats.)
Beyond this, by etymological connection with *grex* (herd), "disgregation"
signifies "unherding," the dissociation of the dull mass Nietzsche again and
again denounces as being subject to a will not its own. As his odd discussion
of its disgregation implies, the will is itself the herd. The herd—the will's
unity and wholeness, its organic totality—comprises the form in which the
will ventures upon its overflow of force. Only in the will's degenerescence,
when the herd, *will*, scatters apart, do the will's individual moments gain

sovereignty and disperse, "outlived" as herding phenomena, into singular molecules of force that no type and no *arche* can gather together.

This emancipation of moments of the will—which can only be called such inauthentically, since they are no longer moments of one will—owes itself to the dissolution of the will itself and of the will's generative and regenerative force. The will's degeneration, its deviation from the form of the species and of the species' homogeneity, frees it of its herd form, of its form *tout court*, and frees it not in order to allow it to realize itself in its unconstrained power but rather in order to open it onto what, always at work within it, withdraws itself from the will's power: the heterogeneity of individuals who do not will, who do not will the will, and who cannot will or want the will; for even the will would still be a form of unification. The disgregation of the will into the singular and smallest signifies—as in the laying by of "little precious objects" in Wagner's melancholy music—a possibility of the will to escape the compulsions of self-relation and form proper to its own figure, to get free of its technical-spectacular style and totalitarian self-presentation. The will experiences this freedom not in itself and not as a will, but in the passivity of a disgregation that, subjectless, succumbs to the laws of the will as little as to those of the concept. That the will experiences disgregation does not mean that it can be sure of or that it can secure this disgregation, for here the will is no longer a subject, and disgregation is the mode of withdrawal from all objectification. It is without closure or determination.

Thus although Nietzsche again and again refers to the degeneration of the will as a descent, he also terms it an "ascent." The will's disgregation does not, however, become the beginning of a new unity, of a realm of freedom, license, and figureless raving. Because of its interminability and incompleteness, it becomes the possible beginning of the new ideologies of the freedom, equality, and destiny of man, indeed of the democratic and communist ideologies Nietzsche never tired of condemning as symptoms of Nihilism. These ideologies preach the equality of individuals who, in the disgregation of the whole, have lost all common measure and who as in-commensurable singularities can no longer have any social form that would be more than a juridical fiction, that is, a play. But the contextual coherence of those who have forfeited or are about to forfeit all organic context can only be imagined through the fiction of a contextual coherence: for exam-ple, through the fiction of the concept "individual," which maintains that these incomparable singularities are all in equal measure individuals.

The economy of this coherence—a coherence that expresses itself in the

juridical, moral, and political fictions of the sameness, freedom, and personality of individuals and that is an economy of outliving, as aphorism 268
of *Beyond Good and Evil* displays—operates even for the disgregation of
the will, so long as determinations of language and in general of communication are in play. The will does prosecute its own disgregation, and yet,
so long as it submits to this disgregation as a will, the image of its objectivity, unity, and possible substantiality remains active in the disgregation
(as in the specular subject-object bond of submission). Disgregation takes
part in the histrionics of the will, and since disgregation is interminable, its
partaking of the play of images or representations has no end. But even in
the representations of this play, disgregation has no end; it is not limited by
them and is never what they present. Instead of being itself a theatrical play
of the will in which the ideas of equality and freedom appear on stage,
disgregation discredits these ideas as theatrical play. Its taking part in the
play's representations takes away a part of them—their stability, consistency, and technical character—and thus delivers them up to a movement
that is restrained by neither political nor moral, neither linguistic nor phenomenological, determinations.

In the epoch of the disgregation of the will—and this epoch is for
Nietzsche the epoch of epochs, for it has always already begun—the individual speaks in that it leaves behind linguistic conventions; it shows itself
in that it retreats from the scene of generality and includes its own generality
in this retreat. This process—this secession—is without destination or destiny not only in the sense that it meets no limit and comes to no end in a new
unity but also in the sense that it has no addressee who would not be
susceptible to the process itself. Nietzsche expressed this thought long before *The Case of Wagner*, in aphorism 367 of *The Gay Science*, in loose
connection with his criticism of Wagner's music and in particular of its
histrionics of totality. There he links his distinction between the art of the
actor and the strictly individual art of the unseemly with the motif of the
death of God:

> Everything that is thought, written, painted, composed, built, or
> in any way given form belongs either to monological art or to
> witnessed art. Even all the seemingly monological art that in-
> volves the belief in God, all of prayerful lyric poetry, falls within
> witnessed art: for the pious, there is no solitude—we, the god-
> less, were the first to come up with this invention. I know of no
> distinction in all the optics of the artist more profound than the
> following: whether the artist views his work in progress (and

"himself") with the eye of the witness or whether he "has forgotten the world." The latter is the essence of all monological art—such art is based on *forgetfulness*; it is the music of forgetfulness.

There can be no distinction in all artistic optics more profound than that between an art intended for a spectator—even if this be a transcendent spectator—and an art without regard for the view of another, even an utterly other, because of the distinction between an art of phenomenality—one which submits to the criteria for perceiving and being perceived—and nonphenomenal art. More precisely, since this distinction has to do not merely with sensual perception but also and more importantly with ideal perception (Nietzsche includes explicitly "everything thought"), it separates an art for another from an art that concerns no one and nothing else: neither a visual spectator nor a listener, neither an earthly public nor a god in whose eyes, according to the doctrine of *The Genealogy of Morals*, human suffering might, as theater, appear justified and fulfilled by meaning.

All art and all philosophy, all thought and all discourse that concern an addressee arise out of the belief in God and unfold as either conscious or involuntary theodicy. In opposition to the social and finally theological art of the dialogue, monological art (including philosophy) is theocidal. It knows no other and recognizes no God who could betoken its determinate destiny. Dialogical thought, action, or life is a form of prayer. The only life capable of monologue is life become godless, no longer in need of an addressee who would bestow sense on it to enable it to bear its own suffering. Only such a life would be able to accept its solitude without the illusion of a transcendental roof over its head and to accept its individuation without need of hope for its generalization. Only the life into whose solitude no God reaches is individual; only the life that gives (itself) up (as) the essential tenor of life is self-reliant. As long as God is not dead, there is no individuality. Individuality exists only as the project of its abandonment.

The solitude of monologue is, however, not the natural form of a discourse that would finally have reflected upon its own truth and self-reliance and rejected all supportive illusions. Even this solitude is, as Nietzsche explicitly states, an invention; even the death of God is—as was God himself—an invention, indeed, an invention made not by an individual in his solitude but by a community in view of its solitude: "We, the godless, were the first to come up with this invention." Even the monologue must bear witness to a community of the we, and even the absence of its addressee, its indeterminacy, takes part in the play of the will's representations. But the indeterminacy of monologue distinguishes its invention as being prior to all other possible inventions in the realms of thought, speech, and action: what is in this manner indeterminate can never become the positive product of the imagination or of the pedagogical force that forms images ("der Einbildungs- oder Bildungskraft"), and it can never be represented as the here and now of an accomplished realization. Indeterminate it remains, despite the most various determinations it may experience, open to all futurity and withdrawn from the constatation of the propositional discourse.

In aphorism 125 of *The Gay Science*, in which Nietzsche lets the madman announce the sentence "God is dead!," one reads: "This monstrous event is still on the way and wanders—it has not yet forced its way to people's ears." Since it is merely still on the way and wandering, since it has not yet forced its way to people's ears, the speech of the madman changes nothing. It remains uncomprehended. But in his speech, this monstrous event is on the way and wandering and rendering this speech, however dialogically it may have been intended, monological—without referent and without addressee, withdrawn from constative knowledge. The monologue, always still on the way and coming on, never already wholly there and present, is nothing other than the progressive indetermination within the dialectical structures of both language and determination. In this progression God dies. In the monologue, the monstrous enters into the secure space of the conventions of language and thought to turn that space gradually into the unenclosable space of solitude. The monologue of individuality is on the way.

Since it is both outside and inside discourse, the monologue is still not already there ("immer noch nicht schon da"). And since it is the discourse of the departure from the obligatory and communal form of the *logos*, it is "the 'still' of the 'no longer' " ("das Immer-Noch des Nicht-Mehr") of this *logos*, the outliving of individuality in a masklike, posthumous figure foreign to the individuality outlived. The monologue, which is always the discourse of the death of God or his representative—life, the will, the subject—is spoken as posthumous discourse and as the discourse of the posthumous human. Such discourse still has to do with humans; it visits them, but its visitation is that of a ghost. Aphorism 365 in *The Gay Science*, entitled "The Hermit Speaks Again," deals with this matter:

> We too associate with, visit, "humans." We too modestly assume the dress in which (*as* which) one knows, respects, seeks us, and we betake ourselves thus to society—that is, among the

disguised who do not want to be considered such—we too act
like all smart masks and politely show the way out to each
curiosity that does not concern our "dress." But there are also
other manners and cunning devices for visiting among humans:
for example, as a ghost—which is highly advisable if one wants
to get rid of them soon, to frighten them away. Test: . . . we
come . . . after we have already died. The latter is the cunning
device of the *posthumous* humans *par excellence*."

Dead during their lifetimes because hidden beneath masks of conventional
manners and alive only after their deaths—as script, rumor, remembrance,
and delayed aftereffect—posthumous humans announce their individuality
only as the living dead, as the survivors of outliving, as ghosts. They present
themselves as disarrangement.

This form stands under the sign of withholding and subsequent sup-
plementation; the survivors are not at liberty not to disguise themselves or
to present themselves in the *oratio recta* of their authentic and proper being.
Their language is, like every language, a mask; they themselves, like those
hidden beneath masks, live only as those departed from their masks. The
individual is the departed par excellence. Therefore Nietzsche lets the hermit
speak as his mask instead of speaking in person, and he lets the hermit speak
of his solitude, which is for him a metaphor for death. The individual has
departed not only from a life that promises community with others but, by
"outliving," from death and from the community of the dead. In the intermediate realm of indeterminacy between life and death, the individual's
language is social synthesis only insofar as it is an agent of disgregation,
communication only insofar as it preserves a most extreme discretion. Language conceals. It conceals, not a determinate something that might just as
well be expressed or caught in a nonlinguistic form of communication, but,
as language, what slips away from all determination, the indeterminacy of
departedness itself, which can be brought neither to language nor simply to
silence since it belongs to no realm of logical distinctions, neither that of life
nor that of death.

By concealing yet always presenting the mask of the indeterminate
within it, language—as language—announces that it breaks down before
the indeterminate, that it changes the indeterminate, through the form of its
reference, into one of the departed, and that it itself is departure. Language
is departure—from every deep or hidden sense, from the subject that means
to express itself in such a sense but takes the fiction of its substantiality only
from the linguistic play of masks, and from the addressee toward whose

comprehension language turns only in turning away from him as from a possible site of its determination. Individuals partake of one another and begin, under the sign of their nonsynthesis, to communicate exclusively in the moment of departure language marks. The sociality of language fulfills itself when language politely shows the way out to everything that seeks a relation to what it intends, be this a meaning or a person. The site of society as also the site of the individual is this departure, in which the two never cease to part both from each other and from themselves. In this manner, society and individual partake of community with themselves and others without making themselves common or mean. This is the only manner in which there can be any community: as the social visitation (*Umgehen*) of those departed from each other and from their common medium, from life and from death.

As is sufficiently well known but cannot be sufficiently thought out, Nietzsche accords special status to the emblem of the mask in his remarks on language and individuality. In the consideration of this emblem, despite the extent to which it offers itself to controversial interpretations because of its indeterminacy, the relationship of both language and individuality to phenomenality, wholeness, and necessity can be pointed out with particular precision. These problematic concepts—phenomenality, wholeness, and necessity—are in turn bound up with one another in the problem of determination or destiny in all of its dimensions, to which Nietzsche devoted much attention. Beginning at the very latest with *On Truth and Lie in an Extra-Moral Sense*, he views language as morphologizing a world that otherwise would be a sheer chaos of infinitely differentiated moments of impression. Even the individual, which Nietzsche invokes in this context primarily against the power of the concept incapable of gaining possession of it, proves to be a morphological, indeed anthropomorphic construction on whose real content no judgment is possible, since the title "reality" is itself taken from and partakes of this morphologizing:

> The overseeing, outseeing, or oversight [*Übersehen*] of the individual and the real gives us the Concept as it gives us also From, yet nature knows neither forms nor concepts, and therefore no species, but only an X as inaccessible to us as it is indefinable by us. For even our opposition of individual and species is anthropomorphic and does not arise from the essence of things. Although we also do not dare say that it does not correspond to this essence, for that would be a dogmatic proposition and quite as insusceptible of proof as its contrary.

If even the individual is anthropomorphically schematized and if therefore only the overseeing, outseeing, or oversight of the individual gives rise to the "individual," then only the inaccessible, that which differs from whatever is grasped, is individual, whereas what can be caught by the concept of the individual remains a mere figure. Nietzsche later expanded this thought, acquired from his readings of Kant and Schopenhauer, to the question of the self-relation of human individuals and drew from it the consequence for consciousness that "consciousness doesn't actually belong to the individual-existence of humans . . . and it follows that, even with the best of wills, each of us, in the attempt to *understand* himself as individually as possible, to 'know himself,' will always bring only the nonindividual to consciousness, its own meanness." The consciousness of a self that is "incomparably personal, singular, unlimitedly individual," can, as consciousness—that is, as subject to the criterion of communicability—always conceive this self only as "a world of surfaces and signs," hence only in such a manner that it masks this self. And the mask can have no point of correspondence with what it hides, for this hidden instance withdraws from all designation and all appearance. The designation phenomenalizes individual difference into something shown. It universalizes its communication in accordance with the measure of an economy of representability that is foreign to the unlimitedly individual. The "phenomenalism and perspectivism" of "communicative signs," of "signs of the herd," rests then on the systematic restriction of difference and on a morphologizing of what has neither shape nor self, neither substance nor positive subjectivity. The sign of the herd, consciousness (including even the most individual consciousness), is a mask.

This phenomenalism of consciousness and language is irreducible insofar as what lies hidden beneath the mask of its forms can always only appear yet again masked both in and for consciousness and language. For us, there is nothing behind the mask but masks—ideas, essentialities, meanings—nothing behind the mask but an X. As Kant insists that the barrier before the individual, before the thoroughly determinate *ens entium*, is for finite reason insurmountable, so Nietzsche insists that the unlimitedly individual, which is for him indeterminable, can only be grasped by consciousness and language as a determinate term and thus, beyond all correction, as disfigured. In the phenomenal and morphological determinations to which language and consciousness subject the indeterminable, an original difference from all origin, idea, and substance continues to disfigure the forms of consciousness. Only for this reason is it possible and proper to speak of the indeterminate as the individual and to determine it as the indeterminable.

In the same aphorism of *The Gay Science* in which he analyzes the "signs of the herd" of consciousness, Nietzsche speaks of a "surplus of this force and art of communication," of the surplus of a faculty or of an inheritance the artist and philosopher receive in "expending it wastefully." But this surplus of the capacity of designation and communication, this hypertrophy of form and consciousness—to reformulate Nietzsche's genealogical argument in structural terms—must contribute, always already and as overdetermination, to the determinations of the forms of consciousness and language, indetermining them, making their stiffened distinctions move, and convulsing the opposition between the signs of the herd and the individual-existence insusceptible of designation, between the phenomenalism of consciousness and the unshowing [*Aphanisis*] of its objects.

If the appropriateness or inappropriateness of linguistic signs cannot be measured against what they determine, if, therefore, they lack all transcendental ground of determination, and if their immanent law is subject to unforeseeable alterations, then the universal proposition that all universal propositions are mere appearance denies itself as appearance. By being different from itself, it thus mobilizes, in the economy of universal determinations that work to restrict individual difference, an economy of another sort: the economy of wasteful expenditure, of giving up the determinations themselves, of affirming difference. Since no determination can become an object of a determination in such a manner as to guarantee their strict correspondence, each determination, however general and susceptible of consensus it may appear, is nonetheless an unrepeatable, singular event. Its singularity—the singularity even of the most universal—consists in its destiny of indeterminacy. Singularity is incapable of attaining to a universally valid truth because it has neither a transcendent nor an immanent guarantee of the appropriateness of its forms at its disposal. The indeterminacy of its determinate destiny is its sole law, the law of singularity.

The waste of the "force and art of communication" that art pursues is an articulation of the law of indeterminacy to which every communication, every sign, is subject. Art is never form, shape, or image without at the same time, in its morphological surplus, leaving form behind, disfiguring shape, and surrendering the claim of the image to reproduce or produce a reality. If art wastes the *force and art of communication*, then it does so by partitioning what it imparts in sharing it, partitioning the part it takes both in what it imparts and in the addressee of the imparted. ("Wenn sie die *Kraft und Kunst der Mitteilung* verschwendet, so durch die Teilung jenes Mit, in dem sie ihre Gemeinsamkeit mit der von ihr gemeinten Sache und den von ihr angesprochenen Adressaten hat.") The phenomenalism of the sign opens itself in art onto the unseemly. If anything there still gets shown, presented, lit up, then it is the extinction of phenomenality, of the *eidos*, and of meaning itself; Wagner composed this extinction in the "secrecies of dying light." In art, communication (*Mitteilung*) denies both its claim to be able to operate in the space of appearances and forms as in the homogeneous sphere of the given and its claim to be able to belong immediately to this sphere itself. Art is nothing but the wasting of its appearance, and the expenditure of its communicative riches is also the internal communication of its moments. It is not a whole, but the whole that reveals itself as mask. Its form— which is not the form of a particular genus or genre but that of art insofar as it is art, of philosophy insofar as it is philosophy—is the form of the *aphorism* in its broadest sense: what is cut off, differentiated, and singled out. The site of art and of philosophy—the inexplicit site of every communication and of consciousness—is departure, for the organic totality that these discourses attempt to project in each of their acts begins where it is cut off from every foundation of determination, even if this foundation should be the definitive absence of foundation. The whole and each of its moments carry the trace of this severance, which makes each into a *singulare tantum*. Nietzsche plays out their associative possibilities in his books of aphorisms. Indeed, one could designate these aphorisms *metaphorisms*, if the word existed: particles that extend their particularity out beyond themselves and therein, *metaphorice*, impart themselves to one another as the im-parted.

If communication denies its claim to totality, then it also simultaneously denies its claim to the necessity of its forms. As an example of this, Nietzsche again and again chooses causality as the figure of explanation. Against the teleological assumption that all appearances have to be thought with reference to a common purpose, Nietzsche had already called up, in his early notes "Teleology since Kant," the "coordinated possibility" of chance to maintain the rights of the incalculably individual against the universal law of a final destiny. In contrast to the necessity that every totality of representation requires, the individuality of the individual—which only stands out more clearly in art than in other communicative forms—is contingent and is the affirmation of contingency. Only contingency can accomplish what is denied to any rule, any decision of the will, and any act of consciousness as such; as the groundless, contingency can ground the singularity of the individual. Whereas the logical determinism and the determinist ideology of religious systems place the individual immediately before God, the thought of indetermination leaves it alone before the impossibility of deciding the existence or nonexistence of God, alone before the undecidability of its own substantial subjectivity. Exposed to the contingencies of randomness, the individual is never destined for wholeness either in itself, or in a nonproblematically accessible other, or in the history it would dominate. Randomness is not the other of the self, but rather the indeterminacy that governs the self—which has no power to determine it in turn—and that can be represented in forms of thought and life only as disfigured, incomprehensible, broken off. Not merely the appearance of the individual, rendered indeterminate by randomness, but its being is a mask.

Indeed the mask is for Nietzsche never arbitrarily selected and worn by one who could also choose to wear none. The mask—much like the desert—grows. "Every deep spirit needs a mask: further still, about every deep spirit there grows incessantly a mask, thanks to the permanently false, that is, *flat*, interpretation of every word, every step, every sign of life such a spirit gives." But the mask grows on the individual and on each of the individual's words not only because of the leveling interpretation others give it and not only because they are incapable of keeping their eyes on the face or the backgrounds and the grounds of the mask—rather, each word is already a mask for the one who speaks it and for the word that it is denied him to speak. "Every philosophy also *conceals* a philosophy, every opinion is also a hiding place, every word also a mask." The mask stands before no face that would not itself be a mask; the word conceals—or designates—no sense that would not itself be a mask; the grounds of the mask can be followed back to no ultimate ground that would not be an abyss.

Nietzsche lets the hermit speak one more time: "The hermit doesn't believe that a philosopher *could* ever have—assuming that a philosopher has always been a hermit first . . . 'final and authentic' opinions at all, if for him behind every cave there were not another, would not have to be another, deeper cave . . . an abyss beneath every ground, beneath every 'grounding.'" The mask is a structural end for all knowledge and self-knowledge, for every word and every communication, because all forms of knowledge and representation must run aground in the attempt to secure the ground of their determination. Determinate types of representation in philosophy, art, and practical life may be historically, sociologically, or psychologically reducible to determinate motifs, but their own relation to the possibility of their groundlessness and indeterminacy remains indeterminable and irreducible. The mask, and therefore the entire realm of signs of phenomenality and forms of consciousness, lies over an abyss whose cavity can be filled by no form and no thought. Thanks to the mask, the illusion of a face can take form, that of a subject thoroughly in control of itself yet hidden by the mask it has put on to protect its grounds and itself as ground. The possibility of such a ground is an effect of the mask, and this effect is always accompanied and suspended by the effect—equally powerful yet incomparably more difficult to seize—of this ground's impossibility. The mask shows itself, Janus-faced, to be the opening of both of these possibilities, of grounding and groundlessness. It shows no determinate something and hides no showing, but shows instead its hiding. In opposition to image and simile, which still nourish the referential, semantic illusion that they show something determinate or at least determinable, "all that is deep loves the mask; indeed, the deepest of things hate images and similes."

Form of appearance and thought though it be, the mask offers in its self-denials a space for the suspension of appearance and thought. If each language is structured like a mask, then each speaks out of its incapacity to be, to hide, or to reveal its own foundation; it speaks out of the impossibility of determining definitively either itself or what it means. The determination by indeterminacy precedes in each language any possibility of determination. The deep ambiguity of language—its Nihilism, if one wishes—is that it finds with each of its traits its determination, which it nonetheless cannot secure with a second trait as its own.

The mask, then, takes itself off. In that the universality of its form offers itself as detachable from every individual difference, in that it offers itself as universality, it leaves room for the possibility that it is without ground and background. In that it sets itself off from itself, the mask makes space for the individual in its difference from its presentational function. The site of the individual is neither before nor beyond the mask, but only in its differential self-relation. The individual is only what is exposed to the possibility of its groundlessness. It speaks in the gap between determination and the absence of determination, out of the "pathos of distance," out of the pathos of the progressive "expansion of distance within the soul itself" and its signs of life. It speaks not as the substance of indivisible subjectivity but rather out of the distance and interminable expansion of distance that divides substantial subjectivity as the form of universality from itself.

The individual shows itself only in the breach of its sign—where its showing gives itself up. If it can still be said, this can be only in a saying that unsays ("in einem Aussagen, das versagt"). Individuality unsays itself. It is, in a formula for the sublime that Nietzsche applies to the "free spirit," "what remains hidden beneath the cloaks of light," and—in a less biblical turn of phrase—at once "night owl" and "scarecrow": the Hegelian bird of absolute knowledge and what holds this bird at a distance (auto-apotropaism, the process of the self's taking self-distance, of conceptual withdrawal, of estrangement). Individuality unsays itself in the differential self-relation of saying; it is unsaid in all constatations, hence it says only in the mode of the not, the no longer, or the not yet. Because it is still to come, individuality is always only promised.

It is not, but comes. Since it remains, however, without determination or addressee, hence also without goal and direction, it never comes as that which is destined for me, as my due, my own; rather it remains still to come, comes without end—it is the open distance out of which a substantial self never results. As promise, the monologue of my singularity must itself renounce me; other than as thus promised yet self-withholding, it cannot be. The future of this monologue is not the programmed one into which I prolong my present self in order to sustain it and retain it as my own, but chance that strikes me without being destined for me and without being able to become mine. It is not I who speak the monologue of my futurity, but rather what in it, unarriving, indefinite, withdraws itself from my will: fate as a law that owes itself to no subjective positing act but to the speech of an instance, of a distance, of a disgregation that cannot be controlled by a subject—be it immanent or transcendent, conscious or unconscious—and that is never sufficiently spoken, never spoken as whole and as law itself, but that can only be perceived fragmentarily, in pieces.

"The individual is a piece of fate from the front and from the back, one more law, one more necessity for all that is coming and shall be." But if this law of the individual, the law of its individuality, is fate "from the front and from the back," fate out of the past and out of the future, then the individual is individual and a law for all only after the entire future has been exhausted and the circle of recurrence has closed an infinite number of times. Even then, it is not the whole but a piece of fate that has become law for all. The individual is a fragment of the decree of fate that only in its entirety could ground the individual's autonomy; for only that entirety would allow the individual to be exclusively determined by what it determines. But as this fragment it becomes the law "for all that is coming and shall be," and for all that has been. The individual, a broken piece, is a law for the totality that alone could determine the piece as piece and fit it together into a whole—into the whole the individual itself would be. But a whole that is, even as a whole, a mere piece, a whole that stands, in its moral and social coherence and in its temporal extension, beneath the law of the piece, hence beneath a law in pieces—such a whole can offer to the individual as consolation neither the internal determination of an identical self that would have itself at its disposal, nor social totalization in the historical process. For the individual, there remains, without consolation, the freedom: to assume himself, under the law of disgregation, as indeterminate.

RICHARD RORTY

The Contingency of Selfhood

As I was starting to write this I came across a poem by Philip Larkin, the last part of which reads:

> And once you have walked the length of your mind, what
> You command is as clear as a lading-list.
> Anything else must not, for you, be thought
>   To exist.
>
> And what's the profit? Only that, in time
> We half-identify the blind impress
> All our behavings bear, may trace it home.
>   But to confess,
>
> On that green evening when our death begins,
> Just what it was, is hardly satisfying,
> Since it applied only to one man once,
>   And that one dying.

This poem is about the fear of dying, of extinction, to which Larkin confessed in interviews. But "fear of extinction" is an unhelpful phrase, and needs unpacking. There is no such thing as fear of inexistence as such, but only fear of some concrete loss. It is not enough to say that poets, like everybody else, fear death, or that they fear nothingness. "Death" and "nothingness" are equally resounding, equally empty terms. To say one fears either is as unhelpful as Epicurus's attempt to say why one should not

From *London Review of Books* 8, no. 8 (May 8, 1986). © 1986 by *London Review of Books*.

fear them. Epicurus said, "When I am, death is not, and when death is, I am not," thus exchanging one vacuity for another. For the word "I" is quite as hollow as the word "death." To unpack such words one has to fill in the details about the "I" in question, specify precisely what it is that will not be.

Larkin's poem suggests a way of unpacking what Larkin feared. What he fears will be extinguished is his idiosyncratic lading-list, his individual sense of what was possible and important. That is what made his "I" different from all the other "I's." To lose that difference is, I take it, what any poet—any maker, anyone who hoped to create something—fears. Anyone who spends his life trying to formulate an answer to the question of what is possible and important fears the extinction of that answer. But this does not mean simply that one fears that one's poems may not be read. For that fear blends into the fear that, even if they are read, nobody will find anything distinctive in them. The words that were marshalled to one's command may seem merely stock items, rearranged in routine ways. One will not have impressed one's mark on the language, but rather have spent one's life shoving about already-coined pieces. So one will not really have had an "I" at all. One's poems, and one's self, will just be better or worse instances of familiar types. This is what Harold Bloom calls "the strong poet's anxiety of influence," his or her "horror of finding oneself to be only a copy or a replica."

On this reading of Larkin's poem, what would it be to have succeeded in tracing home the "blind impress" which all one's "behavings bear"? Presumably it would be to have figured out what was distinctive about oneself—the difference between one's own lading-list and other people's. If one could get this recognition down on paper—if one could find distinctive words for one's own distinctivness—then one would have demonstrated that one was not a copy, or a replica. One would have been as strong as any poet has ever been, which means having been as strong as any human being could possibly be. For one would know exactly what it is that will die, and thus know what one has succeeded in becoming.

But the end of Larkin's poem seems to reject this Bloomian reading. There we are told that it is "hardly satisfying" to trace home one's own distinctiveness. This seems to mean that it is hardly satisfying to have become an individual—in the strong sense in which the strong poet is the paradigm of individuality. Larkin is affecting to despise his own vocation, on the ground that to succeed in it would merely be to have put down on paper something which "applied only to one man once,/And that one dying."

I call this "affectation" because I doubt that any poet could seriously think trivial his own success in tracing home the blind impress borne by all his behavings—all his previous poems. Since the example of the Romantics, since the time when, with Hegel, we began to think of self-consciousness as self-creation, no poet has seriously thought of idiosyncrasy as an objection to his work. But in this poem Larkin is pretending that blind impresses, those particular contingencies which make each of us "I" rather than a copy or replica of somebody else, do not really matter. He is suggesting that unless one finds something common to all men at all times, not just to one man once, one cannot die satisfied. He is pretending that to be a strong poet is not enough: that he would have attained satisfaction only from being, of all things, a philosopher.

I think Larkin's poem owes its interest and its strength to this reminder of the quarrel between poetry and philosophy, the tension between an effort to achieve self-creation by the recognition of contingency and an effort to achieve universality by the transcendence of contingency. The same tension has haunted philosophy since Hegel's time, and particularly since Nietzsche. The important philosophers of our own century are those who have tried to follow through on the Romantic poets by breaking with Plato and seeing freedom as the recognition of contingency. These are the philosophers who try to detach Hegel's insistence on historicity from his pantheistic idealism. They try to retain Nietzsche's identification of the strong poet, rather than the scientist, as the paradigm of humanity, while discarding what Heidegger called Nietzsche's "metaphysics of the will to power." More generally, they have tried to avoid anything that smacks of philosophy as contemplation, as the attempt to see life steady and see it whole, in order to insist on the sheer contingency of individual existence.

They thus find themselves in the same sort of awkward, but interesting position as Larkin. Larkin writes a poem about the unsatisfactoriness, compared with what philosophers hoped to do, of doing the only thing that poets can do. Post-Nietzschean philosophers like Wittgenstein and Heidegger write philosophy in order to exhibit the universality and necessity of the individual and contingent. Both of these philosophers became caught up in the quarrel between philosophy and poetry which Plato began, and both ended by trying to work out honourable terms on which philosophy might surrender to poetry. Both gave us ways of thinking of the creator of metaphor, rather than the contemplator of literal truth, as the paradigm of humanity.

Consider Larkin's suggestion that one might get more satisfaction out of finding a "blind impress" which did not apply only to "one man once" but to all human beings. Think of finding such an impress as being the discovery of the universal conditions of human existence, the permanent, ahistorical context of human life. This is what the priests once claimed to have done. Later the Greek philosophers, still later the empirical scientists, and later still the German idealists, made the same claim. They were going to explain to us the ultimate locus of power, the nature of reality. They would thereby inform us what we really are, what we are compelled to be by powers not ourselves. They would exhibit the stamp which had been impressed on *all* of us. This impress would not be blind, because it would not be a matter of chance, a mere contingency. It would be necessary, essential, telic, constitutive of what it is to be a human. It would give us a goal, the only possible goal—namely, the full recognition of that very necessity, the self-consciousness of our essence.

By comparison to this universal impress, so the pre-Nietzschean philosopher's story goes, the particular contingencies of individual lives are unimportant. The mistake of the poets is to waste words on idiosyncrasies, on contingencies—to tell us about accidental appearance rather than essential reality. To admit that mere spatio-temporal location, mere contingent circumstance, mattered would be to reduce us to the level of a dying animal. To understand the context in which we necessarily live, by contrast, would be to give us a mind exactly as long as the universe itself, a lading-list which was a copy of the universe's own list. What counted as existing, as possible, or as important, for us, would be what really *is* possible or important. Having copied this list, one could die with satisfaction, having accomplished the only task laid upon humanity: to know the truth, to be in touch with what is "out there." There would be nothing more to do, and thus no possible loss to be feared. Extinction would not matter, for one would have become identical with the truth, and truth, on this traditional view, is imperishable. What was extinguished would be merely idiosyncratic animality. The poets, who are not interested in truth, merely distract us from this paradigmatically human task, and thereby degrade us.

It was Nietzsche who first explicitly suggested that we drop the whole idea of "knowing the truth." His definition of truth as a "mobile army of metaphors" amounted to saying that the whole idea of "representing reality" by means of language, and thus the idea of finding a single context for all human lives, should be abandoned. His perspectivism amounted to the claim that the universe had no lading-list to be known, no determinate length. He hoped that, once we realized that Plato's "true world" was just a fable, we would seek consolation, at the moment of death, not in having transcended the animal condition but in being that peculiar sort of dying animal who, by describing himself in his own terms, had created himself.

More exactly, he would have created the only part of himself that mattered by constructing his own mind. To create one's mind is to create one's own language, rather than letting the length of one's mind be set by the language other human beings have left behind. [My account of Nietzsche in what follows owes a great deal to Alexander Nehamas's original and penetrating *Nietzsche: Life as Literature* (Harvard University Press, 1985).]

But in abandoning the traditional notion of truth, Nietzsche did not abandon the idea of discovering the causes of our being what we are. He did not give up the idea that an individual might track home the blind impress all his behavings bore. He only rejected the idea that this tracing was a process of discovery. On his view, in achieving this sort of self-knowledge we are not coming to know a truth which was out there (or in here) all the time. Rather, he saw self-knowledge as self-creation. The process of coming to know oneself, confronting one's contingency, tracking one's causes home, is identical with the process of inventing a new language—that is, of thinking up some new metaphors. For any literal description of one's individuality, which is to say any use of an inherited language-game for this purpose, will necessarily fail. One will not have traced that idiosyncrasy home, but merely have managed to see it as not idiosyncratic after all, as a specimen reiterating a type, a copy or replica of something which has already been identified. To fail as a poet—and thus, for Nietzsche, to fail as a human being—is to accept somebody else's description of oneself, to execute a previously-prepared programme, to write, at best, elegant variations on previously-written poems. So the only way to trace home the causes of one's being as one is would be to tell a story about one's causes in a new language.

This may sound paradoxical, because we think of causes as discovered rather than invented. We think of telling a causal story as a paradigm of the literal use of language. Metaphor, linguistic novelty, seems out of place when one turns from simply relishing such novelty to explaining why these novelties, and not others, occurred. But even in the natural sciences we occasionally get genuinely new causal stories, the sort of story produced by what Kuhn calls "revolutionary science." Even in the sciences, metaphoric redescriptions are the mark of genius and of progress. If we follow up this Kuhnian point by thinking, with Davidson, of the literal-metaphorical distinction as the distinction between old language and new language rather than in terms of a distinction between words which latch onto the world and those which do not, the paradox vanishes. If, with Davidson, we drop the notion of language as fitting the world, we can see the point of Bloom's and Nietzsche's claim that only the strong poet, only the person who uses words as they have never before been used, is able to appreciate her own contingency. For only she sees her language as contingent in the way that her parents or her historical epoch are contingent. She is the only one who can appreciate the force of the claim that "truth is a mobile army of metaphors" because she is the only one who has, by her own sheer strength, broken out of one perspective, one metaphoric, into another.

Only poets, Nietzsche thought, can grasp contingency. The rest of us are doomed to remain philosophers, to insist that there is really only one true lading-list, one true description of the human situation, one universal context to our lives. We are doomed to spend our conscious lives trying to escape from contingency rather than, like the strong poet, acknowledging and appropriating contingency. For Nietzsche, therefore, the line between the strong poet and the rest of the human race has the moral significance which Plato and Christianity attached to the distinction between the human and the animal. For though strong poets are, like all other animals, causal products of natural forces, they are products capable of telling the story of their own production in words never used before. The line between weakness and strength is thus the line between using language which is familiar and universal and producing language which, though initially unfamiliar and idiosyncratic, somehow makes tangible the blind impress all one's behavings bear. With luck—the sort of luck which makes the difference between genius and eccentricity—that language will also strike the next generation as inevitable. *Their* behavings will bear that impress.

To put the same point in another way, the Western philosophical tradition thinks of a human life as a triumph just insofar as it breaks out of the world of time, appearance and idiosyncratic opinion into another world—into the world of enduring truth. Nietzsche, in contrast, thinks the important boundary to cross is not the one separating time from atemporal truth but rather the one which divides the old from the new. He thinks a human life triumphant just insofar as it escapes from inherited descriptions of the contingencies of its existence and finds new descriptions. This is the difference between the will to truth and the will to self-overcoming. It is the difference between thinking of redemption as making contact with something larger and more enduring than oneself and redemption as Nietzsche describes it: "recreating all 'it was' into a 'thus I willed it.' " The drama of an individual human life, or of the history of humanity as a whole, is not one in which a preexistent goal is triumphantly reached or tragically not reached. Neither a constant external reality nor an unfailing interior source of inspiration forms a background for such dramas. Instead, to see one's life, or the life of one's community, as a dramatic narrative is to see it as a process of Nietzschean self-overcoming. The paradigm of such a narrative is the life of the genius who can say of the relevant portion of the past "thus I willed it" because she has found a way to describe that past which the past never knew, and thereby found a self to be which her precursors never knew was possible.

On this Nietzschean view, the impulse to think, to inquire, to reweave oneself ever more thoroughly, is not wonder but terror. It is, once again, Bloom's "horror of finding oneself to be only a copy or replica." The wonder in which Aristotle believed philosophy to begin was wonder at finding oneself in a world larger, stronger, nobler than oneself. The fear in which Bloom's poets begin is the fear that one might end one's days in such a world, a world one never made, an inherited world. The hope of such a poet is that what the past tried to do to her she will succeed in doing to the past: to make the past itself, including those very causal processes which blindly impressed all her own behavings, bear *her* impress. Success in that enterprise—the enterprise of saying "Thus I willed it" to the past—is success in what Bloom calls "giving birth to oneself."

I turn to the way in which Freud helps us accept, and put to work, this Nietzschean and Bloomian sense of what it is to be a fully-fledged human being. "Freud is inescapable." Bloom says in *Agon*, "since more even than Proust he is the mythopoeic mind of our age, as much our theologian and our moral philosopher as he was our psychologist and our prime maker of fictions." I think that Bloom is right about this, and that one can get a start on grasping Freud's importance by seeing him as the moralist who helped de-divinise the self by tracking home conscience to its origin in the contingencies of our upbringings.

To see Freud this way is to see him against the background of Kant. The Kantian notion of conscience divinises the self. Once we give up, as Kant did, on the idea that scientific knowledge of hard facts is our point of contact with a power not ourselves, it is natural to do what Kant did: to turn inward, to find that point of contact in our moral consciousness—in our search for righteousness rather than our search for truth. Righteousness "deep within us" takes the place, for Kant, of empirical truth "out there." Kant was willing to let the starry heavens above be merely a symbol of the moral law within: an optional metaphor, cast in merely phenomenal terms, for the illimitableness, the sublimity, the unconditioned character of the moral self, of that part of us which was not phenomenal, not a product of time and chance, not an effect of natural, spatio-temporal causes.

This Kantian turn helped set the stage for the Romantic appropriation of the inwardness of the divine, but Kant himself was appalled at Romantic attempts to make idiosyncratic poetic imagination, rather than what he called "the common moral consciousness," the centre of the self. Ever since Kant's day, however, romanticism and moralism, the insistence on individual spontaneity and private perfection and the insistence on universally-shared social responsibility have warred with one another. Freud helps us to end this war. He de-universalises the moral sense, making it as idiosyncratic as the poet's inventions. He thus lets us see the moral consciousness as historically conditioned—as much a product of time and chance as political or aesthetic consciousness.

Freud ends his essay on da Vinci with a passage from which I quoted a fragment at the end of "The Contingency of Community."

> If one considers chance to be unworthy of determining our fate, that is simply a relapse into the pious view of the universe which Leonardo himself was on the way to overcoming when he wrote that the sun does not move. . . . We are all too ready to forget that in fact everything to do with our lives is chance, from our origin out of the meeting of spermatozoon and ovum onwards. . . . We all still show too little respect for Nature, which (in the obscure words of Leonardo which recall Hamlet's lines) "is full of countless causes [*ragioni*] that never enter experience."
>
> Every one of us human beings corresponds to one of the countless experiments in which these *ragioni* of nature force their way into experience.

The common-sense Freudianism of contemporary culture makes it easy to see our conscience as such an experiment, to identify conscience with guilt over repressed infantile sexual impulses—repressions which are the products of countless contingencies that never enter experience. It is hard nowadays to recapture how startling it must have been when Freud first began to describe conscience as an ego ideal set up by those who, as he put it in the essay "On Narcissism," are "not willing to forgo the narcissistic perfection of childhood." To illustrate this novelty, I shall contrast a passage from Freud in which it is absent from one in which it is present. In the first passage Freud says: "What prompted the individual to form an ego ideal, on whose behalf his conscience acts as watchman, arose from the critical influence of his parents . . . to whom were added, as time went on, those who trained and taught him and the innumerable and indefinable host of all the other people in his environment—his fellow men—and public opinion." If Freud had made only this sort of large, abstract, quasi-philosophical claim, he would have had said little that was particularly new or useful. The idea that the voice of conscience is the internalised voice of parents and society is suggested by Thrasymachus in Plato's *Republic*, and developed by reductionist writers like Hobbes. What is new in Freud are the details which he gives us about the sort of thing which goes into the formation of conscience, his explanations of why certain very concrete situations and persons excite unbearable guilt, intense anxiety or smouldering rage. Contrast the passage I just quoted with the following description of the latency period: "In addition to the destruction of the Oedipus complex a regressive degradation of the libido takes place, the super-ego becomes exceptionally severe and unkind, and the ego, in obedience to the super-ego, produces strong reaction-formations in the shape of conscientiousness, pity, and cleanliness. . . . But here too obsessional neurosis is only overdoing the normal method of getting rid of the Oedipus complex."

This passage, and others which discuss what Freud calls "the narcissistic origin of compassion," give us a way of thinking of the sense of pity, not as an identification with the common human core which we share with all other members of our species, but as channelled in very specific ways towards very specific sorts of people and very particular vicissitudes. He thus helps us understand how we can take endless pains to help one friend and be entirely oblivious to the greater pain of another, one whom we think we love quite as dearly. He helps explain how someone can be both a tender mother and a merciless concentration camp guard, or be a just and temperate magistrate and also a chilly, rejecting father. By associating conscientiousness with cleanliness, and by associating both not only with obsessional neurosis but also (as he does elsewhere) with the religious impulse and with the urge to construct philosophical systems, he breaks down all the traditional distinctions between the higher and the lower, the essential and the accidental, the central and the peripheral. He leaves us with a self which is a tissue of contingencies, rather than an (at least potentially) well-ordered system of faculties.

Freud shows us why we deplore cruelty in some cases and relish it in others. He shows us why our ability to love is restricted to some very particular shapes and sizes and colours of people, things or ideas. He shows us why our sense of guilt is aroused by certain very specific, and in theory quite minor, events, and not by others which, on any familiar moral theory, would loom much larger. Further, he gives each of us the equipment to construct our own private vocabulary of moral deliberation. For terms like "infantile" or "sadistic" or "obsessional" or "paranoid," unlike the names of vices and virtues which we inherit from the Greeks and the Christians, have very specific and very different resonances for each individual who uses them: they bring to our minds resemblances and differences between ourselves and very particular people (our parents, for example) and between the present situation and very particular situations of our past. They enable us to sketch a narrative of our own development, our idiosyncratic moral struggle, which is far more finely-textured, far more custom-tailored to our individual case, than the moral vocabulary which the philosophical tradition offered us.

One can sum up this point by saying that Freud makes moral deliberation just as finely-grained, just as detailed and as multiform, as prudential calculation has always been. He thereby helps break down the distinction between moral guilt and practical inadvisability, blurring the prudence-morality distinction into invisibility. The latter distinction is the one on which Plato's and Kant's moral philosophy centres. Kant splits us into two parts, one called "reason" which is identical in all of us, and another—empirical sensation and desire—which is a matter of blind, contingent, idiosyncratic impressions. In contrast, Freud treats rationality as a mechanism which adjusts contingencies to other contingencies. But his mechanisation of reason is not just more abstract philosophical reductionism, not just more "inverted Platonism." Rather than discussing rationality in the abstract, simplistic and reductionist way in which Hobbes and Hume discuss it (a way which retains Plato's original dualisms for the sake of inverting them), Freud spends his time exhibiting the extraordinary sophistication, subtlety and wit of our unconscious strategies. He thereby makes it possible for us to see science and poetry, genius and psychosis—and, most important, morality and prudence—not as products of distinct faculties but as alternative modes of adaptation.

He thus helps us take seriously the possibility that there is no central faculty, no central self, called "reason"—and thus to take Nietzschean pragmatism and perspectivism seriously. Freudian moral psychology gives us a vocabulary for self-description which is radically different from Plato's, and also radically different from that side of Nietzsche which Heidegger rightly condemned as one more example of inverted Platonism: the romantic attempt to exalt the flesh over the spirit, the heart over the head, a mythical faculty called "will" over an equally mythical one called "reason." The Platonic and Kantian idea of rationality centres on the idea that we need to bring particular actions under general principles if we are to be moral. Freud, by contrast, suggests that we need to return to the particular: to see particular present situations and options as similar to or different from particular past actions or events. He thinks that only by catching hold of crucial idiosyncratic contingencies in our past are we going to be able to make something worthwhile out of ourselves, to create present selves whom we can respect. He taught us to interpret what we are doing, or thinking of doing, in terms of, for example, our past reaction to particular authority figures, or in terms of constellations of behaviour which were forced upon us in infancy. He suggested that we praise ourselves by weaving idiosyncratic narratives—case histories, as it were—of our success in self-creation, our ability to break free from an idiosyncratic past. He suggests we condemn ourselves for failure to break free of that past rather than for failure to live up to universal standards.

Another way of putting this point is that Freud gave up Plato's attempt to bring together the public and the private, the parts of the state and the parts of the soul, the search for social justice and the search for individual perfection. Freud gave equal respect to the appeals of moralism and romanticism, but refused either to grant one of these priority over the other or to attempt a synthesis of them. He distinguished sharply between a private ethic of self-creation and a public ethic of mutual accommodation, and persuades us that there is no bridge between them provided by universally shared beliefs or desires—beliefs or desires which belong to us qua human and which unite us to our fellow humans simply as human. On Freud's account, our conscious private goals are as idiosyncratic as the unconscious obsessions and phobias from which they have branched off. Despite the efforts of such writers as Fromm and Marcuse, Freudian moral psychology cannot be used to define social goals, goals for humanity as opposed to goals for individuals. There is no way to force Freud into a Platonic mould by treating him as a moral philosopher who supplies universal criteria for goodness or rightness or true happiness. His only utility lies in his ability to turn us away from the universal to the concrete, from the attempt to find necessary truths, ineliminable beliefs, to the idiosyncratic contingencies of our individual pasts, to the blind impress all our behavings bear. He has provided us with a moral psychology which coheres with Nietzsche's and Bloom's attempt to see the strong poet as the archetypal human being.

For those who share this sense of the poet as paradigmatic, Freud will seem liberating and inspiring. But suppose that, like Kant, one instead sees the unselfish, unself-conscious, unimaginative, decent honest dutiful person as paradigmatic. These are the people in praise of whom Kant wrote: people who, unlike Plato's philosopher, have no special acuity of mind nor intellectual curiosity, and who, unlike the Christian saint, are not aflame to sacrifice themselves for love of the crucified Jesus. It is for the sake of such persons that Kant distinguished practical from pure reason, and rational religion from enthusiasm. It was for their sake that he invented the idea of a single imperative under which morality could be subsumed. For, he thought the glory of such people is that they recognise themselves as under an unconditional obligation: an obligation which can be carried out without recourse to prudential calculation, imaginative projection, or metaphoric redescription. So Kant developed not only a novel and imaginative moral psychology but a sweeping metaphoric redescription of every facet of life and culture, precisely in order to make the intellectual world safe for such people. In his words, he denied knowledge in order to make room for faith, the faith of such people that in doing their duty they are doing all they need do, that they are paradigmatic human beings.

It has often seemed necessary to choose between Kant and Nietzsche, to make up one's mind—at least to *that* extent—about the point of being human. But Freud gives us a way of looking at human beings which helps us evade the choice. After reading Freud we shall see neither Bloom's strong poet nor Kant's dutiful fulfiller of universal obligations as paradigmatic. For Freud eschews the very idea of a paradigm human being. He drops the idea of humanity as a natural kind with a intrinsic nature, an intrinsic set of powers to be developed or left undeveloped. By breaking with both Kant's residual Platonism and Nietzsche's inverted Platonism, he lets us see both Nietzsche's superman and Kant's common moral consciousness as exemplifying two out of many forms of adaptation, two out of many strategies of coping with the contingencies of one's upbringing, of coming to terms with a blind impress. There is much to be said for both. Each has advantages and disadvantages. Decent people are, notoriously, dull. Great minds are sure to madness near allied. Freud stands in awe before the poet, but describes him as infantile. He is bored by the merely moral man, but describes him as mature. He does not enthuse over either, nor does he ask us to choose between them. He does not think we have a faculty which can make such choices. He does not see a need to erect a theory of human nature which will safeguard the interests of the one or the other. He sees both sorts of person as doing the best they can with the materials at their disposal, and neither as "more truly human" than the other.

To abjure the notion of "the truly human" is to abjure the Kantian attempt to divinise the self as a replacement for a divinised world. It is to get rid of the last citadel of necessity, the last attempt to see us as all confronting the same imperatives, the same unconditional claims. What ties Nietzsche and Freud together is this attempt; the attempt to see a blind impress as not unworthy of programming our lives or our poems. But there is a difference between Nietzsche and Freud which my description of Freud's view of the moral man as decent but dull does not capture. Freud shows us that, if we look inside the bien-pensant conformist, if we get him on the couch, we will find that he was only dull on the surface. There are, for Freud, no dull people, because there is no such thing as a dull unconscious. What makes Freud more useful and more plausible than Nietzsche is that he does not relegate the vast majority of humanity to the status of dying animals. For Freud's account of unconscious fantasy shows us how to see every human life as a poem—or, more exactly, every human life not so racked by pain as to be unable to learn a language, nor so immersed in toil as to have no leisure in which to generate a self-description. He sees every such life as an attempt to clothe itself in its own metaphors. As Philip Rieff puts it, "Freud democratised genius by giving everyone a creative unconscious." The same point is made by Lionel Trilling, who said that Freud "showed us that poetry is indigenous to the very constitution of the mind; he saw the mind as being, in the greater part of its tendency, exactly a poetry-making faculty." Leo Bersani broadens Rieff's and Trilling's point when he says: "Psychoanalytic theory has made the notion of fantasy so richly programmatic that we should no longer be able to take for granted the distinction between art and life."

To say with Trilling that the mind is a poetry-making faculty may seem to return us to philosophy, and to the idea of an intrinsic human nature. Specifically, it may seem to return us to a Romantic theory of human nature in which Imagination plays the role which the Greeks assigned to Reason. But it does not. For the Romantics, Imagination was a link with something not ourselves, a proof that we were here as from another world. It was a faculty of expression. But what Freud takes to be shared by all relatively leisured language-users—all of us who have the equipment and the time for fantasy—is a faculty for creating metaphors. On the Davidsonian account, when a metaphor is created it does not express something which previously existed, though of course it is caused by something that previously existed. On Freud's account, this cause is not the recollection of another world but rather some particular obsession-generating cathexis of some particular person or object or word early in life. By seeing every human being as consciously or unconsciously acting out an idiosyncratic fantasy, we can see the distinctively human, as opposed to animal, portion of each human life as the use of every particular person, object, situation, event, and word encountered in later life for symbolic purposes. This process amounts to redescribing them, thereby saying of them all: "thus I willed it."

Seen from this angle, the poet, the person who uses *words* for this purpose, is just a special case—just somebody who does with noises and inscriptions what other people do with their spouses and children, their fellow workers, the tools of their trade, the cash accounts of their businesses, the possessions they accumulate in their homes, the music they listen to, the sports they play or watch, or the trees they pass on their way to work. Anything from the sound of a word to the colour of a leaf to the feel of a piece of skin can, as Freud showed us, serve to dramatise and crystallise a human being's sense of self-identity. For any such thing can play the role in an individual life which philosophers have thought could, or at least should, be played only by things which were universal, common to us all. It can symbolise the blind impress all our behavings bear. Any seemingly random constellation of such things can set the tone of a life. Any such constellation can set up an unconditional commandment to whose service a life may be devoted—a commandment no less unconditional because it may be intelligible to, at best, only one person.

Another way of making this point is to say that the social process of literalising a metaphor is duplicated in the fantasy life of an individual. We call something "fantasy" rather than "poetry" or "philosophy" when it revolves around metaphors which do not catch on with other people—that is, around ways of speaking or acting which the rest of us cannot find a use for. But Freud shows us how something which seems pointless or ridiculous or vile to society can become the crucial element in the individual's sense of who she is, her own way of tracing home the blind impress all her behavings bear. Conversely, when some private obsession produces a metaphor which we *can* find a use for, we speak of genius rather than of eccentricity or perversity. The difference between fantasy and genius is not the difference between fantasies which do not lock onto something universal, some antecedent reality out there in the world or deep within the self, and those which do. Rather, it is the difference between fantasies which just happen to catch on with other people—happen because of the contingencies of some historical situation, some particular need which a given community happens to have at a given time.

To sum up, poetic, philosophical, scientific or political progress results from the accidental coincidence of a private obsession with a public need. Strong poetry, common-sense morality, revolutionary morality, normal science, revolutionary science, and the sort of idiosyncratic fantasy which is intelligible to only one person, are all, from a Freudian point of view, different ways of dealing with blind impresses: or, more precisely, ways of dealing with different blind impresses—impresses which may be unique to an individual or common to the members of some historically-conditioned community. None of these strategies is privileged over others in the sense of expressing human nature better. No such strategy is more or less human than any other, any more than the pen is more truly a tool than the butcher's knife, or the hybridised orchid less a flower than the wild rose.

To appreciate Freud's point would be to overcome what William James called "a certain blindness in human beings." James's example of this blindness was his own reaction, during a trip through the Appalachian Mountains, to a clearing in which the forest had been hacked down and replaced with a muddy garden, a log cabin and some pigpens. "The forest had been destroyed; and what had 'improved' it out of existence was hideous, a sort of ulcer, without a single element of artificial grace to make up for the loss of Nature's beauty." But, James continues, when a farmer comes out of the cabin and tells him that "we ain't happy here unless we're getting one of those coves under cultivation," he realises that:

> I had been losing the whole inward significance of the situation. Because to me the clearings spoke of naught but denudation, I thought that to those whose sturdy arms and obedient axes had made them they could tell no other story. But, when *they* looked on the hideous stumps, what they thought of was personal victory. . . . In short, the clearing which to me was a mere ugly picture on the retina, was to them a symbol redolent with moral memories and sang a very paean of duty, struggle, and success.
>
> I had been as blind to the peculiar ideality of their conditions as they certainly would also have been to the ideality of mine, had they had a peep at my strange indoor academic ways of life at Cambridge.

I have been interpreting Freud as having spelled out James's point in more detail, helping us overcome particularly intractable cases of blindness by letting us see the "peculiar" ideality of events which exemplify, for example, sexual perversion, extreme cruelty, ludicrous obsession and manic delusion. He lets us see each of these as the private poem of the pervert, the sadist or the lunatic: as richly-textured and "redolent of moral memories" as our own life. He lets us see as continuous with our own activity what moral philosophy describes as the extreme, inhuman and unnatural. But, and this is the crucial point, he does not do so in the traditional philosophical, reductionist way. He does not tell us that art is really sublimation, or philosophical system-building merely paranoia, or religion merely a confused memory of the fierce father. He is not saying that human life is merely a continuous rechannelling of libidinal energy. He is not interested in invoking a reality-appearance distinction, in saying that anything is "merely" or "really" something quite different. He just wants to give us one more

redescription of things to be filed alongside all the others, one more vocabulary, one more set of metaphors which he thinks have a chance of being
used and thereby literalised.

Insofar as one can attribute philosophical views to Freud, one can say
that he is as much a pragmatist as James and as much a perspectivist as
Nietzsche—or, one might also say, as much a modernist as Proust. For it
somehow became possible, towards the end of the 19th century, to take the
activity of redescription more lightly than it had ever been taken before in
the history of Europe. It became possible to see a new vocabulary, not as
something which was supposed to replace all other vocabularies, something
which claimed to represent reality, but simply as one more vocabulary, one
more human project, one person's chosen metaphoric. It is unlikely that
Freud's metaphors could have been picked up, used, and literalised at any
earlier period. But, conversely, it is unlikely that without Freud's metaphors
we should have been able to assimilate Nietzsche's, James's, Wittgenstein's
or Heidegger's as easily as we have, or to have read Proust with the relish
we did. All the figures of this period play into each other's hands. They feed
each other lines. Their metaphors rejoice in one another's company. This is
the sort of phenomenon which it is tempting to describe in terms of the
march of the World-Spirit towards clearer self-consciousness, or as the
length of man's mind gradually coming to match that of the universe. But
any such description would betray the spirit of playfulness and irony which
links the figures I have been describing.

This playfulness is the product of their shared ability to appreciate the
power of redescribing, the power of language to make new and different
things possible and important—an appreciation which becomes possible
only when one's aim becomes an expanding repertoire of alternative descriptions rather than the One Right Description. Such a shift in aim is
possible only to the extent that both the world and the self have been
de-divinised. To say that both are de-divinised is to say that one no longer
thinks of either as speaking to us, as having a language of its own, as a rival
poet. Neither are quasi-persons, neither wants to be expressed or represented in a certain way.

Both, however, have power over us—for example, the power to kill us.
The world can blindly and inarticulately crush us; mute despair, intense
mental pain, can cause us to blot ourselves out. But that sort of power is not
the sort we can appropriate by adopting and then transforming its language,
thereby becoming identical with the threatening power and subsuming it
under our own more powerful selves. This latter strategy is appropriate only
for coping with other persons—for example, with parents, gods, and poetic

precursors. But our relation to the world, to brute power and to naked pain, is not of the sort we have to persons. Faced with the non-human, the non-linguistic, we no longer have the ability to overcome contingency and pain by appropriation and transformation, but only the ability to recognise contingency and pain. The final victory of poetry in its ancient quarrel with philosophy—the final victory of metaphors of self-creation over metaphors of discovery—would consist in our becoming reconciled to the thought that this is the only sort of power over the world which we can hope to have. For that would be the final abjuration of the notion that truth, and not just power and pain, is to be found "out there."

It is tempting to suggest that in a culture in which poetry had publicly and explicitly triumphed over philosophy, a culture in which recognition of contingency rather than of necessity was the accepted definition of freedom, Larkin's poem would fall flat. There would be no pathos in finitude. But there probably cannot be such a culture. This pathos is probably ineliminable. It is as hard to imagine a culture dominated by exuberant Nietzschean playfulness as to imagine the reign of the philosopher-kings, or the withering away of the state. It is equally hard to imagine a human life which felt itself complete, a human being who dies happy because all that he or she ever wanted has been attained. This is true even for Bloom's strong poet. Even if we drop the philosophical ideal of seeing ourselves steady and whole against a permanent backdrop of "literal" unchangeable fact, and substitute the ideal of seeing ourselves in our own terms, of redemption through saying to the past, "thus I willed it," it will remain true that this willing will always be a project rather than a result, a project which life does not last long enough to complete.

The strong poet's fear of death as the fear of incompletion is a function of the fact that no project of redescribing the world and the past, no project of self-creation through imposition of one's own idiosyncratic metaphoric, can avoid being marginal and parasitic. Metaphors are unfamiliar uses of old words, but such uses are possible only against the backdrop of other old words being used in old familiar ways. A language which was "all metaphor" would be a language which had no use, hence not a language but just babble. For even if we agree that languages are not media of representation or expression they will remain media of communication, tools for social interaction, ways of tying oneself up with other human beings.

This needed corrective to Nietzsche's attempt to divinise the poet, this dependence of even the strongest poet on others, is summed up by Bloom in *Kabbalah and Criticism*:

> The sad truth is that poems *don't have* presence, unity, form or meaning. . . . What then does a poem possess or create? Alas, a poem *has* nothing and *creates* nothing. Its presence is a promise, part of the substance of things hoped for, the evidence of things not seen. Its unity is in the good will of the reader. . . . Its meaning is just that there is, or rather *was*, another poem.

In this passage Bloom de-divinises the poem, and thereby the poet, in the same way in which Nietzsche de-divinised truth and in which Freud de-divinised conscience. He does for romanticism what Freud did for moralism. The strategy is the same in all these cases: it is to substitute a tissue of contingent relations, a web which stretches backward and forward through past and future time, for a formed, unified, present, self-contained substance, something capable of being seen steady and whole. Bloom reminds us that just as even the strongest poet is parasitic on her precursors, just as even she can give birth only to a small part of herself, so she is dependent on the kindness of all those strangers out there in the future.

This amounts to a reminder of Wittgenstein's point that there are no private languages: his argument that you cannot give meaning to a word or a poem by confronting it with a non-linguistic meaning, with something other than a bunch of other words or a bunch of other poems. Every poem, to paraphrase Wittgenstein, presupposes a lot of stage-setting in the culture, for the same reason that every sparkling metaphor requires a lot of stodgy literal talk to serve as its foil. Shifting from the written poem to the life-as-poem, one may say that there can be no fully Nietzschean lives, lives which are pure action rather than reaction: no lives which are not largely parasitical on an un-redescribed past and dependent on the charity of as yet unborn generations. There is no stronger claim even the strongest poet can make than the one Keats made: that he "would be among the English poets," construing "among them" in a Bloomian way as "in the midst of them," future poets living out of Keats's pocket as he lived out of those of his precursors. Analogously, there is no stronger claim which even the Superman can make than that his differences from the past, inevitably minor and marginal as they are, will nevertheless be carried over into the future: that his metaphoric redescriptions of small parts of the past will be among the future's stock of literal truths.

The best way to understand the pathos of finitude which Larkin invokes is to interpret it, not as the failure to achieve what philosophy hoped to achieve—something non-idiosyncratic, atemporal and universal—but as the realisation that at a certain point one has to trust to the good will of those who will live other lives and write other poems. Nabokov built his best book, *Pale Fire*, around the phrase: "Man's life as commentary to abstruse unfinished poem." That phrase serves both as a summary of Freud's claim that every human life is the working-out of a sophisticated idiosyncratic fantasy, and as a reminder that no such working-out gets completed before death interrupts. It cannot get completed because there is nothing to complete: there is only a web of relations to be rewoven, a web which time lengthens every day.

But if we avoid Nietzsche's inverted Platonism—his suggestion that a life of self-creation can be as complete and as autonomous as Plato thought a life of contemplation might be—then we shall be content to think of any human life as the always incomplete, yet sometimes heroic reweaving of such a web. We shall see the conscious need of the strong poet to demonstrate, to make public, the fact that he is not a copy or replica as merely a special, optional form of the unconscious need which everyone has to come to terms with the blind impress which chance has given him, to make a self for himself by redescribing that impress in terms which are, if only marginally, his own.

RICHARD DRAKE

Shepherd and Serpent:
Zarathustra's Phantasmagoria

While the principal motors of human action are sensual pleasure, the lust for power, and selfishness, a more searching analysis is necessary if Zarathustra is himself to understand his own dilemma. The much delayed confrontation with the forces behind Zarathustra's vision of the shepherd and the serpent begins with the effort in "Of the Spirit of Gravity" to define narcissism. Although it is not clear what kind of answer the riddle of Zarathustra's phantasmagoria calls for, the vision demands an intense effort of self-analysis. The prophet approaches that task indirectly:

> He who will one day teach men to fly will have moved all boundary-stones; all boundary-stones will themselves fly into the air to him, he will baptize the earth anew—as "the weightless."
>
> The ostrich runs faster than any horse, but even he sticks his head heavily into heavy earth: that is what the man who cannot yet fly is like.
>
> He calls earth and life heavy: and so will the Spirit of Gravity have it! But he who wants to become light and a bird must love himself—thus do I teach.
>
> Not with the love of the sick and diseased, to be sure: for with them even self-love stinks!
>
> One must learn to love oneself with a sound and healthy love, so that one may endure it with oneself and not go roaming about—thus do I teach.

© 1987 by Richard F. Drake. Published for the first time in this volume.

Although Zarathustra proclaims in his "Prologue" that the superman is the sense of the earth, the Spirit of Gravity has made the earth epitomize the burdensome character of life. Throughout part 1, the prophet argues against all "afterwordly" philosophy and theology by insisting that only the earth and not a transcendental realm can generate the meaningfulness of life. Since the superman has the task of interpreting the earth, the superman is in no sense autonomous or self-justifying. Our indebtedness to and dependence on the earth are so total that it becomes the central concept of Zarathustra's system.

Unlike Protagoras, Zarathustra argues that the earth, not man, is the measure of all things and that values help man determine the various and conflicting ways in which the earth addresses him. In part 3 Zarathustra has to refine his earlier sense of the earth because he understands that our sense of the earth parallels our sense of self. Man's desire to fly images an aspiration for freedom from the weight of gravity. The ability to fly stands for a healthy self-love which would provide perspective on and relief from the suffering associated with the earth. By setting up the earth as a measure of meaningfulness, Zarathustra almost falls into an idolatry of the natural. However, since the prophet refuses to abandon his critique of nihilism by revaluing the transcendental in positive terms, his thinking turns inward to the psychological bases for anxiety and unhappiness. Zarathustra holds out the promise that once we have learned to love ourselves, we can esteem the earth as weightless.

Narcissism is put forward as a quality to be learned because socialization suppresses whatever innate impulses of self-love we have. In its approach to self-love *Thus Spake Zarathustra* finds an important precursor in Goethe's *Faust*. At the beginning of the play Faust feels disgust and revulsion for himself since he believes he has wasted his life. His wager with Mephistopheles implies the conviction that he can never enjoy a healthy affection for himself:

> If ever I lay myself contented upon a bed of ease,
> Let it be over for me immediately!
> If you can ever deceive me
> Into liking myself,
> If you can deceive me with pleasure,
> Let that day be for me my last.
> This wager I offer.

In the adventures that follow, Faust gives himself over to sensual pleasure, the lust for power, and increasing selfishness without knowing any harmony with himself. When Faust finally accepts death, he does so because he has redefined his own egoism in terms of a solidarity with future generations of men. Throughout his life, Goethe's hero restlessly roams about because he cannot endure himself. At the death of Faust, the slowing down of time betokens an increasing harmony between the individual and the collectivity which accompanies the hero's reconciliation with himself.

Of course, by a summary of *Faust* we indicate as many differences as similarities between the two works. For Goethe the redefinition of self in terms of social obligation allows a relaxation of an ever driving and restless will fueled by self-dislike. While Faust never exalts or pleads for a release from restlessness, he comes to experience in his last moments a compromise between an aggressive willfulness and easy acceptance of death because he has made peace with the mankind that he had previously victimized. A treaty with humanity is not open to Zarathustra:

> And truly, to learn to love oneself is no commandment for today or for tomorrow. Rather is this art the finest, subtlest, ultimate, and most patient of all.
>
> For all his possessions are well concealed from the possessor; and of all treasure pits, one's own is the last to be digged—the Spirit of Gravity is the cause of that.
>
> Almost in the cradle are we presented with heavy words and values: this dowry calls itself "Good" and "Evil." For its sake we are forgiven for being alive.
>
> And we suffer little children to come to us, to prevent them in good time from loving themselves: the Spirit of Gravity is the cause of that.

To prevent the development of self-love, culture assaults the newborn infant with its values of good and evil. Socialization depends upon society's effort to wound narcissism permanently. In the wake of Freud we can see that what for Zarathustra has the form of a malicious attack on the infant is society's attempt to create a superego, to hasten the transition from a primordial narcissism—the love we feel for the body that gives us pleasure— to a more advanced narcissism—the love or perhaps respect we feel for ourselves when we have carried out the norms of society. While Freud insists that socialization demands the heavy price of wounded narcissism, Zarathustra is unwilling to make peace with the Spirit of Gravity. In his previous avatars, the Spirit of Gravity stood for the aspect of Zarathustra's personality most in tune with Schopenhauerian nihilism, an attraction to the center of the earth easily interpreted as melancholy, the weight of the past, the fear of death, and finally the impulse to oedipal violence. Here the Spirit of Gravity personifies the efforts of society to impede the gaining of perspective on the education that forces an identity upon the individual.

Section 380 of *The Gay Science* makes the point more discursively and clearly than Zarathustra's imagery:

> In the main the question is how light or heavy we are—the problem of our "specific gravity." One has to be very light to drive one's will to knowledge into such a distance and, as it were, beyond one's time, to create for oneself eyes to survey millennia and, moreover, clear skies in these eyes. One must have liberated oneself from many things that oppress, inhibit, hold down, and make heavy precisely us Europeans today.

If values do accompany the injunction to children not to love themselves, the perspective of flight is necessary not so much to survey millenia, as section 380 asserts, as to wonder about the place of forgiveness in life. If the forces of culture from the family to the state can offer nothing better than forgiveness for the sin of an infant's survival, Zarathustra has a more than Rousseauistic vision of society's corruption. Since the community of man has no generous impulses, the individual is dependent on his own damaged resources. Faced with such a hostile set of circumstances, the individual expresses dissatisfaction with life as a whole: "Yes, life is hard (or heavy—*schwer*) to bear." To one generalization, Zarathustra responds with another: "But only man is hard to bear." A dissatisfaction with man as he is rather than with life as a whole makes easier the possibility of corrective action. A series of shell metaphors suggests a more hopeful assessment which rests on the basis of a dissatisfaction limited to man:

> And truly! Many things that are one's own are hard to bear, too! And much that is intrinsic in man is like the oyster, that is loathsome and slippery and hard to grasp—
>
>   so that a noble shell with noble embellishments must intercede for it. But one has to learn this art as well: to have a shell and a fair appearance and a prudent blindness!
>
>   Again, it is deceptive about many things in man that many a shell is inferior and wretched and too much of a shell. Much hidden goodness and power is never guessed at; the most exquisite dainties find no tasters!

In his resemblance to the oyster, man contains much that is "loathsome and slippery and hard to grasp." Since all three phrases describe responses to the vision of the serpent and the shepherd, the eternal return lies inside man. If the individual can bring himself to swallow the eternal return, he will have moved beyond the shell of identity, found the exquisite dainty therein, and forgiven himself for what he is. The "hidden goodness and power" that Zarathustra is convinced we will find in ourselves brings about a reconciliation in which the individual can affirm first himself and, subsequently, the earth.

In a passage that looks forward to the transformation of the shepherd after he has overcome the serpent, "Of Reading and Writing" speaks of Zarathustra's desire to murder the Spirit of Gravity through laughter, not anger. The violence of the prophet's imagery lessens when he puts a higher value on self-understanding:

> Man is difficult to discover, most of all to himself; the spirit often tells lies about the soul. The Spirit of Gravity is the cause of that.
>   But he has discovered himself who says: This is my good and evil: he has silenced thereby the mole and the dwarf who says: "Good for all, evil for all."

Since the Spirit of Gravity is half mole and half dwarf, the individual conquers the Spirit of Gravity by freeing himself from society's demand for uniformity of values. While the mole cannot see at all, the "prudent blindness" that goes with having a "shell and a fair appearance" does not impede self-discovery. Oedipus prudently blinds himself because he does not want to see his father and mother in the underworld or his children in life. If Zarathustra understands his own primal scene as an emblem of the antagonism between parents and children on one hand and between individual and society on the other, he can avoid the violence that periodically emerges in his rhetoric and explore reconciliation as an alternative.

Zarathustra begins part 3 by remarking that "in the final analysis one experiences only oneself." When involuntary bliss deprives Zarathustra of the desired confrontation with the hidden powers of his own psyche, the deepening self-involvement brought on by the crisis of the eternal return abates. In "Of the Spirit of Gravity" the prophet gropes his way back to the theme of narcissism until finally "The Convalescent" shows Zarathustra reliving the traumas of his phantasmagorical vision. Upon awakening one morning, Zarathustra behaves as if someone else were lying in the bed and could not rise from it. By imagining a catatonic double, the prophet shows one fearful way of responding to the idea of the eternal return. Zarathustra's spirit of affirmation rejects paralysis as a defensible response to the doctrine:

> Up, abysmal thought, up from my depths! I am your cockerel
> and dawn, sleepy worm: up! up! My voice shall soon crow you
> awake!
>
> Loosen the fetters of your ears: listen! For I want to hear you!
> Up! Up! Here is thunder enough to make even the graves listen!
>
> And wipe the sleep and all the dimness and blindness from
> your eyes! Hear me with your eyes, too: my voice is a medicine
> even for those born blind.

Since he addresses the catatonic sleeper as the personification of the eternal
return, Zarathustra's self-conception has become inextricably involved in
the idea even though he has not brought himself to accept the doctrine. The
affirmation of the eternal return wouild consequently be a gesture of self-
acceptance. In his effort to arouse the sleepy serpent, Zarathustra insists
upon a dialogue of a specific kind. By simultaneously ordering the thought
to loosen the fetters of its ears and affirming his desire to hear, the prophet
must be telling himself to open his own ears so that he can listen to an aspect
of himself. Since the union of sight and sound suggests reading rather than
self-examination, the synesthetic effect of "Hear me with your eyes" may
break the circle of self-involvement. But although the "sleepy worm" de-
fensively reduces the snake from"Of the Vision and the Riddle," the therapeutic urgency of the voice reflects a desperate need for the sight or the
understanding that could heal the blindness afflicting the serpent and by
extension Zarathustra.

The true power of the sleeping worm becomes evident when Zarathustra
takes on the role of the conjuring magus. As the snake awakens, it reinstills
the fear of dying by strangulation:

> Are you moving, stretching, rattling? Up! Up! You shall not
> rattle, you shall—speak to me! Zarathustra the Godless calls
> you!
>
> I, Zarathustra, the advocate of life, the advocate of suffering,
> the advocate of the circle—I call you, my most abysmal thought!
>
> Ah! you are coming—I hear you! My abyss speaks, I have
> turned my ultimate depth into the light!
>
> Ah! Come here! Give me your hand—ha! don't! Ha, ha!—
> Disgust, disgust, disgust—woe is me!

In German, the word "rattle" (röcheln) refers to the difficulty of breathing
that the dying experience in their final moments. Although Zarathustra does
not use the same word to describe the "young shepherd writhing, choking,

convulsed," the two moments mirror each other especially since the word "writhe" in German (*sich winden*) describes the action of a snake. Where the shepherd was previously choking on the serpentine aspects of his character, Zarathustra now identifies himself with the wakening snake. The bravado with which the prophet declares himself the godless advocate of life, suffering, and the circle establishes another link between Zarathustra and Faust who attempts to summon the earth-spirit both vainly and vaingloriously. Although Zarathustra prematurely boasts that he has brought the abysmal thought into light, the action of the summoning becomes unclear. When he says "Give me your hand," the prophet behaves as if he were offering a handshake of friendship or seeking to help someone out of a pit. Perhaps when Zarathustra says "don't" or "stop" or "let go" (*lass!*), we are to understand that the devil of the eternal return is trying to pull Zarathustra into the pit. Whatever the figure of the eternal return seeks to do, disgust and pity overcome Zarathustra just as the phantasmagorical vision of serpent and shepherd revolted him. In light of his collapse, Zarathustra's claim to be the spokesman of life, suffering, and the circle rings hollow.

Whenever Zarathustra has had a nightmare or a vision that calls for but resists explanation, it becomes the object of interpretative energies which may or may not succeed in puzzling out the mystery. "The Prophet" is the most striking example of this pattern. The rest of "The Convalescent" presents a dialogue between Zarathustra and his animals about the correct way to interpret both the latest moment of crisis and the eternal return. Our problem in interpreting the dialogue is compounded because the allusive texture of Zarathustra's phantasmagoria has already suggested a reading of the eternal return which in no way coincides with what either the animals or the prophet will say.

After his nightmare Zarathustra collapses like a dead man and remains immobile for several days as if to repeat the catatonia he tried to arouse his double from. During his trance the eagle fetches the goods of the earth—edible and inedible items which arouse both appetite and the sense of beauty. After seven days Zarathustra awakens, takes a rosy apple in his hand, finds its smell pleasant, but does not eat it. The refusal to eat contrasts with the penance of a good meal the prophet had imposed upon himself at the end of "The Prophet." When his animals finally speak, they urge him to an involvement in life of which eating serves as a symbol:

> "O Zarathustra," they said, "now you have lain like that seven days, with heavy eyes: will you not now get to your feet again?

"Step out of your cave: the world awaits you like a garden.
The wind is laden with heavy fragrance that longs for you; and
all the brooks would like to run after you.

"All things long for you, since you have been alone seven
days—step out of your cave! All things want to be your physi-
cians!"

Their first question restates in a milder tone Zarathustra's command to his
catatonic double: "Up, . . . up from [the] depths!" By urging Zarathustra to
"step out of [his] cave" (*Höhle*), they perhaps pun on an ascent from hell
(*Hölle*) since the German words are homophonic. In looking at the rosy
apple, Zarathustra reminds the animals of Adam in Eden. While continuing
the image, they re-write Genesis by insisting that all the world is a garden.
The suggested harmony of man and nature implies the renovation of
Zarathustra and the earth, both of whom can once more become young.

Since the detail of the brooks running after Zarathustra suggests the
sympathy between natural objects and Orpheus, the garden image takes on
a Greek aspect. When they assert that all things want to be physician to
Zarathustra, the animals implicitly rehabilitate the notion of the earth
which had lost importance because of its association with gravity. "Of the
Spirit of Gravity" had implied that the earth is secondary to self-
understanding since our attitude towards the earth depends upon the health
or sickness of our narcissism. By making a case for the earth, the animals
return us to the ambiguity of the "The Wanderer." During that section
Zarathustra seemed to accept the need for a more profound self-
understanding by stating that "in the final analysis one experiences only
oneself." However, the prophet is soon contradicted by his hour: "In order
to see much one must learn to look away from oneself." The tension
between the internal and the external is difficult to resolve because we do
not know how to interpret figuratively the claim that all things want to be
physician to Zarathustra. Are the animals saying that a glance at the apple
ought to convince Zarathustra that the larger sphere of the earth is
fundamentally beautiful and thus generally open to the initiatives of man?
Once we note in passing that *Thus Spake Zarathustra* does not develop a
sense of nature's enmity towards man, it may make more sense to follow
the reference to Orpheus towards the understanding that art enlists nature
in man's behalf by creating the benevolent fiction that nature is reaching
out to help.

In his reply Zarathustra insists upon the contribution language makes
to our sense of the earth:

"O my animals," answered Zarathustra, "go on talking and let me listen! Your talking is such refreshment: where there is talking, the world is like a garden to me. How sweet it is, that words and sounds of music exist: are words and music not rainbows and seeming bridges between things eternally separated?"

Although Zarathustra's tone seems friendly, he rejects the notion of nature's benevolence since words and sounds make no literal statements about the external world. While words and music are "rainbows and seeming bridges," they provide no real access to phenomena; man and nature remain eternally separate. Zarathustra's unfavorable and patronizing view of language overlooks the way in which the body involves us in the world. Had Zarathustra eaten the rosy apple, the divorce between man and nature would be much less convincing since appetite involves us in the external world. Whereas Genesis explains the gulf between man and nature and even the ruthlessness of nature as the result of man's eating, the gap between man and nature which Zarathustra asserts rests on a refusal to eat.

According to part 1, the failure to take the body into account characterizes traditional metaphysics. As Zarathustra goes on, his position reminds us more and more of those inherited habits of thoughts which he had previously rejected:

"Every soul is a world of its own; for every soul every other soul is an afterworld.

"Appearance lies most beautifully among the most alike; for the smallest gap is the most difficult to bridge.

"For me—how could there be an outside-of-me? There is no outside! But we forget that, when we hear music; how sweet it is, that we forget!"

"Afterworld" recalls Zarathustra's critique of metaphysicians and theologians who imagine another world beyond phenomena and on the other side of death. If we accept the correctness of his earlier position, the prophet's use of the word to describe intersubjectivity suggests that he has fallen into error. Within the context Zarathustra's opinion is ambiguous since we cannot be sure whether he is emphasizing that he is an afterworld to others or that others are afterworlds to him. Wherever the accent falls, the statement suggests his oppressive sense of isolation. By definition, afterworlds are concealed and inaccessible since neither Kantian noumena nor realms beyond death are available to either the senses or the intellect. Ironically, we do have access to Zarathustra's afterworld since he has shared his vision of shepherd and serpent. The pessimism about the isolation between human beings recalls *The Birth of Tragedy* where Nietzsche describes individuation as a torment to be overcome through Dionysian music. The appearance that "lies most beautifully" suggests Apollonian differentiation, but since Zarathustra can recognize no outside, his hypertrophied interiority has lost a sharp sense for the boundaries between subject and object while continuing to share the isolation and detachment that Apollo brings. Only the words of his animals and music in general can bring the oblivion that eases the suffering of isolation. Zarathustra's earlier claim that "in the final analysis one experiences only oneself" has received its most extreme expression.

The rhetoric of praise for both language and music should not blind us to the evasion that Zarathustra ostensibly praises:

> "Are things not given names and musical sounds, so that man may refresh himself with things? Speech is a beautiful foolery: with it man dances over all things.
> "How sweet is all speech and all the falsehoods of music! With music does our love dance upon many-coloured rainbows."

Dancing "over all things" contrasts with the dance "upon many-colored rainbows." While the first phrase implies that language and music never touch reality, the second emphasizes how illusory our reconciliation with life must be. Although names and musical sounds seem to refer to things, their primary function is to grant relief from the isolation that afflicts an exaggerated sense of self. The freedom to dance over all things with language and music parodies Dionysian exuberance with a superficial gaiety that can never be in touch with the referential or the experiential world. While Zarathustra seems to be praising his animals, his rhetoric reveals how false and insubstantial the success of music and language is. However, the criticism of music and language under the ironic guise of praise may be misdirected polemicism since Zarathustra may be putting words in the mouths of his animals. How reliable can Zarathustra's judgment of either language of his animals be if the shock of his recent trauma has convinced him that the individual lives in a solipsistic isolation?

The structure of dialogue presupposes that at best each party can make only a partial claim to the truth. In reading the response of the animals to Zarathustra, we have to ask whether they can add something to their master's understanding of what the eternal return can contribute to convalescence:

> "O Zarathustra," said the animals then, "all things themselves
> dance for such as think as we: they come and offer their hand
> and laugh and flee—and return.
>
> "Everything goes, everything returns; the wheel of existence
> rolls forever. Everything dies, everything blossoms anew; the
> year of existence runs on forever.
>
> "Everything breaks, everything is joined anew; the same house
> of existence builds itself forever. Everything departs, everything
> meets again; the ring of existence is true to itself forever.
>
> "Existence begins in every instant; the ball There rolls around
> every Here. The middle is everywhere. The path of eternity is
> crooked."

While Zarathustra argues that music makes "our love dance upon many-colored rainbows," the animals insist that "all things themselves dance for such as think as we." Where Zarathustra underlines the importance of the subjective element in "our love," the animals put a stronger emphasis on the self-disclosure of the earth as an antidote for the alienation and isolation that afflict the prophet. Although the animals turn towards the objective world, the healing power of nature depends upon the stance observers adopt. The stress the animals place upon the way they think reflects the conviction that the self-disclosure of the earth runs parallel to the opening of man towards nature.

By so correcting the imbalance between the objective and the subjective, the animals prepare the way for a restatement of the eternal return in natural, not psychological terms. Since the animals see nature as a garden, their "wheel of existence" is not so much an imagined possibility in the context of which an individual hypothetically assents to relive his life as the cycle of the seasons which mixes blooming and decay, growth and death in a reassuring circularity. The "house of existence" has an eternal newness and a ubiquitous centrality which the animals urge Zarathustra to participate in. By interpreting the eternal return naturalistically, Zarathustra's animals literalize their master's teaching in order to reveal its therapeutic power.

Zarathustra begins his reply in the same mild and ostensibly complimentary tone that characterized his earlier response:

> "O you buffoons and barrel-organs!" answered Zarathustra
> and smiled again; "how well you know what had to be fulfilled
> in seven days:
>
> "and how that monster crept into my throat and choked me!
> But I bit its head off and spat it away."

RICHARD DRAKE

Since the animals "know what had to be fulfilled in seven days," they understand his catatonic trance as a recreation of the world, which, Zarathustra says, has ended in the defeat of the serpent. The animals are called barrel-organs because they too can repeat only one song or tune without any variation. The nastiness in this comparison soon becomes explicit as Zarathustra's tone becomes bitter:

> "And you—have already made a hurdy-gurdy song of it? I, however, lie here now, still weary from this biting and spitting away, still sick with my own redemption.
>
> "And you looked on at it all? O my animals, are you, too, cruel? Did you desire to be spectators of my great pain, as men do? For man is the cruellest animal.
>
> "More than anything on earth he enjoys tragedies, bullfights, and crucifixions; and when he invented Hell for himself, behold, it was his heaven on earth."

The prophet charges that his animals have trivialized the teaching of the eternal return while he himself is still sick with his own redemption. Whether or not the charge is fair, the passage dramatizes Zarathustra's sickness by calling in question for no good reason the motivation of the animals. The paranoid turn in the prophet's answer suggests no redemption has taken place since Zarathustra does not have the energy for the unconditional affirmation of life. Instead, Zarathustra laments how cruelty cleverly takes the form of pity.

While his insight is painfully just, it may miss the point which the animals wished to make about the earth's beauty. The best clue we have to explain the twist in Zarathustra's argument is undoubtedly the shock Zarathustra registers at the animals for having looked on at the scene of redemption. However, although the eagle and the serpent were present for the latest crisis, they did not see the shepherd biting off and spitting away the head of the serpent. Besides the dog, the only observer of the visionary moment is Zarathustra who now identifies himself with the shepherd. When Zarathustra lashes out at his animals, he displaces anger at himself for what he diagnoses as cruelty hiding under pity. Perhaps Zarathustra's anger acknowledges his pleasure at the suffering of the shepherd who figures not only the prophet but also the original and surrogate fathers. The passion of the oedipal trauma fuses the son and all of his fathers into one figure.

To some extent, Zarathustra is aware how contradictory and convoluted he has become. After blasting the "accusers of life," who take sensual delight in proclaiming the worthlessness of existence, Zarathustra asks "do

I want to be the accuser of man?" Despite his awareness of the parallelism between himself and the accusers of life, the prophet imagines himself tied to a "torture-stake" where he calls out not that "Man is wicked" but that "Alas, that his wickedest is so very small." Since the word for "torture-stake" in German (*Marterholz*) suggests the crucifixion, Zarathustra's paranoia transforms him into Christ who dies from man's powerlessness:

> "The great disgust at man—it choked me and had crept into my throat: and what the prophet prophesied: 'It is all one, nothing is worthwhile, knowledge chokes.'
>
> 'A long twilight limps in front of me, a mortally-weary, death-intoxicated sadness which speaks with a yawn.
>
> " 'The man of whom you are weary, the little man, recurs eternally'—thus my sadness yawned and dragged its feet and could not fall asleep.
>
> "The human earth became to me a cave, its chest caved in, everything living became to me human decay and bones and mouldering past."

Here Zarathustra offers his own reinterpretation of the eternal return. Besides being identified with the Schopenhauerian figure of the prophet, the snake that attacks the shepherd is defined as a disgust that results from the knowledge that man cannot be overcome and that the superman cannot be realized. As a result of these insights, the "human earth" comes to resemble both the castle in which Zarathustra dreamt he found himself after first hearing the words of the prophet and a decaying corpse. For Zarathustra, his central doctrine undergoes an extreme impoverishment so that the eternal return comes to mean only that "the little man recurs eternally."

How much credence should we lend to Zarathustra's rereading of his own doctrine? If the interpretation of the animals erred in glossing over the negative aspects of the eternal return, Zarathustra may betray his teaching by underscoring the negative too sharply. The prophet's emphasis results from the feeling of his own powerlessness. Although Zarathustra seems to be pulling back from the Hades of his own unconscious while talking with his animals, he is in fact turning more inward. For instance, the sadism that he is too quick to see in the solicitude of his animals reflects frustration about his own lack of strength. Furthermore, by making brutally explicit the most dismaying implications of the eternal return, he puts forth a reinterpretation which amounts to a victory for Schopenhauerian pessimism. When Zarathustra says that the "long twilight limps" in front of him, the mutilation of Oedipus pervades the setting of the dialogue. The inadequacy Zarathustra feels to the task of affirming the eternal return finds expression in the prophet's sadness "which yawned and dragged its feet and could not fall asleep." Since his polemic against the sublime ones, Zarathustra has been aware of the dangers which excessive self-involvement pose. The hope that a healthy self-love would lead to a perspective beyond the self seems more pertinent now than ever before.

When Zarathustra's nausea appears again, the biography of Nietzsche once more enters into consideration:

> "I had seen them both naked, the greatest man and the small-est man: all too similar to one another, even the greatest all too human!
>
> "The greatest all too small!—that was my disgust at man! And eternal recurrence even for the smallest! that was my disgust at all existence!
>
> "Ah, disgust! Disgust! Disgust!" Thus spoke Zarathustra and sighed and shuddered; for he remembered his sickness. But his animals would not let him speak further.

The phrase "all too human" recalls the title of the first book Nietzsche published after his break with Wagner—*Human, All Too Human*. Probably the title refers to Nietzsche's disillusionment with the many petty features of Wagner's personality. If even the titanic artist-hero can be flawed by anti-semitism, vanity, and intellectual shallowness, the realization of the super-man fades as a possibility. Nietzsche's traumatic struggle to free himself from the throttling influence of Wagner lingers on to impede any clear resolution of the oedipal dilemma. In railing against the smallest man and his return, Zarathustra sounds like the would-be disciple whose contempt for the ordinary man in "Of Passing-By" first overwhelms and then repels Zarathustra. The prophet's analysis of the fool may well apply to Zarathustra himself:

> What, then, was it that started you grunting? That nobody had flattered you enough: therefore you sat down beside this filth, so that you might have cause for much grunting—
>
> so that you might have cause for much revenge! For all your frothing, you vain fool, is revenged; I have divined you well!
>
> But your foolish teaching is harmful to me, even when you are right! And if Zarathustra's teaching were a hundred times justi-fied, you would still—use my teaching falsely!

Offended vanity produces the spirit of revenge which in turn distorts a correct teaching.

In the dialogue with his animals, Zarathustra may use his own teaching falsely as an excuse to avoid strategies of convalescence. Although Zarathustra had reached an honest recognition that his doctrine entails the eternal return of the smallest, his words only worsen and prolong the crisis. The refusal of his animals to let him speak further contrasts with his earlier exhortation to them: "go on talking and let me listen! Your talking is such refreshment." Since Zarathustra's earlier assessment of language as an indispensable ingredient in convalescence has proven incorrect, the advice of the animals to go into nature receives new support. When Zarathustra remembers his sickness, we recall his earlier praise of forgetting as another ingredient of convalescence and judge that remedy also as inadequate. By calling out "Disgust! Disgust!" Zarathustra returns full circle to his response when he saw the serpent attack the shepherd.

While the reply of the animals seems merely to repeat their earlier advice, they do make one significant variation in their theme:

> "Go out to the roses and bees and flocks of doves! But go out especially to the song-birds, so that you may learn singing for them!
>
> "For convalescents should sing; let the healthy talk. And when the healthy man, too, desires song, he desires other songs than the convalescent."

As soon as Zarathustra enters the garden of the world, he should pay special attention to the song-birds since the prophet needs music more than speech. When Zarathustra says that the animals know what comfort he devised for himself in seven days, he indirectly admits for the first time that no redemption has taken place. Instead of his asking for animals to continue talking, he insists "do be quiet" because, while he knows that he does need the musical consolation, he fears that his animals will make another "hurdy-gurdy song" (*Leierlied*) out of his convalescence. In response, the animals agree that there is no further need for words:

> "Speak no further," his animals answered once more; "rather first prepare yourself a lyre, convalescent, a new lyre!
>
> "For behold, O Zarathustra! New lyres are needed for your new songs.
>
> "Sing and bubble over, O Zarathustra, heal your soul with

new songs, so that you may bear your great destiny, that was
never yet the destiny of any man!"

Because the word "hurdy-gurdy song"in German means literally "song for
a lyre," the animals can make a pun which suggests both the continuing
presence of Wagner and a need for balance between Apollonian art and
Dionysian insight. With the lyre as instrument and weapon, Zarathustra can
hope to battle the Spirit of Gravity just as Nietzsche fights Wagner who
forges in his music an alliance between pessimism and aesthetics. By taking
up his vocation as singer of the eternal return against nihilism, Zarathustra
can heal himself. Because he has not seen the necessary connection between
his wounded narcissism and the healing of the wound through the enunci-
ation of the eternal return, Zarathustra has been a reluctant prophet. The
art of Apollo will make life and the insight of the eternal return bearable
even though we never escape the dual tyranny of the past and death. By
invoking Apollo as the principle of redemption, the animals surprisingly
vindicate *The Birth of Tragedy*, a work written in Nietzsche's Schopenhauerian phase which insists in Section 24 that art alone justifies life. When the
naturalism of looking upon the world as a garden reveals its dependence on
art, the animals show that they have accepted at least one of Zarathustra's
reservations about their therapeutic strategy.

The animals understand how intense Zarathustra's suffering is because they circumspectly raise the issue of suicide by imagining what
Zarathustra would say if he were to die now. Without holding out the false
hope of a reincarnation that might lead to a higher stage of existence,
the eternal return tries to thwart the desire to die. When the animals put
words into Zarathustra's mouth, they more or less repeat the major
features of the eternal return, but one formulation does deserve special
attention:

> " 'But the complex of causes in which I am entangled will
> recur—it will create me again! I myself am part of these causes
> of the eternal recurrence.' "

"Entangled" translates correctly the past participle *verschlungen* whose in-
finitive means to swallow and to eat. Perhaps the word distantly recalls the
entangling of serpent and shepherd with all the murky misgivings about
appetite which the vision expresses. The passage additionally suggests a
recognition of those forces or causes that make up necessity. At the moment
of death, Zarathustra ought to have the courage of submission. By refusing
to celebrate the eternal return, the prophet revolts against the unchangeable

and inevitable facticity of the past. The energy and wisdom to consent to the "complex" (or knot—*Knoten*) of causes must be found since the past is a Gordian knot which no sword can cut.

When Zarathustra knows that he himself is a "part of these causes" or even "belongs to these causes" (*gehören*), he no longer has to expend energy in resisting what he himself is. The hour can then come "when he who is going down shall bless himself." After cursing the smallest men and by implication himself, Zarathustra, the animals suggest, must take up the difficult task of blessing. Ideally, the moment of death transcends the need to attack one's own weaknesses, to rail against destiny or to otherwise offer futile protest. Zarathustra's animals must imagine a hypothetical confrontation with death because the prophet has not yet overcome his self-disgust. To accept one's helplessness before death may not seem titanic or heroic, but it does demand more of Zarathustra than he is capable of doing. Although Zarathustra can accept his duty to proclaim the superman, he does not yet have the power of the superman to will the eternal return. The silence with which Zarathustra responds to the imagined moment of death indicates a higher degree of understanding than anything he has said in "The Convalescent." The dialogue ends in a silence where Zarathustra takes to heart the criticism and advice of his animals.

Zarathustra's animals have urged him "heal your soul with new songs." Although the prophet does not immediately reply, he does eventually respond with "The Second Dance Song" addressed to the woman Life. By examining various passages from this section, we can determine the nature and the difficulties of the reconciliation Zarathustra attempts to achieve. While dancing sublimates eros, Zarathustra's song portrays the ambivalence of his sexual attraction to life.

> At my feet, my dancing-made feet, you threw a glance, a laughing, questioning, melting tossing glance:
>
> Twice only did you raise your castanets in your little hands—then my feet were already tossing in a mad dance.
>
> My heels raised themselves, my toes listened for what you should propose: for the dancer wears his ears—in his toes!
>
> I sprang to your side: then you fled back from my spring; towards me the tongues of your fleeing, flying hair came hissing!
>
> Away from you and from your serpents did I retire: then at once you stood, half turned, your eyes full of desire.
>
> With your crooked smile—you teach me crooked ways, upon crooked ways my feet learn—guile!

The scene is a flamenco dance which begins by fixing the attention of the participants on the feet. Since Zarathustra fully participates in the dance, we know that he is finally convalescing. When he does aggressively approach Life, she leaps back to assume the posture of Medusa whose serpentine hair turns all men into stone. The subsequent retreat of the male from the sexual threat that the Medusa stands for elicits the erotic longing of Life because the rhythms of attraction and repulsion reflect the ambivalence Zarathustra's sexualization of life entails. The "crooked smile" of Life teaches Zarathustra the "crooked ways" on which the circularity of time forces him to walk. The "crookedness" of the entire scene may signal Zarathustra's new image of himself as Perseus, a hero who cannot or perhaps should not directly attack either the Medusa or the monster attacking Andromeda. Other literary antecedents may also reflect the effort of Zarathustra to free himself from his self-image as Oedipus. Since Eve in Hebrew means life, the prophet may see himself as a new Adam forced to face a woman with much serpent in her nature. Nietzsche may also be referring to Walpurgisnacht in Goethe's *Faust* where sexual guilt leads the hero to imagine that he sees Gretchen. In an effort to calm Faust, Mephistopheles identifies the woman as the Medusa.

As the song progresses, it leaves the dance floor to become a hunt, a metaphor which maintains the ambivalence of affection and hostility. When Zarathustra asks Life "will you be my hound or will you be my kill?" he assumes the superior stance of the hunter who thinks he has little to fear. The smugness betrays him into imagining a scene of pastoral bliss:

> Are you now weary? There yonder are sheep and evening: let us end our pursuit: is it not sweet to sleep when the shepherd plays his flute?
>
> Are you so very weary? I will carry you there, just let your arms sink! And if you are thirsty—I should have something, but you would not like it to drink!—
>
> Oh this accursed, nimble, supple snake and slippery witch! Where have you gone? But on my face I feel from your hand two spots and blotches itch!
>
> I am truly weary of being your shepherd, always sheepish and meek! You witch, if I have hitherto sung for you, now for me you shall—shriek!

Life is not a sweet young girl who can be safely flirted with. Instead, as she is depicted here, she combines the features of a serpent and Circe. The two spots and the blotch show the effect of a snake bite. Throughout the hunt Life shows all the nimbleness of Proteus as she successively becomes bat, owl, dog, and finally serpent. The erotic metaphor of the song induces a sentimental view of Life until she reveals herself as a Circe who wants to change the would-be shepherd into a sheep. Like Odysseus in book 10 of the *Odyssey*, Zarathustra reacts with anger and subdues her.

Once the prophet has put aside his naiveté about Life, their relationship enters a more serious phase which the second part of the section describes. When Life does first speak, she betrays none of Zarathustra's sentimental exhilaration. In a mood of harsh realism, Life states directly that Zarathustra and she do not love each other "from the very heart." Although she claims that "tender thoughts" are coming to her, Life makes her love for Zarathustra dependent upon her jealousy for that other woman, Wisdom. With this reference "The Second Dance Song" recalls the first "Dance Song" where Zarathustra unsuccessfully plays the god of love as he tries to mediate between these two women. The tense and hostile relationship Life has with Wisdom is in fact necessary because the love between Zarathustra and Life could not continue without the competition. Within the complicated erotic triangle, Life proposes a truce or a pact with Zarathustra whom she accuses of infidelity. Every night when the prophet listens to the "heavy booming bell," he thinks of leaving life. The language here is ambiguous because it may mean that an ascetic wisdom devoted to the contempt of the earth attracts Zarathustra or that the suffering in the prophet's life makes suicide attractive. Whichever interpretation we opt for, Zarathustra admits the charge, but goes on to whisper to her a secret which Life says no one knows. After he speaks the thought of the eternal return, they weep together because of its sadness. The wisdom of Zarathustra has told him a truth which Life thought only she knew. Ironically, Wisdom has overcome the animosity between Zarathustra and Life and effected the long-delayed reconciliation.

Life has been reticent about her secret because she knows how much devotion to the eternal return costs. The first "Dance Song" ended with Zarathustra disheartened at the thought that both Life and Wisdom are ungraspable. In that conclusion, the Spirit of Gravity shows himself a much more formidable foe than Zarathustra had suspected. The sadness of the reconciliation between Life and Zarathustra gives way as we listen to the "heavy booming bell" of midnight count from one to twelve. The reconciliation of Life and the prophet rests on the outcome of a struggle between Woe and Joy. When Woe says "Fade away," it urges the acceptance of time's evanescence and death. In response, Joy urges that life be prolonged into eternity. At a similar climactic moment in his career, Faust takes a middle course by paradoxically asking a moment to linger away and accepting that moment as his last. Within *Thus Spake Zarathustra* Joy and the prophet defeat Woe but only after recognizing that woe is indeed deep. Just as Life wins an ambiguous victory over Wisdom for Zarathustra's affection, so too Joy defeats Woe in a close contest.

When Zarathustra achieves a reconciliation with Life, he simultaneously defeats Schopenhauerian pessimism and deflates the oppressive influence of Wagner. However, that victory and all victories over the Spirit of Gravity are never clear-cut and always tentative. Any effort, including Nietzsche's own, to make Zarathustra's affirmation of life categorical amounts to a serious distortion of the text. The defeat of the composite precursors Schopenhauer-Wagner depends upon the affirmation of Nietzsche's own sexuality. Since ascetic Wisdom will always be tempting to Zarathustra, his affirmation of Life and with her his own masculinity does not resound with a definitive tone. The rest of Nietzsche's philosophical career traces his attempt to preserve his fidelity to life.

Chronology

1844   Born in Rocken bei Lützen, Saxony, Prussia, on October 15.

1864   Enters University of Bonn to study theology.

1865   Leaves Bonn to enter University to Leipzig in classical philology, following his Bonn philology professor Friedrich Ritschl.

1867   First paper, "Zur Geschichte der Theognideischen Spruchsammlung," published.

1868   Publishes articles on Greek lyric poets and Diogenes Laertes.

1869   Receives doctorate from Leipzig, without usual examination or defense, based on published articles. Given chair in Greek language and literature at University of Basel. First lecture courses are on Aeschylus, Greek lyric poets, and Latin grammar. Publishes Basel inaugural lecture, *Homer and Classical Philology*.

1871   Publishes *Socrates and Greek Tragedy* privately.

1872   First lecture course on rhetoric. Delivers lecture series *On the Future of Our Educational Institutions*. Writes but does not publish *On Truth and Lie in an Extra-Moral Sense* and "On the Pathos of Truth." Publishes *The Birth of Tragedy*.

1873   Publishes *Untimely Meditation* 1 on Strauss.

1874   Publishes *Untimely Meditations* 2 and 3, *The Use and Abuse of History for Life* and *Schopenhauer as Educator*.

1876   Publishes *Untimely Meditation* 4, *Richard Wagner in Bayreuth*. Writes but does not publish *Philosophy in the Tragic Age of the Greeks*. Takes a year's leave from Basel for health reasons.

1877   First translation of *Richard Wagner in Bayreuth* published in French.

1878   Publishes *Human, All Too Human* 1. Gives last lecture courses on Hesiod, Plato's *Apology*, Greek lyric poets, and Introduction to Plato.

1879   Publishes *Human, All Too Human* 2. Resigns from post at Basel, citing ill health.

1880   Publishes *The Wanderer and His Shadow*.

1881   Publishes *Dawn*. Begins practice of spending summers in Sils-Maria (Switzerland) and winters on the Riviera (Genoa, Rapallo, Nice).

1882   Friendship with Lou-Andreas Salomé. Publishes *The Gay Science*.

1883   Publishes *Thus Spake Zarathustra* 1 and 2.

1884   Publishes *Zarathustra* 3.

1885   Publishes *Zarathustra* 4 privately.

1886   Publishes *Beyond Good and Evil*, and begins publishing new editions of older texts (e.g., *Birth of Tragedy*.)

1887   Publishes *The Genealogy of Morals*.

1888   Publishes *The Case of Wagner*. Writes but does not publish *The Antichrist*, *Twilight of the Idols*, *Nietzsche Contra Wagner*, *Dionysus Dithyrambs*, and *Ecce Homo*. Copenhagen professor Georg Brandes gives first university lectures on Nietzsche.

1889   Collapses in Piazza Carlo Alberto in Torino. Progressive paralysis sets in.

1897   After mother dies, moved to Weimar by sister.

1900   Dies in Weimar on August 25, buried in Rocken.

Contributors

HAROLD BLOOM, Sterling Professor of the Humanities at Yale University, is the author of *The Anxiety of Influence, Poetry and Repression*, and many other volumes of literary criticism. His forthcoming study, *Freud: Transference and Authority*, attempts a full-scale reading of all Freud's major writings. A MacArthur Prize Fellow, he is general editor of five series of literary criticism published by Chelsea House. During 1987–88, he served as Charles Eliot Norton Professor of Poetry at Harvard University.

G. WILSON KNIGHT was Professor of English at the University of Leeds. His many influential books include *The Wheel of Fire, The Imperial Theme, The Burning Oracle, The Mutual Flame, The Christian Renaissance, The Shakespearian Tempest, Christ and Nietzsche*, and *The Starlit Dome*.

MAURICE BLANCHOT has published hundreds of essays and some two dozen books. Those available in English range from novels and shorter fictions (*Thomas the Obscure, Death Sentence, The Madness of the Day*, and *Time Comes*) to works in literary criticism and theory, political theory and analysis, and philosophy (*The Sirens' Song, The Space of Literature, The Writing of the Disaster*, and *The Gaze of Orpheus*).

PIERRE KLOSSOWSKI is a French writer, artist, and translator. His work on Nietzsche includes *Un Si funeste désir, Nietzsche et le cercle vicieux*, and the French translation of Heidegger's two-volume *Nietzsche*. He has also written on Claudel, Gide, and Sade, and his novels, *Roberte ce Soir* and *The Revocation of the Edict of Nantes* have been translated into English.

PAUL DE MAN was, until his death in 1983, Sterling Professor of Comparative Literature at Yale University. He is the author of *Blindness and Insight: Essays in Contemporary Criticism, Allegories of Reading, Figural Language in Rousseau, Nietzsche, Rilke, and Proust*, and *The Rhetoric of*

Romanticism, and posthumously of the forthcoming collections *The Resistance to Theory, Aesthetic Ideology*, and *Fugitive Essays*.

GILLES DELEUZE teaches philosophy at the University of Paris and has written two books on Nietzsche, as well as texts on Bergson, Hume, Sacher-Masoch, Spinoza, and Kafka. His *Nietzsche and Philosophy* has been translated, as have *Proust and Signs, Kant's Critical Philosophy*, and two books written with Felix Guattari, *Anti-Oedipus* and *A Thousand Plateaus*.

JACQUES DERRIDA is Directeur d'Etudes at the Ecole des Hautes Etudes en Sciences Sociales in Paris, Visiting Professor in the Humanities at Yale University, and Andrew D. White Professor-at-large at Cornell University. He has written two books on Nietzsche, *Otobiographies* and *Spurs/Eperons* and is the author of many articles and books including *La Voix et le phenomène (Speech and Phenomena), La Dissemination (Dissemination), Les Marges de la Philosophie (Margins—of Philosophy), Glas*, and *La Carte postale*.

ALEXANDER NEHAMAS is Professor of Philosophy at the University of Pennsylvania. He is the author of *Nietzsche: Life as Literature*.

WERNER HAMACHER teaches in the Humanities Center and the German Department at The Johns Hopkins University. He has written on Kant, Fichte, Schlegel, Schleiermacher, Yeats, and Kleist, and has edited Hegel's *"Der Geist des Christentums": Schriften 1796–1800*.

RICHARD RORTY is Kenan Professor of the Humanities and teaches English and philosophy at the University of Virginia. A MacArthur Prize Fellow, he is the author of *Philosophy and the Mirror of Nature, Consequences of Pragmatism*, and is at work on books about Heidegger and Dewey.

RICHARD DRAKE recently completed work on *Shepherd and Serpent: A Reading of "Thus Spake Zarathustra" and Its Psychogenesis*, and currently works in New York as an international banker.

Bibliography

Adorno, Theodor W. *Negative Dialectics*. Translated by E. B. Ashton. New York: Seabury, 1973.

———. "Wagner, Nietzsche, and Hitler." *Kenyon Review* 9, no. 1 (1947): 155–62.

——— and Max Horkheimer. *The Dialectic of Enlightenment*. Translated by John Cumming. New York: Herder & Herder, 1972.

Alderman, Harold. *Nietzsche's Gift*. Athens: Ohio University Press, 1977.

———. "Origin and Telos." *Research in Phenomenology* 10 (1980): 192–207.

Allen, Christine Garside. "Nietzsche's Ambivalence about Women." In *The Sexism of Social and Political Theory: Women and Reproduction from Plato to Nietzsche*, edited by Lynda Lange and Lorenne M. G. Clark. Toronto: University of Toronto Press, 1979.

Allison, David B. "*Destruction/Deconstruction* in the Text of Nietzsche." *boundary* 2 8, no. 1 (1979): 82–89.

———, ed. *The New Nietzsche: Contemporary Styles of Interpretation*. New York: Dell, 1977.

Arrowsmith, William. "Nietzsche on Classics and Classicists." *Arion* 2 (Spring, Summer, and Winter 1963).

Asher, Kenneth. "Deconstruction's Use and Abuse of Nietzsche." *Telos* 62 (1984–85): 169–78.

Assoun, Paul-Laurent. *Freud et Nietzsche*. Paris: Presses Universitaires de France, 1980.

Bäumler, Alfred. *Nietzsche, der philosoph und politiker*. 3d ed. Leipzig: P. Reclam, 1937 [1931].

Bataille, Georges. "Nietzsche and the Fascists," "Propositions," "Nietzschean Chronicle," and "The Obelisk." In *Visions of Excess: Selected Writings, 1927–1939*, translated and edited by Allan Stoekl. Minneapolis: University of Minnesota Press, 1985.

———. *Sur Nietzsche, volonté de chance*. Paris: Gallimard, 1945.

Birus, Hendrik. "Nietzsche's Concept of Interpretation." *Texte: Revue de Critique et Théorie Littéraire* 3 (1984): 87–102.

Blanchot, Maurice, "Reflexions sur le nihilism" and "Sur un changement d'époque: l'exigence du retour." In *L'entretien infini*. Paris: Gallimard, 1969.

Bolz, Norbert. "Nietzsches Spur in der Ästhetischen Theorie." In *Materialen zur*

Ästhetischen Theorie T. W. Adornos, edited by B. Lindner and W. M. Lüdke. Frankfurt-am-Main: Suhrkamp Verlag, 1980.

Booth, David. "Nietzsche on "The Subject as Multiplicity'." *Man and World* 18, no. 2 (1985): 121–46.

Breazeale, J. Daniel. "The Word, the World, and Nietzsche." *The Philosophical Forum* 6 (Winter-Spring 1974–1975): 301–20.

Cahiers de Royaumont: Nietzsche. Actes du 7ième colloque philosophique international de Royaumont, "Nietzsche," 1964. Paris: Editions du Minuit, 1967.

Camus, Albert. "Absolute Affirmation." In *The Rebel: An Essay on Man in Revolt*, translated by Anthony Bower. New York: Vintage Books, 1956.

Cixous, Helene. "Le Bon Pied, le bon œil." *Cahiers Renaud-Barrault* 87 (1974): 47–75.

Colli, Giorgio. *Scritti su Nietzsche*. Milano: Adelphi, 1980.

Conroy, Mark. "The Artist-Philosopher in Nietzsche's *Jenseits von Gut und Böse*." *MLN* 96 (1983): 615–28.

Corngold, Stanley. "Self and Subject in Nietzsche during the Axial Period" and "Mann as a Reader of Nietzsche." In *The Fate of the Self: German Writers and French Theory*. Princeton: Princeton University Press, 1986.

Danto, Arthur C. *Nietzsche as Philosopher*. New York: Macmillan, 1965; Columbia University Press, 1980.

Deleuze, Gilles. *Nietzsche and Philosophy*. Translated by Hugh Tomlinson. New York: Columbia University Press, 1983.

———. *Nietzsche, sa vie, son oeuvre*. Paris: Presses Universitaires de France, 1965.

de Man, Paul. "Anthropomorphism and Trope in the Lyric." In *The Rhetoric of Romanticism*. New York: Columbia University Press, 1984.

———. "Genesis and Genealogy (Nietzsche)" and "Rhetoric of Persuasion (Nietzsche)." In *Allegories of Reading*. New Haven: Yale University Press, 1979.

Derrida, Jacques. *The Ear of the Other: Otobiography, Transference, Translation*. Edited by Christie V. McDonald and translated by Peggy Kamuf and Avital Ronell. New York: Schocken, 1985.

———. *Spurs: Nietzsche's Styles = Eperons: les styles de Nietzsche*. Bilingual edition. Translated by Barbara Harlow. Chicago: University of Chicago Press, 1979.

———. "White Mythology: Metaphor in the Text of Philosophy." In *Margins—of Philosophy*, translated by Alan Bass. Chicago: University of Chicago Press, 1982.

Donadio, Stephen. *Nietzsche, Henry James, and the Artistic Will*. New York: Oxford University Press, 1978.

Fink, Eugen. *Nietzsches Philosophie*. Stuttgart: W. Kohlhammer, 1960.

Foucault, Michel. "Man and His Doubles." In *The Order of Things*, translated by Alan Sheridan. New York: Random House, 1970.

———. "Nietzsche, Freud, Marx." Translated by Jon Anderson and Gary Hentzi. *Critical Texts* 3, no. 2 (1986): 1–5.

———. "Nietzsche, Genealogy, History" and "Theatrum Philosophicum. In *Language, Counter-Memory, Practice*, translated by Donald F. Bouchard and Sherry Simon. Ithaca, N.Y.: Cornell University Press. 1977.

————. "*Ecce Homo* or the written body." Translated by Judith Still. *Oxford Literary Review* 7, no. 1–2 (1985): 3–24.

Gilman, Sander L. *Nietzschean Parody: An Introduction to Reading Nietzsche.* Bonn: Bouvier Verlag. 1976.

Girard, René. "Dionysus versus the Crucified." *MLN* 99, no. 4 (1984): 816–35.

Glucksmann, André. "Whereby I Am above Everything (Nietzsche for the Lot)." In *The Master Thinkers*, translated by Brian Pearce. New York: Harper & Row, 1980.

Goicoechea, David, ed. *The Great Year of Zarathustra (1881–1981).* Lanham, Md.: University Press of America, 1983.

Goth, Joachim. *Nietzsche und die Rhetorik.* Tübingen: Max Niemeyer Verlag, 1970.

Granier, Jean. *Nietzsche.* Paris: Presses Universitaires de France, 1982.

————. *Le Problème de la vérité dans la philosophie de Nietzsche.* Paris: Editions du Seuil, 1965.

Haar, Michel. "La critique nietzschéenne de la subjectivité." *Nietzsche–Studien* 12 (1983): 80–110.

————. "Heidegger et le surhomme." *Revue de l'enseignement philosophique* 30, no. 3 (1980): 1–17.

————. "Nietzsche and Metaphysical Language." Translated by Cyril and Liliane Welch. *Man and World* 4, no. 4 (1971): 359–95.

Habermas, Jurgen. "The Entwinement of Myth and Enlightenment: Rereading *The Dialectic of Enlightenment.*" Translated by Thomas Y. Levin. *New German Critique* 26 (1982): 13–30.

————. "Nachwort." In *Friedrich Nietzsche: Erkenntnistheoretische Schriften.* Frankfurt-am-Main: Suhrkamp Verlag, 1968.

————. "Psychoanalysis and Social Theory: Nietzsche's Reduction of Cognitive Interests." In *Knowledge and Human Interests*, translated by Jeremy J. Shapiro, 2d ed. London: Heinemann, 1978.

Hamacher, Werner. "Das Versprechen der Auslegung: Überlegungen zum hermeneutischen Imperativ bei Kant und Nietzsche." In *Spiegel und Gleichnis.* Norbert Bolz and Wolfgang Hübener, eds. Würzburg: Königshausen und Neumann, 1983: 252–73.

Harlow, Barbara. "*Ecce Homo*: A Questionable Epigraph." *Nuova Corrente* 68–69 (1975–1976): 585–613.

Harries, Karsten. "Copernican Reflections and the Tasks of Metaphysics." *International Philosophical Quarterly* 23, no. 3 (1983): 235–50.

Hart-Nibbrig, Christian. "Nietzsches Lachen." *Merkur* 37, no. 1 (1983): 82–89.

Hatab, Lawrence. "Nietzsche on Woman." *Southern Journal of Philosophy* 19, no. 3 (1981): 333–45.

Hayman, Ronald, *Nietzsche: A Critical Life.* New York: Oxford University Press, 1980.

Heidegger, Martin. *Nietzsche.* Translated by Frank A. Capuzzi and David Farrell Krell, 4 vols. San Francisco: Harper & Row, 1979. [Vol. 1: *The Will to Power as Art*, Krell trans., 1982; vol. 2: *The Eternal Recurrence of the Same*, Krell trans., 1984; vol. 3: *The Will to Power as Knowledge and as Metaphysics*, Krell trans., forthcoming; vol. 4: *Nihilism*, Capuzzi trans., 1979.]

———. *What Is Called Thinking?* Translated by J. Glenn Gray and Fred D. Wieck. New York: Harper & Row: 1968.

———. "Who Is Nietzsche's Zarathustra?" In *Nietzsche. Volume 2: The Eternal Recurrence of the Same*, translated by David Farrell Krell. San Francisco: Harper & Row, 1984.

———. "The Word of Nietzsche: "God is dead.' " In *The Question Concerning Technology and Other Essays*, translated by William Lovitt. New York: Harper & Row, 1977: 53–112.

Hinman, Lawrence M. "Nietzsche, Metaphor, and Truth." *Philosophy and Phenomenological Research* 43, no. 2 (1982): 179–99.

Hollingdale, R. J. *Nietzsche.* Boston and London: Routledge & Kegan Paul, 1973.

Hoy, David C. "Philosophy as Rigorous Philology? Nietzsche and Poststructuralism." *New York Literary Forum* 8–9 (1981): 171–85.

IJsseling, Samuel. *Rhetoric and Philosophy in Conflict.* Translated by Paul Dunphy. The Hague: Martinus Nijhoff, 1976: 103–14.

International Studies in Philosophy. Papers delivered at annual meetings of North American Nietzsche Society, summer issue of each year since 1983.

Irigary, Luce. *Amante marine: de Friedrich Nietzsche.* Paris: Editions du Minuit, 1980.

Jacobs, Carol. *The Dissimulating Harmony: The Image of Interpretation in Nietzsche, Rilke, Artaud, and Benjamin.* Baltimore: The Johns Hopkins University Press, 1978.

Jaspers, Karl. *Nietzsche: An Introduction to the Understanding of His Philosophical Activity.* Translated by Charles Wallraff and Frederick Schmitz. Tuscon: University of Arizona Press, 1966.

Kaufmann, Walter. *Nietzsche: Philosopher, Psychologist, Antichrist.* 3d ed., rev. and enl. Princeton: Princeton University Press, 1968 [1950].

Kittler, Friedrich. "Nietzsche (1844–1900)." In *Klassiker der Literaturtheorie. Von Boileau bis Barthes*, edited by Horst Turk. Munich: Beck, 1979.

———. "Wie man abschafft, wovon man spricht: Der Autor von *Ecce Homo.*" In *Literaturmagazin* 12 (*Nietzsche*), edited by Nicolas Born, Jürgen Manthey, and Dolf Schmidt. Hamburg: Rowohlt, 1980: 153–78.

Klossowski, Pierre. *Nietzsche et le cercle vicieux.* Paris: Mercure de France, 1969.

———. "Sur quelques thèmes fondamentaux de la *Gaya Scienza* de Nietzsche" and "Nietzsche, le polythéism et la parodie." In *Un Si funeste désir.* Paris: Gallimard, 1963.

Knight, G. Wilson. *Christ and Nietzsche: An Essay in Poetic Wisdom.* London and New York: Staples Press, 1948.

Kofman, Sarah. "Metaphor, Symbol, and Interpretation." Translated by David B. Allison. In *The New Nietzsche*, edited by David B. Allison.

———. *Nietzsche et la métaphore.* 2d ed., rev. Paris: Editions Galilée, 1983 [1972].

———. *Nietzsche et la scène philosophique.* Paris: U.G.E., 1979.

———. "Nietzsche: La chambre des peintres." In *Camera Obscura—de l'idéologie.* Paris: Editions Galilée, 1973: 47–69.

Krell, David Farrell. "Analysis." In Heidegger, *Nietzsche* I: 230–57; II: 237–81; III: forthcoming; and IV: 253–94.

————. "Descensional Reflection." In *Philosophy and Archaic Experience*, edited by John Sallis. Pittsburgh: Duquesne University Press, 1982.

————. "Heidegger, Nietzsche, Hegel." *Nietzsche–Studien* 5 (1976): 255–62.

————. "Heidegger's Reading of Nietzsche: Confrontation and Encounter." *Journal of the British Society for Phenomenology* 14, no. 3 (1983): 271–82.

————. "Der Maulwurf/The Mole: Philosophic Burrowing in Kant, Hegel, and Nietzsche." In *Why Nietzsche Now?*, edited by Daniel O'Hara. Bloomington: Indiana University Press, 1985.

Lacoue-Labarthe, Philippe. "Le détour" and "Nietzsche Apocryphe." In *Le Sujet de la philosophie (Typographies I)*. Paris: Aubier-Flammarion, 1979.

————. "Histoire et mimèsis" and "L'Antagonism." In *L'Imitation des modernes (Typographies II)*. Paris: Editions Galilée, 1986.

Laporte, Roger. "Philosophie d'hier—Nietzsche—Philosophie de demain." *Digraphe* 18–19 (1979).

Laruelle, François. *Nietzsche contre Heidegger. Thèses pour une politique nietzschéenne*. Paris: Editions Payot, 1977.

Lectures de Nietzsche. Special issue of *Critique* 313 (June 1973).

Lefebvre, Henri. *Hegel, Marx, Nietzsche*. Paris: Casterman, 1975.

Lingis, Alphonso. "Differance in the Eternal Recurrence of the Same." *Research in Phenomenology* 8 (1978): 77–91.

————. "The Language of *The Gay Science*." In *The Philosophical Reflection of Man in Literature*. Analecta Husserliana 12, edited by Anna-Teresa Tymieniecka. Dordrecht: D. Reidel Publishing, 1982.

Löwith, Karl. *From Hegel to Nietzsche: The Revolution in Nineteenth-Century Thought*. Translated by David E. Green. New York: Holt, Rinehart & Winston, 1964.

Lukács, György. "Nietzsche as Founder of Irrationalism in the Imperial Period." In *The Destruction of Reason*. Translated by Peter Palmer. Atlantic Highlands, N.J.: Humanities Press, 1981.

Lyotard, Jean-François. "Notes on the Return and Kapital." Translated by Roger McKeon. In *Nietzsche's Return. Semiotext(e)* 3, no. 1 (1978): 44–53.

Magnus, Bernd. *Nietzsche's Existential Imperative*. Bloomington: Indiana University Press, 1978.

————. "Perfectibility and Attitude in Nietzsche's Übermensch." *Review of Metaphysics* 36, no. 3 (1983): 633–59.

Miller, J. Hillis. "Between Practice and Theory." In *The Linguistic Moment: From Wordsworth to Stevens*. Princeton: Princeton University Press, 1985.

————. "The Disarticulation of the Self in Nietzsche." *The Monist* 64, no. 2 (1981): 247–61.

————. "*Gleichnis* in Nietzsche's *Also Sprach Zarathustra*." *International Studies in Philosophy* 17, no. 2 (1985): 3–15.

Minson, Jeffrey. *Genealogies of Morals: Nietzsche, Foucault, Donzelot, and the Eccentricity of Ethics*. London: Macmillan, 1985.

Montinari, Mazzino. *Nietzsche lesen*. Berlin and New York: Walter de Gruyter, 1982.

Nancy, Jean-Luc. "Nietzsche. Mais où sont les yeux pour le voir?" *Esprit* 369 (March 1968): 482–503.

————. " 'Notre Probité!' Sur la verité au sens moral chez Nietzsche." In *L'Impératif catégorique*. Paris: Flammarion, 1983.

————. "La thèse de Nietzsche sur la téléologie." In *Nietzsche aujourd'hui?* I. Paris: U.G.E., 1973.

Nehamas, Alexander. "Immanent and Transcendent Perspectivism in Nietzsche." *Nietzsche–Studien* 12 (1983): 473–90.

————. *Nietzsche: Life as Literature.* Cambridge: Harvard University Press, 1985.

Nietzsche. Special issue of *Nuova Corrente* 68–69 (1975–6).

Nietzsche aujourd'hui? I: Intensités, II: Passion. Colloque de Cérisy, 1972. 2 vols. Paris: U.G.E. 1973.

Nietzsche's Return. Special issue of *Semiotext(e)* 3, no. 1 (1978).

Nietzsche–Studien: Internationales Jahrbuch für die Nietzsche–Forschung. New York and Berlin: Walter de Gruyter, 1972– .

Norris, Christopher. "Nietzsche: Philosophy and Deconstruction" and "Between Marx and Nietzsche: The Politics of Deconstruction." In *Deconstruction: Theory and Practice.* London and New York: Methuen, 1982.

Norris, Margot. "Nietzsche's *Ecce Homo*: Behold the Beast." In *Beasts of the Modern Imagination: Darwin, Nietzsche, Kafka, Ernst, and Lawrence.* Baltimore: The Johns Hopkins University Press, 1985.

O'Hara, Daniel, ed. *Why Nietzsche Now?* [Initially a special issue of *boundary 2* 9, no. 3 and 10, no. 1 (1981).] Bloomington: Indiana University Press, 1985.

Pasley, Malcolm, ed. *Nietzsche: Imagery and Thought. A Collection of Essays.* Berkeley and Los Angeles: University of California Press, 1978.

Pautrat. Bernard. *Versions du soleil: figures et système de Nietzsche.* Paris: Editions du Seuil, 1971.

The Philosophy of Nietzsche. Special issue of *Journal of the British Society for Phenomenology* 14, no. 3 (October 1983).

Pletsch, Karl. "The Self-Sufficient Text in Nietzsche and Kierkegaard." *Yale French Studies* 66 (1984): 160–88.

Reichert, H. W. and Karl Schlechta, eds. *International Nietzsche Bibliography.* Revised and expanded edition. Chapel Hill: University of North Carolina Press, 1968.

Rey, Jean-Michel. *L'Enjeu des signes: lecture de Nietzsche.* Paris: Editions du Seuil, 1971.

Ricoeur, Paul. "Religion, Atheism, and Faith." Charles Frelich, trans. In *The Conflict of Interpretations*, edited by Don Ihde. Evanston, Ill.: Northwestern University Press, 1974.

Ronell, Avital. "Queens of the Night: Nietzsche's Antibodies." *Genre* 16 (1983): 404–22.

Rorty, Richard. "Beyond Nietzsche and Marx." *London Review of Books* 3, no. 3 (19 February–4 March 1981): 5–6.

————. "Unsoundness in Perspective." *Times Literary Supplement* 4185 (17 June 1983): 619–20.

Rupp, Gerhard. *Rhetorische Strukturen und Kommunikative Determinanz: Studien zur Textkonstitution des philosophischen Diskurses im Werk Friedrich Nietzsches.* Bern: Lang, 1976.

Ryan, Michael. "The Act." *Glyph* 2 (1977): 64–89.

Said, Edward. "Conrad and Nietzsche." In *Joseph Conrad: A Commemoration*, edited by Norman Sherry. New York: Harper & Row, 1977.

Schacht, Richard. *Nietzsche*. Boston and London: Routledge & Kegan Paul, 1983.

Schlechta, Karl, ed. *Nietzsche Chronik: Daten zu Leben und Werk*. Munich: Carl Hanser Verlag, 1975.

Schlüppmann, Heide. *Friedrich Nietzsches ästhetische Opposition*. Stuttgart: J. B. Metzler, 1977.

Schrift, Alan D. "Language, Metaphor, Rhetoric: Nietzsche's Deconstruction of Epistemology." *Journal of the History of Philosophy* 23, no. 3 (1985): 371–95."

———. "Nietzsche's Psycho-Genealogy." *Journal of the British Society for Phenomenology* 14, no. 3 (1983): 283–303.

———. "Reading Derrida Reading Heidegger Reading Nietzsche." *Research in Phenomenology* 14 (1984): 87–119.

Shapiro, Gary. "The Rhetoric of Nietzsche's *Zarathustra*." In *Philosophical Style*, edited by Berel Lang. Chicago: Nelson Hall, 1980.

Simmel, Georg. *Schopenhauer und Nietzsche*. Leipzig: Duncker & Humboldt, 1907.

Solomon, Robert C., ed. *Nietzsche: A Collection of Critical Essays*. New York: Anchor Books, 1973.

Stambaugh, Joan. *Nietzsche's Thought of Eternal Return*. Baltimore: The Johns Hopkins University Press, 1972.

———. "Thoughts on a Nachlass Fragment from Nietzsche." *Nietzsche–Studien* 6 (1977): 195–204.

———. "Thoughts on Pity and Revenge." *Nietzsche–Studien* 1 (1972): 27–35.

———. "Thoughts on the Innocence of Becoming." *Nietzsche–Studien* 14 (1985): 164–76.

———. *Untersuchungen zum Problem der Zeit bei der Philosophie Nietzsches*. The Hague: Martinus Nijhoff, 1959.

Stern, J. P. *A Study of Nietzsche*. Cambridge and New York: Cambridge University Press, 1979.

Stevens, Jeffrey. "Nietzsche and Heidegger on Justice and Truth." *Nietzsche–Studien* 9 (1980): 224–38.

Stoekl, Allan. "From *Acéphale* to the Will to Chance: Nietzsche in the Text of Bataille." *Glyph* 6 (1979): 42–67.

Strong, Tracy B. "Comment" [on Nehamas, "Immanent and Transcendent Perspectivism"]. *Nietzsche–Studien* 12 (1983): 491–94.

———. *Friedrich Nietzsche and the Politics of Transfiguration*. Berkeley: University of California Press, 1975.

———. "Nietzsche and Politics." In *Nietzsche: A Collection of Critical Essays*, edited by Robert C. Solomon. New York: Anchor Books, 1973.

———. "Texts and Pretexts: Reflections on Perspectivism in Nietzsche." *Political Theory* 13, no. 2 (1985): 164–82.

Tonnies, Ferdinand. *Der Nietzsche–Kultus*. Leipzig: O. R. Reisland, 1987.

Valéry, Paul. *Quatre lettres de Paul Valéry au sujet de Nietzsche*. Paris: Cahiers de la Quinzaine, 1927.

Vattimo, Gianni. *Ipotesi su Nietzsche*. Torino: Giappichelli, 1967.

———. *Il soggetto e la maschera: Nietzsche e il problema della liberazione*. Milano: Bompiani, 1974.

————. *L'avventura della differenza*. Milano: Garzanti, 1980.

Wahl, Jean A. *L'Avant-dernière pensée de Nietzsche*. Paris: Centre de documentation universitaire, 1961.

————. "Le cas Nietzsche." *Revue de métaphysique et de morale* 66 (1961): 306–11.

————. *La pensée philosophique de Nietzsche des années 1885–1888*. Paris: Centre de documentation universitaire, 1959.

Warminski, Andrezj. "Prefatory Postscript: Interpretation and Reading." In *Readings in Interpretation: Hölderlin, Hegel, Heidegger*. Minneapolis: University of Minnesota Press, forthcoming.

Warren, Mark. "Nietzsche and Political Philosophy." *Political Theory* 13, no. 1 (1985): 183–212.

————. "The Politics of Nietzsche's Philosophy." *Political Studies* 33, no. 3 (1985): 418–38.

————. "The Use and Abuse of Nietzsche." *Canadian Journal of Social and Political Theory* 4, no. 1 (1980): 147–67.

Weber, Samuel. "The Debts of Deconstruction and Other, Related Assumptions." In *Taking Chances: Derrida, Psychoanalysis, and Literature*, edited by Joseph P. Smith and William Kerrigan. Baltimore: The Johns Hopkins University Press, 1984: 33–65.

West, Cornel. "Nietzsche's Prefiguration of Postmodern American Philosophy." In *Why Nietzsche Now?*, edited by Daniel O'Hara. Bloomington: Indiana University Press, 1985.

White, Hayden. "Nietzsche: The Poetic Defense of History in the Metaphorical Mode." In *Metahistory: The Historical Imagination in Nineteenth-Century Europe*. Baltimore: The Johns Hopkins University Press, 1973.

Williams, W. D. "Nietzsche's Masks." In *Nietzsche: Imagery and Thought*, edited by Malcolm Pasley. Berkeley and Los Angeles: University of California Press, 1978.

Wood, David and Robert Bernasconi, eds. *The New Nietzsches*. Coventry: Parousia Press, forthcoming.

Zuckert, Catherine. "Nietzsche's Rereading of Plato." *Political Theory* 13, no. 2 (1985): 213–38.

Acknowledgments

"The Golden Labyrinth: An Introduction to *Thus Spake Zarathustra*" by G. Wilson Knight from *Christ and Nietzsche: An Essay in Poetic Wisdom* by G. Wilson Knight, © 1948 by Staples Press, Inc. Reprinted by permission.

"Reflections on Nihilism: Crossing of the Line" (originally entitled "The Limits of Experience: Nihilism" by Maurice Blanchot from *The New Nietzsche: Contemporary Styles of Interpretations,* edited by David B. Allison, © 1977 by David B. Allison. Reprinted by permission.

"Nietzsche's Experience of the Eternal Return" by Pierre Klossowski from *The New Nietzsche: Contemporary Styles of Interpretation,* edited by David B. Allison, © 1977 by David B. Allison. Reprinted by permission.

"Rhetoric of Tropes (Nietzsche)" by Paul de Man from *Allegories of Reading: Figural Language in Rousseau, Nietzsche, Rilke and Proust* by Paul de Man, © 1979 by Yale University. Reprinted by permission of Yale University Press.

"Active and Reactive" by Gilles Deleuze from *Nietzsche and Philosophy* by Gilles Deleuze, © 1983 by the Athlone Press. Reprinted by permission of Columbia University Press and the Athlone Press.

"Otobiographies: The Teaching of Nietzsche and the Politics of the Proper Name" by Jacques Derrida from *The Ear of the Other: Otobiography, Transference, Translation,* edited by Christie V. McDonald, © 1985 by Schocken Books, Inc. Reprinted by permission of Schocken Books, Inc.

"How One Becomes What One Is" by Alexander Nehamas from *Nietzsche: Life as Literature* by Alexander Nehamas, © 1985 by the President and Fellows of Harvard College. Reprinted by permission of Harvard University Press.

" 'Disgregation of the Will': Nietzsche on the Individual and Individuality" by Werner Hamacher from *Reconstructing Individualism: Autonomy, Individuality, and the Self in Western Thought,* edited by Thomas C. Heller, Morton Sosna, and David E. Wellbery, © 1986 by the Board of Trustees of the Leland Stanford Junior University. Reprinted by permission of the publishers and Stanford University Press.

"The Contigency of Selfhood" by Richard Rorty from *London Review of Books* 8, no. 8 (May 8, 1986), © 1986 by *London Review of Books*. Reprinted by permission.

"Conflicting Interpretation of Zarathustra's Phantasmagoria" by Richard Drake from *Sheperd and Serpent: A Reading of* Thus Spake Zarathustra *and Its Psychogenesis* by Richard Drake, © 1986 by Richard Drake. Reprinted by permission.

Index